Praise for *Why Can't I Meditate?*

"*Why Can't I Meditate?* is, as far as I know, the first in-depth and pragmatic analysis of a key issue that bedevils many people who undertake the practice of meditation. It is not at all uncommon for someone to encounter a deep resistance to meditation even though they are sincerely committed to it. This important study is an invaluable handbook that provides practical guidance and advice for anyone who strives to understand and overcome the obstacles that prevent meditation from becoming an integral part of one's life."
—Stephen Batchelor, author of *Buddhism Without Beliefs* and *Confession of a Buddhist Atheist*

"I am very happy to finally see someone writing about why people can't meditate. I've known Nigel for many years; he's a sincere practitioner who has been thinking about how to untangle the blockages in the human mind for some time now. We had a lot of discussion together about the ideas presented here and I think his book will be very useful. It's helpful to know the underlying causes of meditation problems—this book shows how to work with them."
—Tsoknyi Rinpoche, author of *Open Heart, Open Mind*

"People learning mindfulness often ask, 'I know mindfulness practice is helpful; how can I best establish my meditation practice?' Now I can recommend this wonderful book. Nigel Wellings offers insightful, compassionate, and eminently practical guidance, based on his extensive personal experience as a teacher and practitioner and interviews with some of the most accomplished mindfulness teachers in the field."
—Willem Kuyken, professor of clinical psychology, University of Exeter

Why Can't I Meditate?

Why Can't I
Meditate?

*How to Get Your
Mindfulness Practice on Track*

Nigel Wellings

A TarcherPerigee Book

tarcherperigee

An imprint of Penguin Random House LLC
375 Hudson Street
New York, New York 10014

First published in the United Kingdom by Piatkus Books in 2015

First TarcherPerigee paperback edition published in 2016

Most TarcherPerigee books are available at special quantity discounts for bulk
purchase for sales promotions, premiums, fund-raising, and educational needs.
Special books or book excerpts also can be created to fit specific needs. For details,
write: SpecialMarkets@penguinrandomhouse.com.

ISBN 978-1-101-98327-0

Printed in the United States of America
1   3   5   7   9   10   8   6   4   2

Book design by Jennifer Daddio / Bookmark Design & Media Inc.

Nigel Wellings is a psychoanalytic psychotherapist and author who works within a broadly contemplative perspective. He first attempted to practice mindfulness in his late teens and has been engaged with the relationship between psychotherapy and meditation for the last forty years. With Elizabeth McCormick, he has published several books, including *Nothing to Lose: Psychotherapy, Buddhism and Living Life*. His essay "With Buddha in Mind: Mindfulness-Based Psychotherapy in Practice" was recently published in *Crossroads in Psychoanalysis, Buddhism, and Mindfulness*. He lives in Bath, England, and is a teacher on the Bath and Bristol Mindfulness Courses.

www.mindfulness-psychotherapy.co.uk

www.bath-bristol-mindfulness-courses.co.uk

May this be a bridge, a boat, a ship

for all who struggle with their practice

of mindfulness.

Contents

Foreword

This important book goes to the heart of a crucial area of inquiry for anyone who aspires to bring mindfulness meditation into his or her everyday life. All who have engaged with a personal meditation practice will know that there is often a gap between the aspiration to do it and the reality of trying to practice it each day: everything in our life and values points us toward the importance of our practice, but there seem to be so many barriers that stop us from doing it.

In very skillful ways, Nigel's book brings us back to the humanness of this conundrum. It offers a gentle reminder that it is natural to find practicing mindfulness challenging because it deliberately points us toward the awkward and painful truths, the contradictions, of our existence. When we commit to a daily practice, we find many moments when we waver between doing our chores, taking a bath, having a glass of wine, hanging out with friends and family, or choosing the seemingly crazy and counterintuitive option of sitting on our meditation cushion and settling into sensing the immediacy of our—sometimes painful—experience. How human it is to feel the strong pull toward familiarity, comfort, and pleasure and to avoid what is painful, raw, and tender. Yet through a mindful engagement with our experience, we can know the deep relief that comes from learning to live in accord with the way things really are. The deep, intrinsic sanity in the process of the practice returns us to what is essentially true about ourselves and the world. This book beautifully unpacks and explores this ambivalence and helps us to see it as the real territory of our practice. These moments of hesitation and doubt do not mean that we haven't quite "got it"; they are the heart of our practice. Not wanting to meditate is not something outside of the practice but a natural part of the all-embracing inquiry that our practice essentially is. We mindfully include all our feelings, all our uncertainties, our reluctance to really engage, and settle into our practice, day to day, with a spirit of investigative curiosity.

This experience is true for all, including those of us who teach mindfulness-based programs. Teachers have the additional external injunction of "good practice guidance," which requires us to have an ongoing, daily personal mindfulness practice, interspersed with retreats for periods of intensive meditation. This formal meditation practice gives us the space to see the patterns and processes within us and the ways we inadvertently collaborate in creating our own suffering. We see in ourselves all the times when we are judgmental, nonaccepting, striving, critical, and angry. Of course, this contradicts our ideal of what an embodied mindfulness-based teacher should be like. Yet how could we possibly offer this practice to others unless we were engaged in our own ongoing exploration of its joys and struggles?

Over time, the understanding that emerges through these

insights becomes part of the fabric of our being. Embodying mindfulness isn't then an effortful, self-conscious process but rather a natural expression of our being, moment by moment— an implicit orientation within us that becomes explicit through the visible and tangible expression of what mindfulness looks, feels, and sounds like. Knowing this, embodying it within our life, we are able to teach mindfulness authentically in the classroom.

Nigel's writing, and the words of the practitioners and teachers who speak through the pages of this book, help us to understand and find words for the interior world of thoughts and emotions that our mindfulness reveals: a world of emotional contradictions and conflicts that is usually hidden from view and often harshly judged when seen. In so doing, he encourages us to look into our own inner world in a fresh and curious way— supporting us to come back again and again, with kindness and compassion, to who we are in each moment. This supports us in our practice to form a clear intention, a sense of purpose and direction, and then let the reality of what arises be just the way it is.

This book is easy to read and very accessible, and is delivered with a lightness of touch and humor. Clear chapters that address specific points are enhanced by the many accounts from people's personal practices—these help to normalize and universalize the processes that seem so personal and that give rise to so much internal judging. It is tremendously reassuring to hear what is going on behind the closed eyes of other meditators and to find that it is no different from what we are going through. The book embodies kindness and generosity, and shows that when we begin to bring to our practice clarity and a sense of commonality with other practitioners, our self-judging and self-critical tendencies naturally become quieter.

Committing to a mindfulness meditation practice is an ongoing process, not a one-off event. As I read this book, I sensed anew the motivation arising in me to settle into my practice. It is so helpful to be reminded in a fresh way of how, in essence, my patterns and tendencies are no different from those of others, and to bring to mind, with a renewed clarity, what it is that brings me to my practice each day.

Rebecca Crane, MA
Director, Centre for Mindfulness Research
and Practice
Bangor University

Preface

The idea for this book came about through my experience teaching mindfulness courses. It became clear to me that while many of us enjoyed and valued the courses, perhaps the majority of us never really established enough of a "mindfulness habit" to keep it going for long after the course finished. I was curious and concerned about this—why was it not happening? Speaking to others who teach similar courses and several who teach mindfulness teachers, it seemed my observation was by no means unique. Yes, it was true, lots of good things came out of the courses, but keeping the meditation going was tough, and, despite really wanting to continue, many people didn't.

Thinking about how I'd started meditating a little over forty years ago, then stopped for quite a long time before taking it up again, I realized that there had been a huge discrepancy between my ideas about meditation—its enormous value—and how hard it could be to do. Could other people experience the same gap between what they imagine meditation is about and their actual experience of it?

This is what prompted the interviews that are found throughout this book. The first two—with someone I call here "a struggling meditator" and someone who taught meditation in a psychotherapy training school—were tentative and exploratory: what did they feel got in the way of practicing meditation? Interestingly, both came to largely the same conclusion, based upon their own experience and, in the teacher's case, that of people he taught. What they said was that there is something about meditation that can be deeply unsettling, perhaps threatening in some way, and that even if we are not consciously aware of this, we sense it and are wary. This view coincided with my own, and as the interviews continued it became clear that one way or another everyone agreed—there is an element of meditating that is somehow alarming to our sense of who we are. So, yes, it could help us relax. Yes, it was great for catching thoughts that made us feel depressed and anxious. And, yes, it supported our immune system and gave us choices. But at a certain point, if we kept on doing it, it brought us into a more honest and intimate relationship with ourselves, and this was not always a relationship we were sure we wanted. So we stopped.

I came away from the interviews with an enormous feeling of gratitude and respect. While on the surface the meditators found it difficult to maintain their practices, beneath this, on a personal level, their struggles were full of insight, bravery, and humor. Even though practicing meditation day after day, week after week, sometimes put them in touch with emotions they would rather not have, they met these with a wonderful honesty, and it made them into people who had far fewer illusions about themselves.

Where I have got to now is not the last word. Sixteen

struggling meditators are interviewed here, all of whom appear with names that they have chosen for themselves. A further thirty-one, also with fictional names, and some who are composites, provide the many examples found throughout the book. To this are added the insights of ten meditation teachers who, between them, represent a broad cross-section of disciplines and traditions: mindfulness-based stress reduction, mindfulness-based cognitive therapy, Theravada Buddhism, three varieties of Tibetan Buddhism, Zen, and, finally, Advaita Vedanta (a contemplative nondual tradition with its roots in Hinduism).

Traditionally, their own meditation has been something that meditation practitioners were not meant to speak about. Fortunately, this taboo now seems to be fading away, and as we talk to each other about our practices, what we discover is that we are not alone in our struggles on our meditation journey and that what each of us has experienced is, when communicated, of great value to others. However challenging things have been on our meditation seat or cushion, once shared they become a generous gift. I hope that as you read this book and compare it with your own experience you will embellish, correct, and contradict, taking up its inquiry and making it your own.

Acknowledgments

A very big thank-you to Imogen Batterham, Lesley Dean, Maddy Eterick, Gaynor Evans, Margaret Graham, Annzella Gregg, Rosamund Harwood, Jacqui Hughes, Laurence Jarosy, Jenny Joyce, Jules Latham, Trish Luckett, Jill McEwan, Bas Verplanken, Steven Webster, and Clive Wilson. Each of you gave with great generosity from your own experience—sometimes easy, sometimes hard—of meditation. You are the riches of this book.

Also thank you to the students who contributed their thoughts and experiences: Jo, Amanda, Harry, Penny, Fran, John, Caroline, Jane, Sophie, Kit, Gwen, Julia, Paul, Linda, Connor, Jim, Molly, Jerry, Peter, Christie, Polly, David, Kay, Kate, Jamie, Eva, Felix, Ian, Lisa, Chris, and Jake. These are not your real names, and some of you are made out of more than one person, but collectively you are a treasure trove of wisdom.

And the teachers: Stephen Batchelor, who reminds us that mindfulness is just one part of a path that is a deep engagement with the whole of our life; Rebecca Crane for her foreword and her insight and kindness; Christina Feldman for her transmission; Peter Harvey, my professor of Buddhist studies, for the memorable names for the hindrances and also for correcting my occasional misrepresentation of Buddhism (Peter, any remaining mistakes are my own); Willem Kuyken for finding me the time, even while his daughters were most rightly insistent for his; Franklyn Sills for being the first to confirm my suspicions; Lama Rabsang for his deep knowledge of practice and lovely warmth; Geshe Tashi Tsering for his humility and saintliness; Tsoknyi Rinpoche, my own teacher, for pointing out the nature of mind—for this there are no words that can capture my gratitude; Philippa Vick, *femme inspirée* and *soror mystica*; and, lastly, Martin Wells, also a mystic and a laugh. Thank you all for your contributions—your presence has not only helped us see more deeply into our meditation but has also demonstrated that we have arrived in a world where the sectarian inclinations of religion, spirituality, and psychology can successfully be put aside. What joins us is far more than what separates us.

Thank you also to Dr. Imogen Batterham and Professor Bas Verplanken for reading through the manuscript and making encouraging and helpful comments; to Dr. Elena Antonova for casting an eye over the neuroscience; to my dear friend Liz McCormick for her reading and enthusiasm for the chapter "The Damaged Heart"; and to Philippa Vick, my wife and partner, who is present throughout the entire book in her ideas, insights, and inspirations. Without her this book could not have happened. Thank you also to Christopher Germer and Professor Paul Gilbert for their support; to Julia Crane and Clare Allen for their patient work of transcribing; and lastly to George Miller, gamekeeper turned poacher who, with his publishing expertise, taught me the dark arts of self-promotion, which ultimately attracted the much-welcomed attention of Anne Lawrance and Jillian Stewart, my editors at Piatkus.

Contributors

Stephen Batchelor studied for eight years under the guidance of Tibetan lamas and completed a three-year Zen training in Korea. A former Buddhist monk, he is the author of *Alone with Others, The Faith to Doubt, The Awakening of the West, Buddhism without Beliefs,* and *Verses from the Centre: A Buddhist Vision of the Sublime.* He is a Gaia House guiding teacher and cofounder of Sharpham College for Buddhist Studies. He teaches worldwide and lives in southwest France. Stephen's most recently published book is *Confession of a Buddhist Atheist.*

Rebecca Crane, MA, directs the Centre for Mindfulness Research and Practice at Bangor University and has led the development of the center's training and research areas since it was founded in 2001. She has been practicing and exploring mindfulness meditation since her early twenties and has a professional background in occupational therapy and counseling. She is a certified mindfulness-based stress reduction (MBSR) teacher with the Center for Mindfulness in Massachusetts and has developed her mindfulness-based cognitive therapy (MBCT) teaching skills through working with Mark Williams and other colleagues since 1998. She has written *Mindfulness-Based Cognitive Therapy* (in the CBT Distinctive Features Series) and has published on mindfulness-based teaching competency and implementation.

Christina Feldman is a cofounder of Gaia House and a guiding teacher. She has been leading insight meditation retreats worldwide since 1976 and is committed to the personal retreat program at Gaia House. She is a guiding teacher of the Insight Meditation Society in Barre, Massachusetts. She is the author of a number of books, including *Woman Awake* and *Way of Meditation*, and coauthor of *Soul Food*. Her recent books include *Silence* and *The Buddhist Path to Simplicity*.

Willem Kuyken, PhD, is professor of clinical psychology and cofounder of the Exeter Mindfulness Network at the University of Exeter in England. His work is focused on mood disorders and evidence-based approaches to mood disorders. The aim is to better understand depression and translate this understanding into cost-effective approaches to preventing and treating it. He has been teaching mindfulness-based cognitive therapy since 2001 and has published on mindfulness mechanisms, clinical trials, and implementation. All of his work is informed by a long-standing personal mindfulness practice in the Vipassana tradition.

Chöje Lama Rabsang is the resident teacher at Palpung Changchub Dargyeling, a Tibetan Buddhist meditation center in Wales. After completion of his own studies, a three-year retreat and a further retreat in India at Palpung Sherabling, he came to Britain in 2001. He now teaches at the center, in the surrounding community, and annually in Finland.

Tsoknyi Rinpoche is a meditation master of the Drukpa Kagyü and Nyingma traditions, living in Nepal and teaching extensively in the West since 1991. His publications include *Open Heart, Open Mind: Awakening the Power of Essence Love, Carefree Dignity: Discourses on Training in the Nature of Mind*, and *Fearless Simplicity: The Dzogchen Way of Living Freely in a Complex World*.

Franklyn Sills is a cofounder of the training organization the Karuna Institute, where he has contributed to the development of a Buddhist, mindfulness-based form of psychotherapy: Core Process Psychotherapy. He has worked as a psychotherapist, lecturer, and meditator for at least thirty-five years and has also helped develop a form of complementary medicine called Craniosacral Biodynamics. He is the author of a number of books, including *Being and Becoming: Psychodynamics, Buddhism, and the Origins of Selfhood* and *Foundations in Craniosacral Biodynamics* volumes one and two.

Geshe Tashi Tsering is the resident Tibetan Buddhist teacher at Jamyang Buddhist Centre, London. Since 1994 he has taught at Buddhist centers in the United Kingdom and around the world, and is the creator and teacher of the Foundation of Buddhist Thought, a two-year correspondence and campus course on the basics of Tibetan Buddhism in the Foundation for the Preservation of the Mahayana (FPMT) tradition.

Philippa Vick is a UK Council on Psychotherapy–registered psychotherapist and MBSR/MBCT teacher and supervisor. Initially an acupuncturist and herbalist, she has been working as a psychotherapist for over twenty years, specializing in trauma and mindfulness-based therapy. In 2006 she started the Bath and Bristol Mindfulness Courses.

Martin Wells is a teaching and supervising transactional analyst who has been studying meditation for over thirty years. He works mostly in the National Health Service in the United Kingdom as a consultant psychotherapist, integrating nondual teachings with mindfulness and psychotherapy. He is the founder of TA ~ Spiritual, which provides training that brings together transactional-analysis psychotherapy and spirituality. He has run retreats in Scotland, India, and Spain.

Something on Buddhist Traditions

I n a largely secular and inclusive book like this one, some compromise on clearly differentiating between one school of Buddhism and another is inevitable. What I have tried to do in those parts that are explicitly Buddhist is always to have in mind the sort of Buddhism I am writing about as I pick my way through the labyrinth of subtleties that is Buddhist thought.

To this end, the majority of the Buddhism here is a direct descendant of the Early Buddhism of the Pali *suttas* and their contemporary representative, Theravada Buddhism. References to the Ānāpānasati Sutta (Teaching on In and Out Breathing) and to the Satipaṭṭhāna Sutta (The Four Foundations of Mindfulness), as well as to the hindrances, factors of enlightenment, and so on, all represent this tradition—one which has entered our culture largely through the Insight Meditation Society founded in 1975 by Joseph Goldstein, Jack Kornfield, and Sharon Salzberg and which has particularly influenced many psychotherapists and psychologists involved in bringing mindfulness to the West.

Alongside this I have also included elements from Mahayana

Buddhism. References to the second-century CE Mahāyāna Mahāparinirvāṇa Sūtra (The Great Teaching on the Final Release), the notions of bodhisattva and the path of the perfections, the union of wisdom and compassion, and so on, all represent quintessential elements of this tradition. While Early Buddhism placed great importance on loving kindness and compassion, it is in Mahayana Buddhism that they are brought to the fore and given particular emphasis.

Lastly, there is a pervasive yet not explicit reference to my own school of Buddhism and its principal teaching, Dzogchen. This shows itself in the definition of "how things really are," an idea we repeatedly return to. While the Early Buddhist answer to this is the "three factors of existence"—impermanence, not self, and suffering—the nondual teaching of Dzogchen speaks of an intrinsic awareness, *rigpa*, that is the unimpeded union of emptiness and clarity in which everything spontaneously arises and disappears. Careful reading of the book will find this beautiful vision throughout.

When we can begin to effortlessly rest in this intrinsic awareness, allowing the contents of our mind to appear and disappear without grasping, aversion, or fear, then we begin to understand the comfort and ease that is at the heart of the practice.

Introduction

It is hard for the ego to direct its attention to perceptions and ideas which it has up till now made a rule of avoiding, or to acknowledge as belonging to itself impulses that are the complete opposite of those which it knows as its own.

SIGMUND FREUD

Awareness requires only that we pay attention and see things as they are. It doesn't require we change anything.

JON KABAT-ZINN

In the end, you're always up against you—you can either do it or you don't. Really I don't know that there's any tricks to be learnt; I think it's a question of wanting to do it.

ELLEN

I am talking with Jo. She has just completed a mindfulness meditation course and has had her first week of practicing alone without the support of the course or us, her teachers. She is feeling rather anxious. She is unsure whether she is doing it "right" and, furthermore, as she practices, the practice itself is throwing up lots of new questions. She asks, "If my mind is full of thoughts that are all emotional, what then?" The sense of rising panic is palpable; she describes her meditation practice as "grungy and chaotic." At this moment, her newly born mindfulness meditation is extremely vulnerable. No longer held within the group, and as yet not strong in itself, it could easily dwindle and die. Somehow, she must find a way to take these first steps on her meditation journey.

Why Can't I Meditate?

This is a book for anyone who is thinking about meditating, who wants to meditate but is finding it hard to start and continue, or who has started but has stopped again. This book is also for any- and everyone who is interested in meditation, whether they are coming at it from something like the Jon Kabat-Zinn eight-week mindfulness course or a broader background like Buddhism or perhaps another contemplative tradition. The reason this book can be so inclusive is that whatever our approach, the problems (and successes) are universal. We all struggle to find something really nourishing in our lives and make space for it on a daily basis. We all struggle with keeping that something going and are disappointed when we do not. We all struggle with just trying to relax—that is, deeply, profoundly relax. So how can we start, particularly when we have already tried but feel we have failed?

Perhaps my greatest qualification for writing this book is my own long struggle with meditation. I have felt rather ashamed of this and have at times believed I am just bad at meditating.

However, in recent years I have been greatly heartened by a deeply experienced meditation teacher. Describing her own practice, she said that you would think she would be good at it after thirty years but, in fact, her mind was just as unruly and full of thoughts as ever. She added, though, that in another way she *has* become good at it because she no longer beats herself up for being who she is. She now just stays happily present with however she finds herself—and nothing more. I find this very comforting; it relieves me of punitive self-expectations and says something really important about the central place of kindness and generosity. It is OK to be me, just as I am right now, and this is the very best place to start from. Actually, it is the *only* place to start from.

My problems with meditation started in my late teens when I first joined a meditation group. I remember sitting on the floor next to my bed in an approximation of a crossed-leg position and concentrating very hard on deep breathing. I probably had my eyes crossed. After numerous uncomfortable attempts I began to feel something a bit odd and fuzzy. It was working! However, I later learned that I was hyperventilating and my "spiritual experience" was nothing more than too much oxygen. Silly as this now seems, it was an excellent introduction, if only I could have understood it. It told me that my desire for an altered state of consciousness was misguided—that I was trying to get away from the experience I was having and escape to something I imagined was better. This common and not unreasonable misunderstanding continued for many years. During the seventies, I pursued my interest in meditation, attending first a challenging ten-day meditation retreat and then later becoming involved with Tibetan Buddhism. However, if I am honest, what I was really interested in was becoming a different person, having different emotions. I wanted something better and identified this as something "spiritual" (while others might want something calmer, happier, or more whole). I thought if I could only meditate like the people I read about, everything would be OK. Yet I found this was not so easy. Sitting down to meditate was never as attractive as doing something else, and when I did sit my mind was full of thoughts that would carry me away into daydreams and fantasies, worries and concerns. And when they were not doing this, I would quickly grow drowsy and fall asleep. My meditation was just as someone described—like being stuffed into a telephone box with a large crowd of people all suffering emotional disturbances. I wanted what meditation promised, but the effort to practice it put me off more often than not. It was boring, frustrating, upsetting and seemed to make little difference.

Finally, this began to reach something of a crisis while I was living in India. Each day, in the little house I had rented, I tried to practice the meditation methods I had been taught. However, as I sat there it felt false and unreal. I could by then go through the motions, but felt I was playacting. I was someone in the guise of a meditator, but it was nothing more than that. Within my mind, all was the same. On the one hand, there was the fantasy that if I could only stop thinking and have some sort of enlightening experience, things would be great. On the other were the niggling doubts—why, if this is so good, is it so hard to do? Why each day do I have to force myself? And why, if I can find anything else to do, will I always do that first? These doubts were shaming as they pointed to the reality that I might value the *idea* of meditation, but something inside of me was deeply unwilling to do it.

Sometimes events provide an answer we cannot come to clearly in our minds. My growing meditation crisis, on reflection, seemed to resolve itself when I finally abandoned it for a while in favor of psychotherapy. I gave it all up and spent many years in the labyrinth of my personal history and the greater labyrinth of psychotherapy training. What I finally learned was that while a spiritual life, and particularly meditation, is not the same as psychotherapy (or counseling or analysis), nor does it have the same goals, there are, nonetheless, places of cross-fertilization. Both disciplines are concerned with the ability to be able to stay with our emotional and mental life without drawing back out of fear. Both seek to reduce suffering. My meditation problems were revealed as psychological ones. I was frightened by my own emotions, the vulnerability of intimacy, commitment to myself and others. Psychotherapy revealed this and unearthed its origins, but meditation—the ability to stay consciously aware of my emotions and thoughts from moment to moment—enabled me to make different choices. Meditation, finally, became a way to be right where I was without wanting to change, to find a kindness toward myself that freed me of the compulsion to run. It also freed me from the tyranny of ideals. I still have all these inclinations—I still am almost as neurotic as ever—but now there is space and humor around them. It is OK not to be perfect.

Subsequently, I have had many conversations with people struggling with the same concerns, particularly since I have started teaching mindfulness-based psychotherapy and a mindfulness-based stress-reduction program. People say that they really like the idea of meditation, but they cannot do it. Either they cannot make themselves stop what they are doing and give themselves a few minutes of meditative space, or they do meditate but cannot keep it going, make it part of their daily routine. Ruth tells me that she gets up every morning with the intention to meditate but finds herself putting on the kettle and clearing up a bit, and before she knows it, she is looking at some schoolwork she has to mark and her day has begun. Ellen has none of these pressures, but despite her desire to meditate she can find nowhere in her house to settle. The bedroom is too "bedroomy," the sitting room is too "full of things." Even the little spare room is no good because her husband's clothes are hanging in it and there is a great big sofa and not the right chair. And then there are the dogs, with their big brown eyes, waiting for their walk! Clara does start a meditation practice, but after a few weeks she becomes disheartened; she wonders whether this particular type of meditation does not suit her—maybe she should try something new or go back to something she tried to practice before? For each of these women, the desire to meditate and to keep it going regularly is real. It is something each of them truly wants. Yet for them, as for many others, something unknown but very powerful within them gets in the way, sabotaging all efforts and causing frustration and disappointment. Rebecca Crane, director at the Centre for Mindfulness Research and Practice at Bangor University, says of this unknown something:

> *What really fascinates me is what brings us to the practice and away from the practice, because we may find it incredibly easy*

*to take to the cushion some days and then there are periods
when it just is not what we want to do. I think that's true for all
the people I've spoken to. In our good practice guidance it's very
clearly there, make a daily practice. But actually, it's like a hidden world: we don't really know what goes on and what people
really do, but we do know that it's not easy.*

In this book I am going to try to understand why we have
these sorts of problems with our meditation and what we can do
to resolve them. While I mainly talk about mindfulness
meditation—the type of meditation that is taught by health
professionals during mindfulness-based stress reduction (MBSR)
and mindfulness-based cognitive therapy (MBCT) courses and
by Buddhism, the home of mindfulness—much of what is in the
following pages is equally true for any form of meditation from
any tradition. This is because the focus is not so much on the
meditation as it is on us, the meditators. I will be looking at
the things each of us finds difficult, and also under the surface
to see why this might be so. In this I am helped by two groups of
people who have generously talked about their experiences either
as struggling meditators or as meditation teachers working with
struggling meditators. In the interviews throughout the book
they talk about what has been hard, why that is, and what has
helped. I hope they will shed light on our places of growth and
also help us to realize that what we find hard is, in all likelihood, found just as hard by everyone else, that it is a rare event
for us to have a struggle someone hasn't had before. So we are
not alone!

Mindfulness Meditation

"Why are we doing this?" Amanda asks. We are at the beginning of an eight-week mindfulness course, and we are talking about turning toward our emotions and allowing ourselves to consciously feel them. "Why would I want to do that when I already feel bad?" she insists. It is a good question. It seems to make no sense to enroll in a course that is supposed to make things easier and then be asked to feel things that are stressful. If this is what it is all about, how can mindfulness meditation make things better?

Understanding how mindfulness works is quite difficult because it is so different from anything else we normally do. When we first hear about it, we tend to wrongly associate it with something we already know—like relaxation classes, for example. Listening to the people who come to the eight-week mindfulness courses, I have learned that it takes quite a long time before we really begin to understand what mindfulness is. The problem is that we naturally want to have a different experience from that which we are currently having: if I feel depressed and anxious, for example, I want it to stop, and coming to the course, I believe, will do this. However, the course says something that is so nonsensical, so counterintuitive, that it is at first even difficult to hear, let alone understand. It says that *to change a painful emotional experience, it is first necessary to turn toward it and experience it fully*. Admittedly, this does sound crazy, and even for many of us who, on the surface, may have accepted this idea for some years, it is possible there remain parts of us that still do not really believe it. And why would we? It sounds like putting a burned finger back in the fire to heal it.

The instructions for practicing mindfulness are simple but not easy. Talking about her own first experience of being taught mindfulness, Pema Chödrön, an extremely skillful and compassionate Buddhist meditation teacher, says she was asked to get comfortable, relax, and then rest her attention on her breath. However, she explains, her actual experience was something quite different: getting comfortable was hard, relaxing intentionally was extremely difficult, and just resting her attention on the breath nearly impossible. After starting, the next thing she remembered was the bell sounding the end of the meditation session. She had spent the entire time carried away by her thoughts—entirely mindless.

Pema Chödrön's experience was by no means exceptional. Most of us are simply not used to placing our attention on our breath or the sensations in our bodies. Not having developed our concentration, our minds immediately wander off, looking for something more stimulating, or we quickly fall asleep. When this happens, we may then think that this is just too hard or that we are particularly poor meditators and imagine that someone else, who is good at meditation, sits perfectly still in a relaxed, thought-free, calm state. Attractive as this fantasy is, it is just that—a fantasy. Mindfulness meditation is all about working with an unruly mind: the mind that goes to sleep, seeks distractions, and has all sorts of disturbing and frightening thoughts and emotions. Mindfulness, as strange as this may seem, is not about escaping from our emotions and thoughts but is designed specifically to take us right up to the edge of everything we want to get away from and enable us to stay there comfortably and without fear.

Present, Accepting, Seeing Things as They Really Are

There is a story about a much-loved meditation teacher who died in the early 1970s. Together with his students, he went to start some building work at the top of a hill in the mountains of California. Parking at the bottom, they began their long walk up and eventually reached the top to find that no one had brought the shovel they would need to perform their task. The students started blaming each other and a quarrel broke out—they had come a long way and it was hot. In the meantime, on seeing they had left the shovel behind, the teacher immediately turned round and began to walk back down to the car to fetch it. He just did what was necessary—he went back to get the shovel.

This little story—myth or otherwise—illustrates the three key components of being mindful:

- Mindfulness is being consciously aware of what is happening inside us and around us in the present moment. Here, the meditation teacher saw clearly what was happening in the immediate situation around him. He was undistracted by his students' squabble or what had just happened and did what was needed there and then. This is also called "being present"—being present with our experience just as it is—or sometimes "bare attention." Applying bare attention is to be attentive and nothing more.

- Mindfulness is accepting what we experience without picking or choosing, without judgments about right or wrong, good or bad. Being present and accepting the situation as it is, the teacher simply does what is necessary without adding anything else. His own emotions—perhaps being irritated that it has happened, wanting it to be different, wishing he was somewhere else with more mindful students—are all met with an attitude of nonjudgment and kindness, noticed and let go.

- Mindfulness sees things as they really are. When we no longer cloak our immediate experience with reactive thoughts and emotions we begin to see things as they really are. This sounds rather grand, but it is actually simple: everything, including ourselves, is interconnected and continuously changing. When we resist this it causes suffering. When we can go with the flow we find freedom and ease. Later Buddhism puts this in another way, saying that suffering comes to an end once mindfulness reveals that all our thoughts and emotions, everything we believe ourselves to be, happen within the sphere of awareness that is in itself spacious, clear, and compassionate—our basic awakened nature. Knowing all this, as a real living experience, the teacher is free of conflict.

Formal Meditation: Our Root Practice

Learning to be mindfully present, accepting and seeing things as they really are, is best cultivated during a daily formal mindfulness meditation practice. This means setting some time aside each day, preferably at the same time of day, to practice being mindful. Essentially, when we practice mindfulness we usually choose something to rest our conscious awareness on that is called an "object of mindfulness" or sometimes an "object of meditation." This could be sound, our breath, our physical or emotional sensations, our thoughts, or even awareness itself. Of course, as many of us who have tried this know, what happens next is that we suddenly become aware that we have been distracted by memories, thoughts, and fantasies that have carried us off in a chain of associations. Returning to the present, we realize that perhaps after only one or two breaths we have been away somewhere else. However, the good news is that being mindful is to remember to come back to the present and that awareness is our default position. This means that for however long we are absent, we always come back to where we are, that there has never been a person who sat down to practice mindfulness who forgot forever what they were doing. Rather, after some time we think, "Oh yes, I'm being mindful of my breathing." And then we continue until the next distraction and repeat the process. Jack Kornfield, an insight meditation teacher who has been giving meditation instruction since the 1970s, says we have to be prepared to do this *thousands* of times. The point is not that we are trying to stop thinking, particularly, but rather that we are training in remembering and coming back. Thus the practice of mindfulness meditation *includes* thinking. The whole process is being present with, say, the breath, realizing we have drifted off, and then remembering to return. Every part of it is the practice. Difficult as it is to believe, the thinking part is not wrong. Sean, having completed the eight-week course and then subsequently attended many evenings of group mindfulness practice, surprisingly came out with the belief that he should have no thoughts while he was meditating. Where had he got this from? At no time had he been asked to try to achieve this, nor had he been told that it was something to aim for. Quite simply, he had made it up and turned it into an impossible goal. The point is, we all drift off; otherwise we could not practice remembering to come back.

Motivation

We start our daily practice of mindfulness by making our motivation conscious. Many years ago my own meditation teacher said that the first step on the path is to know why we want to start meditating. I understood this to mean that I should ask myself what I wanted to get out of it. Now, quite a long time on, I feel I have part of the answer to this question: like everyone else, I want to feel better, less driven and less scared; I want something meaningful in my life. Traditionally, Buddhism has answered this question by talking about finding out "how things really are." We enter the meditation hall because by finding out how things really are we will begin to calm and resolve the difficult and painful aspects of our life. Buddhism also says that the motivation to know the truth of things can be on two levels: we can find out just for ourselves or for everyone else as well—so I see my mindfulness meditation as something that can help me personally but can also help others. Again, from my experience, I have observed that most of us start off with the more limited motivation. It is generally our own suffering that motivates us, rather than that of others. However, I think it is also true that as we come to know what hurts us and no longer shy away from it but become capable of staying with our vulnerability, we also become aware that the same things hurt others too. Knowing this then leads naturally to a deeper sympathy with those around us and the wish that they too should not suffer. When this realization dawns, Buddhism says, we have begun to become a bodhisattva, a person who practices mindfulness for the well-being of all sentient beings. We could also say we have begun moving beyond our own narcissism and into a greater community spirit.

Peter Harvey, a meditation teacher in the Theravada tradition at the Samatha Trust and a Buddhist scholar, says that by starting with just five minutes of meditation a day and working up to forty, we may increase our calm and awareness, become more patient, better with ups and downs, more clearheaded and energetic, more open, confident, and authoritative. This is my experience also. Participants in the eight-week mindfulness courses regularly report a growing ability to be present with their difficult emotions, finding a means to be with themselves in a more open and accepting way, no longer so self-denigrating and critical. This has often surprised me, as these changes seem to have come about with very little mindfulness practice. It is perhaps the first insight in a group that learns mindfulness together: we realize that the hard time we have been giving ourselves for being especially and uniquely useless is exactly the same hard time everyone else has been giving themselves for the same thing. In this way, quite naturally, our motivation to find something that helps ourselves opens out to something bigger, something that clearly sees that we are all in the same boat and could all do with some help.

Kindness and Compassion

Those who have attended our eight-week mindfulness courses often mention how important the emphasis on acceptance, kindness, and compassion was for them. Harry says, laughing, that however puny and faltering his attempts to meditate have been, the course has always provided something encouraging to build on. It is as if many of us have never received complete, positive support for our efforts, and entering a course in which one of the premises is that there is more right with us than wrong comes as a big (and welcome) surprise.

Along with kindness and compassion also comes generosity. This is particularly necessary when we feel our meditation is failing or if we have started meditating and then stopped. At these moments it is all too easy to feel self-critical and shamed, two very negative and corrosive emotions. That we should feel worse as a result of something that is about making things better seems all wrong, and when this happens it helps to find a generosity of spirit that can say, "Yes, we all wobble and stop in our practice, but that does not mean I cannot start again." Being compassionate, understanding of our common frailties and extending kindness toward ourselves when we need support is the feeling atmosphere in which mindfulness flourishes. In fact, it would not be too extreme to say that the struggle to meditate is, at times, so hard that it forces us to be kind and compassionate toward ourselves and that this is one of its biggest benefits. It also requires a sense of humor.

Sources of Mindfulness

We can now learn mindfulness from a variety of different sources, some secular, some Buddhist, and some from other contemplative traditions that have adopted it. Mindfulness-based stress reduction (MBSR) teaches us that what makes the stresses in our life particularly damaging is how we mismanage them. The tendency to resist or willfully ignore our situation, misperceive and have fixed ideas about who we are and the reality we inhabit, is slowly replaced with mindfulness and the attitudes associated with it: nonjudgment, patience, beginner's mind, trust, nonstriving, acceptance, and letting go. These begin to help us disengage from our established destructive coping mechanisms—ways of surviving that come with great physical and emotional costs. Once we are more mindful, we can then integrate this into daily life, bringing mindfulness into our communication with others, particularly when stressful, and into the choices we make about what is important for us. Finally, the vision of MBSR is a radical reorientation of how we engage with our lives. As Jon Kabat-Zinn says:

> The ultimate promise of mindfulness is much larger, much more profound, than simply cultivating attentiveness. It helps us understand that our conventional view of ourselves and even what we mean by "self" is incomplete in some important ways. Mindfulness helps us to recognize how and why we mistake the actuality of things for some story we create. It then makes it possible for us to chart a path toward greater sanity, well-being, and purpose.

Mindfulness-based cognitive therapy (MBCT) specifically targets the experience of recurrent depression, though in practice its value extends well beyond this narrower remit. It teaches how destructive and unrecognized patterns of thinking and acting can be lifted into consciousness. These patterns are experienced as depression, anxiety, and a dissatisfaction with who we are and what we are doing, and by mindfully noticing them we have a choice to do something different, something less harmful. Breathing mindfully gives us an alternative way to be in ourselves, the refuge of a "breathing space": a place where instead of being enmeshed in emotional reactivity to unwanted situations we are more accepting of our experience as it is. In this way we recognize that thoughts are just thoughts, that they are fleeting events that pass through our awareness. When this is practiced over an extended period, within an atmosphere of kindness and compassion, it produces well-being and the ability to choose what heals. Like MBSR, the final goal of MBCT is profound, as its creators, Zindel Segal, Mark Williams, and John Teasdale, say: "The ultimate aim of the MBCT program is to help individuals make a radical shift in their relationship to the thoughts, feelings, and body sensations that contribute to depressive relapse."

Buddhism is the original home of mindfulness. It was first practiced almost two and a half thousand years ago. Buddhism's starting point is the observation that our experience is full of many different types of unsatisfactory and painful experiences, many of which we bring upon ourselves by the way we think and act. It seeks to alleviate this unhappiness by finding a place of calm fearlessness in the midst of conflicting and reactive emotions and establishing a deep insight into the true nature of reality. Being mindfully present with whatever arises, experiencing it with equanimity, acceptance, nonidentification, kindness, and compassion, develops the wisdom to see things as they really are, not just as they appear to be, and with this understanding comes the end of suffering.

Calm and Insight

What is now generally called "mindfulness meditation" is, in fact, a combination of two types of meditation that in Buddhism are always practiced in tandem: calm abiding (*samatha*) and insight (*vipassanā*). The Buddha is said to have achieved his awakening by these combined means, and although they have been much embellished during the evolution of Buddhist meditation, all schools of Buddhism still use this original template in one way or another. The basic idea is that when we concentrate gently and patiently upon one thing the mind becomes still and pleasurably calm. Once the mind has acquired this skill it can then be used to look deeply into the mind itself, and this will give insight into how things really are—which is the "purpose" of meditation. We could think of this as holding a glass of murky water. While it is agitated it remains murky, but when held still it calms down, and as the murk settles, it becomes clear. There are slightly different accounts of this process, depending on who is teaching mindfulness. Traditionally, the discussion has emphasized the need to calm the mind before we begin to practice insight meditation. The consensus seems to be that we need to achieve a sufficiently calm and steady attention that will then enable insight to become possible. This is sometimes achieved by practicing concentration until the mind stills and then changing over to whatever style of insight meditation our tradition teaches. However, it is equally common to find (reflecting the earliest teaching) that the two practices are done simultaneously. Here each practice balances the other: our calm and concentrated mind supporting our insight and our insight facilitating deeper levels of calm. In this way of seeing things, calm and insight are two sides of the same practice, each supporting the other to reach their final destination: the end of conflicted and turbulent emotions and ignorance of how things really are.

There is also the slightly confusing issue of whether mindfulness plays a part in the cultivation of both concentration and insight. The answer to this seems to depend on how we understand mindfulness. The earliest teaching is clear that mindfulness is at the heart of both calm-abiding and insight meditations. When our minds wander, it is mindfulness that remembers to recall us to our practice.

However, in some later traditions mindfulness has become associated with insight meditation alone and is used as a synonym for it: mindfulness meditation = insight meditation. Furthermore, in some traditions, mindfulness has also become linked with a quality of nondual awareness and is called "innate mindfulness" because it need no longer be maintained through intention. Entirely relaxed, this "kingly mindfulness" just minds itself.

For those of us who have learned mindfulness through MBSR, MBCT, or a similar approach, the relationship of calm-abiding and insight meditation will not be an issue. While probably not being mentioned, both will be present and in conjunction. In the eight-week mindfulness course, two of the principal practices are a body scan, which is frequently associated with insight meditation, and mindfulness of breathing, which, when practiced, develops both. Furthermore, the subjects we explore in each of the sessions—such as "not buying into our story," "thoughts are not facts," and the driven and impermanent nature of emotions—are all deeply related to the issue of how things really are.

Given that the heart of all this is becoming more able to remain present with experience as it presents itself to us—mindful of our thoughts, emotions, and sensations—it seems that the only real difference in the *practice* of calm and insight meditation is the emphasis. If the emphasis is on deepening concentration, then it is the path of calm. But if it is about recognizing that everything in me is always changing, that this also includes what I call "me," and that when I try to resist this change it hurts, then it is insight. What comes out for me, here, is the importance of recognizing that our drifting away and remembering to come back is the core of the practice: being present with whatever we are experiencing, with a kind and compassionate acceptance, while seeing how things are fluid and changing and relaxing in the flow. (See "Something on Buddhist Traditions," page xxvii), for a little more about this.)

Informal Meditation: Integration

Mindfulness is a way of relating to ourselves and the world around us, and with practice it can slowly become something that is always present. This integration of mindfulness into our daily lives is called "informal meditation," and it depends upon the roots of our formal meditation practice to feed it and help it grow. Those who have come to mindfulness through an eight-week course will remember at the end of the first evening being invited to bring mindfulness to a small daily task such as brushing teeth or eating a meal. This is the first step in integrating the mindfulness cultivated during formal practice into our lives. In this book almost the entire emphasis is on our formal sitting practice: how we get it started, established, resolve its problems, and encourage it to grow. This is because without the foundation of formal meditation it is unlikely that we will successfully begin to really solidly establish mindfulness within the relentlessly busy lives we lead, and the deep habit of working on automatic pilot will remain intact. However, this is not to diminish the importance of informal meditation practices (such as the three-minute breathing space taught in MBSR and MBCT courses) that help us integrate mindfulness into our day. Getting the balance right is very helpful. For our mindfulness to really grow and prosper, it needs to be replenished daily by our sitting meditation. However, if we do this and only this, it will not become part of our everyday existence. So we need to stitch our practice into the fabric of our life, learning how to be present with ourselves, moment to moment, on our meditation seat and off.

How This Book Unfolds

Chapter 1, "Why Do We Want to Meditate?," asks an important question for each of us to find the answer to. Some motivations are profoundly helpful, while others can stop our meditation practice in its tracks. Being motivated to remain mindfully present with our chaotic minds and difficult emotions is often hard, but once we begin to feel the benefits of this, our practice becomes more self-sustaining.

Chapter 2, "Taking Our Seat," concerns the practical issues of starting and maintaining a meditation practice: creating a routine, choosing a time to practice and for how long, fitting in around family, finding a place to sit, and making a ritual. It also invites us to clarify for ourselves exactly what method we are practicing.

Chapter 3, "The Guardian at the Gate," looks at the distractions we experience when we begin to meditate. They may be because we are unused to trying to concentrate for sustained periods of time, but they can also be because they defend us against going close to thoughts and emotions we do not want to feel. Defenses are not bad, but maintaining them once they are unnecessary works against us.

Chapter 4, "Meeting Ourselves," explores what might be going on behind our defenses. We are primarily emotional beings who, when threatened, respond by grasping, resisting, or cutting off. We increase our unhappiness when we attack ourselves for being who we are, which introduces several different ways of understanding why we seem so divided within ourselves. This all points toward patterns of hurt accumulated during childhood that may be unconsciously affecting our ability to meditate. Finally, there is the suggestion that we unknowingly sense that our meditation threatens our sense of self and this is why we hesitate to practice.

Chapter 5, "Grabby, Grumpy, Sleepy, Jumpy, and Maybe," takes the Buddhist notion of the five hindrances and uses it to understand in detail why our meditation may not be working and exactly what to do about it. You'll find lots of practical suggestions here.

Chapter 6, "A Deeper Insight," is a longer chapter. Sometimes when our meditation gets really stuck, it may be because something in our personal history is keeping it locked. Traditionally, Buddhism has paid little attention to our personal stories, but sometimes it can be invaluable to understand our psychological history, so we can identify if there is something about meditation that is threatening us and causing an "amygdala meltdown" (see pages 209–11). When this is the case, we can work with it by "acknowledging, doing something different, and doing it again"—a three-stage way to heal our traumas and get back on track.

Kindness and compassion provide the essential atmosphere in which mindfulness prospers. In chapter 7, "The Damaged Heart," we look at why these may sometimes be too painful to directly approach. We consider our first experience of love and the barriers that grow up around it and also wounds to the heart that we receive from life. Finally, we have no choice but to open to kindness and compassion because they naturally flow as our practice of mindfulness unfolds.

Chapter 8, "It's Not All Pain," reminds us that mindfulness is not all sitting with what is difficult and painful. We can face what scares us and find the courage to be fully present with what we experience. Joy, happiness, contentment, calm, and many other deeply healing experiences all flow from our mindfulness practice.

Chapter 9, "Final Words": beyond our meditation practice is a wider path that takes the insights found through meditation and weaves them into wise and compassionate interactions with those around us and the world in which we live. Whether we decide to formally meditate or not, this ethical and meaningful engagement can still be at the center of our life.

How to Use This Book

As you read each chapter, you will find accounts of the problems and the solutions that ordinary meditators have worked with. I hope these will make it clear that our difficulties are really the essential part of the practice and that we all struggle in the same way. Alongside these personal accounts are suggestions and observations from meditation teachers representing each of the secular and Buddhist mindfulness traditions. Some are psychologists, some Buddhists, some both.

In each chapter you will also find exercises that help make the material more personal. These exercises combined may show us what our resistance to meditation has been about. They give us insight into the defenses and barriers that protect us from feeling the pain of difficult emotional experiences from our past. In this way we may be able to answer for ourselves the question, why can't I meditate? I can't meditate because . . .

Lastly, there are many specific strategies we can use to put our practice back on track once what has been blocking us has been identified. These are scattered throughout the book but are found primarily in chapters 5, 6, and 7. However, to make this as simple as possible, the single most important thing is learning to identify our "felt sense," our emotions as felt in our bodies, and to stay mindfully present with them. From this, all else can open. (Instructions for this are found on pages 143–47.)

At the back of the book you will find a "Quick-Fix Chart for the Struggling Meditator," where (hopefully) you can diagnose your meditation problem and find a solution. And if you have yet to learn mindfulness meditation, you'll find instructions on how to begin (see page 341), but bear in mind that you will need a live teacher at some stage.

Much of this book is about turning toward emotions that may have their origins in our past. I have tried to find and offer a variety of ways we can help ourselves understand and become freer and more at ease with these feelings. However, it may be that in some instances we can benefit from being accompanied, for at least part of our journey, by a wise and compassionate counselor or psychotherapist. Seeing ourselves is always hard, and it is particularly hard to see things we have been avoiding looking at for a long time. Therapy may have some usefulness here, supporting being present with our experience just as it is, from moment to moment, and with great kindness. This is not to say that therapy is always necessary, but rather that it is an optional and valuable resource that can help if needed. I say more about this in "On Mindfulness and Psychological Trauma" (see page 339).

Not Losing Heart

And finally, as you read this book you may sometimes feel your heart sinking as we look a little deeper into the often unknown and hidden emotions that make practicing meditation occasionally hard. All of us feel this at times, and it can all seem just too difficult and complicated. If this happens, try not to let yourself become disheartened. Meeting ourselves is not always easy, but it is extraordinarily worthwhile, bringing into our lives a greater understanding of who we are and an emotional spaciousness and well-being. To be reading this means you have already come a very long way.

Calming Our Anxious Minds—Just Five Breaths

As you read the pages of this book, you will find a great deal about the problems we all face when practicing mindfulness meditation. This could perhaps be a little disheartening, and so it helps to remember that, even for the most novice meditator, finding a way to calm an anxious and agitated mind is actually entirely possible and only five conscious breaths away. This is how:

Rest your attention on your breath and simply follow it as you breathe in and out for five breaths. Let the breath be as relaxed as possible, so you can feel that it breathes itself in and out without you having to do anything to help. It will naturally slow and deepen, but this is its job, not yours. And stick to just five breaths—resist doing more.

Introduction: Key Points

- This is a book for those of us who are thinking about meditating, who want to meditate but are finding it hard to start and continue, or who have started but have stopped again.
- This book focuses more on the meditator than the meditation and so goes beyond any one tradition.
- Mindfulness is initially difficult to understand, as it asks us counterintuitively to turn toward what we would prefer to avoid.
- Mindfulness practice is
  - *– being present with our experience in each moment;*
  - *– meeting this with acceptance, kindness, and compassion;*
  - *– seeing the true nature of how things really are without adding anything extra.*
- We practice mindfulness during formal meditation sessions each day, preferably at the same time. Being fully present with our experience, moment to moment, includes distractions. These are not something to be fought against but are an essential part of the path.
- We need to know what motivates us—the personal motivation of helping ourselves and the wider motivation of helping others as well.
- Kindness, compassion, generosity, and humor are all essential for our meditation to prosper and grow.
- Mindfulness may be learned in a variety of ways; here

we focus on MBSR, MBCT, and Buddhism, but there are others.

- Mindfulness is the key component in the union of calm and insight meditation, which together create an unwavering attention that enables insight into how things really are.

- Mindfulness is something we bring to the whole of our lives. Through our daily formal meditation, we begin to integrate mindfulness into everyday activities.

- Along with many personal stories and ideas, this book offers exercises that show how what was once felt as a problem may, when approached mindfully, become a gift. So take heart!

CHAPTER 1

Why Do We Want to Meditate?

We think it's easy to be at peace with our own mind and body, our own emotional world, and yet apparently it is not.

CHRISTINA FELDMAN

People come because they're struggling with themselves and their experience in some way. The learning process asks us to turn towards the very things we really don't want to take a look at—because that's where the reactive patterns that we're struggling with are happening, and if we don't take a look there, then we haven't got a starting place.

REBECCA CRANE

Yesterday I dropped off towards the end of the forty minutes and felt a bit cross with myself. You just have to accept that really, don't you?

SAM

What moves us to start practicing mindfulness meditation? Motivation is at the heart of our practice; it gives us the enthusiasm, the vision, the impetus to start and then keep going, even when it becomes difficult. For those of us who approach mindfulness through MBSR and MBCT roots (see page 16), it is likely that our motivation may be explicitly linked to our need to heal stress, anxiety, and depression. For those who approach it through Buddhism, the desire for a spiritual path may be more present. Traditionally, Buddhism has seen motivation at two levels. The first is a personal motivation, wanting to make our own lives better, while the second, more altruistically, is the desire to help everyone else as well. Whatever the approach, our own suffering lies at the center and is the universal starting point—whether the very apparent suffering of mental and physical unhappiness or the more subtle yet equally profound pain of spiritual longing.

Starting Out

When we first start out, it seems that our motivation is quite clear and simple. We feel something is wrong with us and we want to change it. This "wrongness" comes in many forms. Rebecca Crane, director at the Centre for Mindfulness Research and Practice at Bangor University, highlights depression, chronic pain, and stress:

> Many of the people who come on our eight-week courses are motivated because they want something in their lives to be better. They don't want to get depressed again, or they want to find a better way of working with pain, or they want to manage "overwhelm" at work, all of these sorts of things. There's a kind of hook that people arrive with and it's a really good starting place; it's a great motivator.

Asked what originally motivated them, a whole variety of reasons are forthcoming from people who have been through the courses we teach. Ellen says:

There is a longing not to do the busy busy. Busyness in one's life isn't the answer, especially as I'm in the last decade of my life. Really I suppose that one wants to get to the essence of one's self and be true to one's self.

And Ann:

I suppose I must have been looking for something, but I wasn't aware what it was I was looking for. I think I was looking for a way to be calmer and less reactive. I've always had problems with my daughter, well, since she was in her late teens, and I can remember one morning when she was living at home, thinking, "Right, I'm going to be calm; I'm going to try to meditate," and then encountering her in the kitchen and exploding. So I think it was an attempt to gain some control over myself. Over my emotions and reactions. I think that's maybe it.

Ann's desire for less emotional reactivity and a greater sense of calm is shared by most of us as we struggle with busy lives. Sam says of this:

I had some notion of getting my mind into order I suppose, and I was attracted to the idea that you could find some sort of stillness through meditation. I suppose the whole idea of calming thoughts down and reaching some still, inward point appealed to me. Of course, then I realized it wasn't as easy as all that.

For some, it takes something painful to motivate them: loss of job security, a relationship breaking down, perhaps someone dying. Traditionally, these liminal events are seen as a gateway into a deeper relationship with ourselves—a threshold where events require that we stretch. For Ben, it was a divorce:

> *When I separated and divorced from my wife, I realized that I needed to work hard on myself, that there were all sorts of reasons to sit down and see where I was. I did some sessions with a therapist, but I wasn't happy with that. I realized that I needed something to work with on myself. I needed a tool.*

For others, it is not so much outer events that initiate meditation practice as psychological problems—feeling overwhelmed, experiencing chronic misery, never being able to settle, feeling socially inadequate—the list is almost endless. Nicky talks about her experience of recurrent depression and how this led her to do a mindfulness meditation course:

> *This is probably the third or fourth time I've suffered from depression for a length of time. . . . Well, I think I've probably been depressed for quite a lot of my life really, but not noticed it . . . or maybe I fight it most of the time, . . . I'd had another episode of depression, and I think I've always sort of known what's good for me but never done it. People had suggested meditation to me before, but I never thought it was the right thing for me; then my counselor thought it would be good and, unlike the past when I had felt resistance, it obviously was just the right thing to do at the right time. I don't think I've ever thought of doing a course as such. I'd been to the Buddhist meditating thing in town, and I'd done guided meditations with people. But I suppose it was just the right time for me to do it,*

*and I knew what was good for me and I needed the course just
to keep me focused.*

Nicky's experience is in no way exceptional. Depression is
almost endemic in our society as we struggle to survive in a
world that at times becomes alien and threatening. For many of
us, having tried a variety of "cures," we reach a point where we
have nowhere else to turn except back toward ourselves. Willem
Kuyken, professor of clinical psychology and cofounder of the
Exeter Mindfulness Network at the University of Exeter, says
of this:

> *I think with recurrent depression, the reason people take up
> mindfulness is because the other option is to repeatedly be
> dragged into depression involuntarily. They've tried running,
> they've tried hiding, they've tried antidepressants, they've tried
> CBT [cognitive behavioral therapy], they've tried changing
> marriage, they've tried changing country, and they're still faced
> with their stuff. So we've got to do something different, right? So
> if somebody says, "Well, come and just sit in here and let's look
> and see whether actually it is what you think it is; we'll just stay
> with this and . . . actually these are just thoughts . . . these are
> just experiences," then we are willing to have a go.*

However, even motivations as powerful as these, from a
mindfulness point of view, have a hidden danger if they set up a
goal that we must then achieve or fail. Put another way: we need
to be motivated by some powerful need to get started and keep
going, but when we start practicing, we must, during each

mindfulness meditation session, let this need go. If we do not, we are in danger of damaging our mindfulness before it is established, by looking for the fruit before the plant has even begun to grow. Wanting to feel better is fine, but checking whether we feel fine yet, every time we practice mindfulness, will only take us away from being present with how we actually are, now, to the hope that we might be better in the future. Tess describes this tension; starting out on her practice she discovered that her motivation to make things "sorted" and "perfect" was, in fact, a hindrance to being present with her experience just as it was—that her motivation had become a goal that worked against her.

> I'd had psychotherapy for several years and found it messy and hard work, but it was very good at the same time. But then when it ended I found I actually needed something else as a focus that made me return to myself, rather than being out there, struggling. . . . Then I read a book by Pema Chödrön, called The Wisdom of No Escape, and that was like, "Ah! Yeah—that's what I'm trying to do!" She named my always looking for things that are actually a way of escaping the reality of how things really are, my always wanting things to be different. It's true. I'm always wanting things to be different. I don't want it to be like it is now. I want it to be like everything is sorted—this perfect thing.

Tess's story is not so very different from just about everyone else's. We all want to feel better, more happy, more at ease with ourselves and other people. While this makes a powerful motivator for change, it also is one of the things that our mindfulness meditation reveals as a subtle nonacceptance of ourselves. Wanting to be different means we do not want to be who we are now. Mindfulness enables us to recognize this and turn toward ourselves with greater kindness and acceptance. Here there is something about getting the balance right. Rebecca Crane again:

> *If our motivation is an idea of how things should be, an idea of a future possibility where I'll be able to manage my pain in a beautiful, kind, and peaceful way, then this really gets in the way of being able to sense into our experience just as it is, in this moment. However, I also feel that we would never sit on the cushion if we didn't have a motivation. So it isn't a question of throwing motivations out of the window, but more a question of holding them in a light-touch way.*

Holding our motivations lightly—not letting them obscure being accepting and present with our experience just as it is—may enable them to change and evolve. Rebecca continues:

> *I think there's also a thing about motivation evolving as we stay with the practice. The sorts of motivations that bring us into an eight-week course, that are often things around wanting something in everyday life to be better or more easy or less stressful, remain things that get us onto the cushion perhaps for the rest of our lives. But I also sense that they're eventually not enough—that our motivation inevitably shifts as we've been with the practice over time. For people who have been practicing for a longer period of time, mindfulness becomes embedded within them as a way of being; there's a congruence between*

the practice and their core beliefs about their views about life, their world and the nature of things. So it actually is in synchrony with the whole person. It's no longer a kind of an add-on to make one aspect of your life a little bit more easy.

Acceptance

Acceptance is to see things as they really are in the present. It is the opposite of denying what is, wanting things to be different, or resisting things as they are. When we accept ourselves as we are in our meditation, we are present with whatever our experience is—physical sensations, thoughts, and emotions—without the intention of changing it for something we believe will feel better. By being accepting of what is, we see that it is always changing.

Acceptance does not mean having to like what we experience, nor is it a passivity that means we'll never change anything. By accepting what is, we place ourselves in the best position for making wise changes. Acceptance makes space for the most appropriate actions.

Acceptance does not mean that we drift into unconscious indifference to our meditation, either allowing ourselves to be continuously caught up in a torrent of thinking or sliding along dull, sleepy, and disengaged. Mindfulness is awareness of where we are in our meditation and leads us back kindly to our object of mindfulness. Mindfulness is noticing when we have lost acceptance and have fallen into unhelpful judgments.

Approaching Ourselves Differently

In the eight-week mindfulness course, there is often a marked difference in the emotional atmosphere in the room between the first and second weeks. The first week feels exciting; we are keen to get started and are full of expectations that this will help us. However, when we return a week later, having been invited to practice the body scan meditation daily for six consecutive days, many of us feel we have taken on more than we can manage, and doubts have crept in that perhaps this is not for us after all. It is the same if our introduction to meditation has been through Buddhism or another contemplative tradition. Exciting as these teachings initially sound, the experience of putting them into practice on our meditation cushion or seat is often at first difficult and depressing. It just seems so hard to place our attention on one thing and have it stay there. We quickly realize that there is a big difference between the *idea* of meditating and the actual *experience* of having a go. When this discrepancy is particularly significant and shows no sign of changing, our original motivation may be threatened. We may want to give up.

Tess's experience above brings out this deep paradox in mindfulness meditation: we start out with the hope that in the future we will feel better, but if we are to practice mindfulness, it will mean accepting ourselves just as we find ourselves in the present moment, giving up the whole enterprise of self-improvement. Furthermore, we must accept parts of ourselves that we would like to get rid of—our out-of-control mind and difficult, conflicting emotions. In fact, mindfulness intentionally turns us toward these parts of ourselves, making them more conscious, more apparent. It is rather like the fairy tale "Beauty and the Beast." Beauty would do anything to get away from the Beast she has been married to, and it is only when she starts to make a relationship with him, to accept and then love what she first felt was ugly and frightening, that he transforms into what is most valuable. Willem Kuyken says of this self-confrontation and acceptance:

> *Why would one voluntarily go into a room where the wallpaper says things like "You're a defective human being," "People don't love you," all that kind of stuff. I can really see how that wallpaper, that kind of mindscape, is not a very nice place to inhabit, so why would you want to inhabit it?*

Rebecca Crane describes this journey of acceptance as being "counterintuitive"—quite the opposite of our normal and largely unconscious inclination to protect ourselves against feeling anything bad or difficult:

> *It's very hard to sit with our experience; it's just very counterintuitive. Our instinct is to want to retreat from feeling the intensity of our experience. All of our instincts take us in the opposite direction. This shows up in many ways.*
>
> *Many people describe that they're too busy to practice, saying that forty-five minutes is too long. My sense of this is that often, when you begin to inquire what's really happening, you find there's a challenge in shifting mode. If we're into the busyness of our everyday life, shifting gear and settling into*

being just present with our experience, rather than into the forward thrust of our lives, is a really challenging shift. It's counterinstinctive—it's not what we're hardwired to do. We're hardwired, somehow, to be on the move, to be moving away from much of what we experience. So my sense is, it's not always the length of the practice that's the challenge; it's that switch that's really challenging—to actually make that move in our lives to say, "This is what I'm going to do right now." Many students say, "There were choices that I had last evening: I could watch TV. I could lie on my bed and eat chocolate. I could have a long bath, I could hang out with my partner or my kids." All of those things, actually, in the moment, are more attractive options than taking one's seat on the cushion and observing the interplay of experience as it is arising. So just in the immediate term, given the choice, it's often a bit of a no-brainer. What's more pleasant? All of those other things are much more pleasant.

Ellen, a meditator who has had a long struggle to start her practice, describes what happens in her mind when she comes up against the resistance that Rebecca describes. Right at the beginning of her journey she only has a faltering belief that meditation will help her, which is no match against a much stronger inclination not to do it:

I start off with the best of intentions. It's almost as if I'm waiting for a switch to be thrown, but you do it or you don't do it. I hope all the advice and encouragement will help, but then when I come to do it, it doesn't. I think I need to convince myself that

*it will be to my advantage, if that's the right word. That it would
be more beneficial to do it than not—like not drinking or not
eating too much butter or not smoking.*

Ellen's "switch" is not "thrown" that easily. Perhaps she intuits that her mindfulness may bring her into a relationship with herself that she is ambivalent about having.

Being with ourselves can sometimes be difficult. We live in a world of increasing distractions, where if we choose, we need never be entirely alone and still. Christina Feldman, meditation teacher and a founder of Gaia House Buddhist Meditation Retreat Centre, talks about this:

Mindfulness meditation is the most difficult, the most challenging, experience for many people because it is the only moment in their lives when they actually sit with their own mind-body-heart process in an unobstructed way—when this process is not always camouflaged by their life, by life distractions, by habits, by all the ways that we order our world to ensure that we feel the most pleasant, the least unpleasant, experience where we feel most in control. When people sit or walk with themselves in silence, so many layers of that camouflage are just put to one side, and people discover they're not that comfortable or at ease in their own skin, with everything that is going on there. It's sometimes almost a startling, even horrifying, awareness that comes into being, of just how chaotic their minds are—how habitual and obsessive their thinking can be, and how difficult, how challenging, it is just to feel at ease in silence, in simplicity, in aloneness. Essentially, that aloneness is something people don't always know what to do with, except knowing that it feels uncomfortable. I notice sometimes people pose the question, why is meditation so difficult? Why is the practice so difficult? I think this is the wrong question. Rather, it's, why is there so much difficulty in just being with myself, just being with this mind and body and everything it does? And I think when people ask that question, then they start looking at some of their habits of a lifetime: their reactivity, their impulsiveness, their tumultuous thoughts—a lack of inner peace essentially. We think it's easy to be at peace with our own mind and body, our own emotional world, and yet apparently it is not.

Tess's experience shows just how frightening this can be. Coming from a family that believed her grandmother to be insane, she feared that her mindfulness practice would reveal seeds of the same in her.

Wanting things to be different, I was aware that my thoughts would dwell on the past and project into the future, but also that there were too many of them. I had too many thoughts, and I wanted to find a way of calming those thoughts because I associated this with my nan who was mentally unwell. As a child, I knew that her head was absolutely full of thoughts; she'd be speaking out loud and she was incredibly unhappy because her thoughts tormented her. So I am afraid for my mental health, especially seeing it in my family and having it drummed into me quite a lot that it jumped a generation. So I need to do something with my mind now, so that I don't have that happen to me when I'm older. So when I am sometimes sitting with a lot of thoughts, I do have a little worry that I could start sitting there, sort of staring and being lost in this world of thought.

Fortunately, mindfulness meditation does not only take us closer to those parts of us that scare us, but also, being a practice that includes the cultivation of "calm abiding," it is a source of deeply replenishing nourishment. Elizabeth's initial interest in mindfulness was not driven particularly by unhappiness but more by simple curiosity:

I knew one or two people who I kind of rated, who had done it, and so I thought, "Yeah, I just want to find out a bit more." So I'd no idea what I was getting myself into. Absolutely no idea. But when I began to be exposed to it, I felt that it possibly could address a bit of me that wasn't getting any attention. What would you call it? I suppose we are talking about a kind of spiritual bit of me, for want of a better word—I can't think of anything else. . . . I didn't have any other practice, if you like; having ditched active Christianity years ago in my twenties . . . there hadn't really been anything in between. So, yes, it was addressing—or it seemed like there was the potential to address—a part of me that had not been taken care of or listened to over a long time.

Elizabeth's experience of coming home to herself and sensing that mindfulness may feed her spirituality is a common one. With practice, mindfulness enables access to a well of deep calm that already exists within us and that opens out into insight into the nature of how things really are. The insight that began to dawn for Elizabeth was personal, and yet it linked her to an interconnected universe:

When I think of spirituality, it is something about the opposite of me in isolation. It is about seeing me, tiny as I am, as part of something. Even as we speak, seeing myself in my mind's eye not quite as big as the universe, because that feels too big at the moment, but the world and the people in it. So when I think of spirituality, or me and my spiritual self, it is something about both the inside bit and the connection of the inside bit with something vast and not really known. . . . I can't know it. I can't know everybody in the world—of course I can't—or the creatures in the world, but I can have a sense of the feeling that I'm not alone. Just a sense of connectedness.

Curiosity

The desire to push beyond where we currently are—particularly when we do not like or want the experience we are having—is countered by curiosity. When we become curious, we slow down and return to the present. Being curious requires that we first accept where we are, dropping our judgments, and that we start to look at and feel into what is really happening now. When we are motivated by wanting to change what we feel, we are easily disappointed and frustrated when what we want does not happen. When we are curious about where we currently are, we have already arrived at our destination. Wanting something different turns our meditation into consumerism. Curiosity makes it into an experiment, an act of creativity.

Kindness and Compassion

It is easy to think of loving kindness and compassion as two things that are essentially the same. However, in Buddhism they are distinct qualities. Loving kindness is the wish that we and others will be happy—not distracted, not amused nor entertained, but truly happy. Compassion is the wish that we and others should not suffer. As such, they are two sides of the same coin. Buddhism also has an idea of the "far and near enemies" of loving kindness and compassion—what destroys and corrupts them. The far enemies are their antitheses, so for kindness it's hatred, and for compassion cruelty. The near enemies are far subtler. The near enemy of kindness is conditional love, and of compassion pity, which implies superiority and separation. Another perspective on this is to think that in kindness we open to ourselves and others, and with compassion we are present with the pain we may find when we do.

Moving from the Idea to the Experience

Whatever our initial motivation, and whether mindfulness brings us closer to our lost spirituality or to parts of our experience we have been unable to stay with, it is necessary at some point to make our commitment to our practice more resilient to the temptation to do it only when we feel like it, and to establish it as a regular resource within our lives. Different teachers talk about this transition in different ways. Tibetan Buddhist monk and meditation teacher Geshe Tashi Tsering, from Jamyang Buddhist Center in London, plots a path from "assumption," based on trust in someone else's authority, via "conviction," based in personal experience, to "aspiration," which acts as a powerful motivator:

> *The first step is developing personal conviction—conviction in the sense of you personally understanding the benefits of doing meditation. Not somebody teaching you the benefits of meditation, which you accept in blind faith, but what you understand from your own experiences of meditation. When we say, "Oh yeah, I do meditation because meditation helps with this and that and so on and so forth," this is not real conviction: this I usually call assumption. Assumption is blind faith; it still helps meditation, but it is not yet conviction. When we start to build something based on assumption, it's not that stable, not that good as a solid base. So while many people feel and want to do meditation, they are unable to start, are unable to continue, because there is no conviction in the meditation. . . . Conviction comes from a little experience of the benefits of doing meditation. This will help make the move from assumption to conviction. Then, when people have got conviction, that conviction will bring a strong aspiration—really wanting to do it.*

The journey that Geshe Tashi describes is not one that runs a straight course. For many of us, it is three steps forward and two back because the habit of not being present with ourselves is so strong. Martin Wells, consultant psychotherapist and meditation teacher, talks about the problems with commitment his students bring to the practice:

> *What people mostly bring is the commitment-to-practice issue, and then what commonly goes with that is a sense of not doing it right, so feeling ashamed of not doing something that they think will benefit them or even know will benefit them. It's a sort of vicious circle that they describe: "I'm not doing it; I must be not a good student." Something that my former teachers helped with was to distinguish between commitment and motivation. They noticed that a lot of people meditate based on emotional motivation. So we wake up in the morning and we might feel like meditating, or there was something that happened to us the day before that we want to sit with. We either meditate when we have a problem or we only meditate when we feel relaxed and OK. Commitment, on the other hand, is just doing the practice irrespective of how we temporarily feel.*

However, this is not to say that emotion has no place in helping us establish a regular meditation practice. Tibetan Buddhist teacher Tsoknyi Rinpoche describes how it is not enough just to think practicing is a good idea; we have to go one step further and feel it in our bodies. Speaking of working with his students, he says:

> *When they connect to basic well-being, which I call essence love, and some calm and clarity, and with a warm heart, then I think they'll start. Until then, it is very difficult. Because emotionally they cannot start. So this creates the emotion to start. Cognitively, they think, "Ah, good, I'm going to start. I*

*want to practice, it's good," but the body's not getting it. If you
write a book where all the explanation is based on the head,
people will go, "Oh yes, good, good," but they might not change.
Of course, you have to go through the head, otherwise how can
you reach the body? But there's something further on from that.*

The means to get started and continue is to move from simply being excited and enthusiastic on the ideas level to really feeling it in the body. When we feel it in the body, there's a kind of a motivation that comes from connection with the Buddha nature, which becomes a deep inspiration that takes over for faith and replaces it with a little bit of experience that then becomes the motivator. Rebecca Crane sees much the same process within the context of MBSR, where the practice of mindfulness (here she calls it "settling with our experience") begins to have a recognizable effect upon our lives, which then becomes a more powerful motivator than the ideas and hopes we started out with. However, she also recognizes that this new motivation remains vulnerable until it becomes stronger by repeatedly reconfirming it through meditative experience.

Many people during the eight-week course do have some tangible experiences that enable them to see that there is a connection between settling with our experience and managing "overwhelm" at work, between settling with our experience and really being able to see what's happening in our reactive patterns and how they interact with our chronic pain. Once people have a tangible sense of these connections, this does form a stronger motivation to do the work. But I think that our memory is very short and there's a lot that takes us in the opposite direction from being in connection with our experience. One of the advantages of the eight-week course, if people really go for it and do the practices, is that it does give us a bank of memory, that even if we lapse from the practice, there is something in our core that can remember how the practice makes a difference. But even so, those kinds of tangible memories do become quite fuzzy if we don't keep practicing on a really consistent basis. It becomes harder over time to decide to practice when we're faced with going to sit on the cushion or all these other tempting choices that we have. That body memory of the connection between doing the practice and its tangible benefits isn't strong enough to make us take that step and put our bottoms on the cushion.

However, once we have begun to establish a regular mindfulness practice that enables us to be present with ourselves in a kind and accepting way, which enables us to find calm in the middle of a busy mind and a busy life and return to that calm over and over again, then we experience the move from our meditation being merely an idea to an experience. It is no longer a cognitive thing but emotionally compelling as well. It is only when we sit down and do the practice that we get the feel of it, that it becomes a pleasure, even though it might be a strange and sometimes difficult pleasure. And once the practice gets to that stage, it starts to motivate itself from the inside. Rebecca Crane again:

I hear students express almost a sense of relief that comes out of being with our experience just as it is, which is very different from the usual mode of manipulating it in some way, trying to make it different or trying to get away from this, towards something else. That sense of even this is OK. It is just how it is, and there's a deep relief that even in the unsatisfactoriness, there's a sense of okayness. That's very settling and becomes a motivation in itself. Because our default is wanting to be fixed and sorted, while it truly never will be that way, somehow this is kind of settling back into realizing that truth and realizing that our lives will always be skidding around and uncertain.

This perhaps is the major insight—the most important milestone on the road to establishing our new mindfulness practice. By moving our practice away from being driven by our "likes and dislikes," experiencing the relief of acceptance and turning it into something we always do, regardless of how we feel, it becomes stable and self-sustaining. It is similar to the good habit of brushing our teeth—we accept that we brush our teeth every day, whether we feel like it or not.

So how do we encourage ourselves to make that shift? Rebecca Crane feels the key is acceptance:

I often share the story about my own practice experience. That for many years, after I'd finished the practice, an automatic process would come in about whether that was a good practice or not—an evaluation, a sort of an assessment of it. You know how innate that is within us, to automatically judge our experience: whether it was productive or whether it would lead to something good in my life. Even if it wasn't pleasant, would it be productive? Finally, there came a time when this just naturally dropped away and there was more of a sense of it was as it was. I've no idea whether it was good or bad, but it certainly was just a practice. . . . So it's really that sense of accepting that you won't necessarily go through this eight-week course and have a nice time with your practice. It may be challenging. Accepting this feels really important.

How Long Does It Take to Form a Meditation Habit?

The answer to this question depends on how single-minded we are and whether we form habits naturally, but if we want to get to the place where we practice every day without having to think about it—where it feels uncomfortable not to do it—then on average it's sixty-six days. This number really is an average though. Drinking a glass of water every day, say, is a much easier habit to form than a daily mindfulness practice, which may take longer to really solidly establish itself.

However, if we sit daily for two months, same time, same place, and only missing a single day infrequently, we will have a meditation habit in just over two months, which is just a fraction longer than an eight-week mindfulness course.

WHY A MINDFULNESS HABIT IS NOT AN ADDICTION

What is the difference between an addiction and a habit? One way of understanding this is that an addiction has something destructively compulsive about it. A habit, on the other hand, can be either bad or good—like drinking too much coffee or brushing our teeth. Regardless of whether a habit is good or bad, there is a difference between these types of habit, which tend to become unconscious once established, and a meditation habit. A meditation "habit" becomes habitual when we need no longer make a daily decision to sit—we just do it. However, once meditating, mindfulness is the opposite of habit—mindfulness is fresh moment-to-moment awareness, completely awake and present.

Nicky's experience of this reveals a bravery that is sometimes required when it comes to facing ourselves: wanting to escape but somewhere knowing that pushing the experience away— burying part of ourselves—does not help. Talking of her recurrent periods of depression, she says:

I certainly know that when I'm feeling down I just have to sit with it. I've always had that. I've always thought, "Well, I may as well see what it's like." While at other times, I just think, "Oh, go away, I don't want anything to do with you at all, thank you"—you know, it's too painful. But when I'm in a good enough space, I think: "Well, if you go with it, then you can only see what it's like, whereas if you push it away, it's going to be going away and it's never going to come up to the surface."

Sam likewise describes the stages of his own process of acceptance, presenting the paradox that when we give something up it may then come toward us.

The experience comes and goes. It can be very pleasant and very delightful, but if you expect it to come along, it may not come along, and I have learnt that you just have to accept what comes along, and sometimes it is boring and sometimes it is pleasant and sometimes it is distracted or sleepy or whatever it is, really.

I see it more as something to do with acceptance of myself and the bits that I don't particularly like and accepting me in the moment, in the body—hook, line, and sinker—with whatever I feel, and trying to be kind and comfortable with that and not sit there in some hot state of judgment and fury with myself. I suppose I expect less of the stillness, and I just try and go with whatever happens in the thirty to forty minutes.

Martin Wells takes this a step further. As we practice mindfulness, a self-awareness grows in us that not only begins to know our habitual patterns of thoughts and emotions but also begins to glimpse that awareness itself—he calls it "stillness"—seems to have its own intention. It is as if stillness wants to know stillness. With this, our motivation moves from being driven by our personal will to bring about change to being an expression of awareness itself.

Like all transitions, it's made through awareness. We start to see through our emotional ups and downs, and see where they lead us to is something consistent in the background. So rather than in any way using will, what makes our practice more stable is an inner energy that helps us to sit. It's more like we relate to the stillness, and then the stillness calls us, and the sitting comes from a wish to be present in that way.

Even a little taste of this deeper motivation can radically alter our perception of our personal situation, the "little room" in which we normally live. Speaking of this little room and discovering how it is situated within the vast expanse of awareness, Willem Kuyken says:

It was indeed a mirage: there is a much bigger awareness; the sky of awareness is much bigger than that little room . . . that's very empowering, because you've done that deliberately: you've anchored your attention, you've cultivated your awareness.

This is a journey Nicky is beginning to make:

Something made me do it again, and so I felt better . . . not immediately, but I suppose after a period of time I did feel better. Calmer. I feel happier with life. I just feel that I don't want so much, or I don't . . . what I've got is good. You know, I'm back at work now, so I don't think . . . well, I know I don't meditate every single day like I "should" do, but . . . I really appreciate my days off and . . . I don't know, I just appreciate things more. Which is lovely!

A Greater Motivation

Most of us are naturally motivated by our own suffering and our desire to find a way to feel better. However, there may come a time when we feel that there is not much coming back from our mindfulness practice—that sitting on our cushion or seat is not really an enjoyable or satisfying experience. When this happens, we may wonder why we are doing it, whether it has any value. Buddhism offers an answer to this that could help. Our practice of mindfulness is not simply about making ourselves feel better—it is a way of taking full responsibility for ourselves and our relationship to the world: how we speak and act, the means by which we survive, what motivates us, and how we understand things are all ways of interacting that affect not only ourselves but everyone else as well. Mindfulness can lift these interactions into consciousness, thereby enabling us to make better and wiser choices. In this way our motivation is broadened from "what am I getting out of this?" to "what can I give as my awareness of myself and others grows?" With this radical shift, our experience of meditation changes; having a far wider perspective, we are no longer primarily fixated on ourselves.

EXERCISE: MOTIVATION

What is my present relationship to my motivation? Here is a set of questions to reflect on, to help you see where you are right now:

What was the feeling of my original motivation? Can I still feel this now?

Do I practice my meditation like I brush my teeth—automatically, regardless of whether I want to or not?

Do I sense a part of me that really longs to meditate? What is this part like?

Do I sense a part that really does not? What does this part
want to do instead?

What would really motivate me now—perhaps after my
initial motivation has faltered?

Why Do We Want to Meditate? Key Points

- We are all initially motivated by personal suffering,
  whether it's emotional unhappiness or a sense of something missing.
- This motivation is necessary to get us going but destructive if it becomes a goal that stops what we are feeling.
  We must hold our motivation lightly.
- Mindfulness is counterintuitive: it asks that we accept
  ourselves—both the painful and the nourishing parts.
- Mindfulness is stabilized and self-sustaining once we
  begin to have a good experience of it that comes from
  the practice itself.

CHAPTER 2

Taking Our Seat

People discover that their life has followed them onto the cushion.
CHRISTINA FELDMAN

Sometimes people are caught within that almost impossible struggle to create a space, to create silence . . . of course it doesn't need to be created—it's there already. Unchanging.
MARTIN WELLS

You can see thoughts come in and then go. That's being calm and relaxed.
LAMA RABSANG

Being in a group of people and being asked to meditate for the first time can be an odd feeling. Sitting there, probably with eyes closed, among a group of strangers can provoke quite a lot of anxiety: how can I relax when it may not be safe? When I first had this experience, I remember sitting on my chair with my legs and arms crossed—the classic defensive posture. I felt distinctly silly and, furthermore, the group seemed to snap so compliantly into meditation postures—eyes closed, feet on the floor, upright—that something inside me wanted to rebel and refuse to do it. It took a long time not to be so defensive, and now, even though it is I who invite groups to meditate, I still occasionally feel a hint of the old anarchic defiance when I imagine everyone is being especially good. However, all of this is nothing compared with the difficulties, both physical and emotional, we can find ourselves in when we first try to meditate in our own home alone.

In this chapter we are going to look at what it means to start and then establish a meditation "habit." Creating a meditation habit is to take the step from doing a little meditation every now and then, depending on what we feel like, to doing it every day, come rain or shine. It is like planting our meditation in rich soil and making sure that each day it has the right amount of light and water to prosper and grow—not just shoving it in anywhere and mostly forgetting about it. Those of us who have tried this may have already discovered that while it seems largely a practical thing—a question of when and where to practice and for how long—it is also hugely emotional, because finding time just for ourselves, and then having to continue day after day however we feel, is hard. In fact, working with our resistance to practicing meditation, our not wanting to do it, which is part of the practice itself, starts immediately. And because of this, it is important that we get the balance right between creating a supportive physical situation and remembering that mindfulness is not so much about striving to create something perfect as helping us to be with things just as they are. So while we do need a place to practice that is relatively undisturbed, there comes a time when we realize it is not our meditation cushion that is at fault when we find it difficult to practice, but rather our ability to sit on it. Knowing this then enables us to settle.

Creating a Routine

None of us really knows before we start exactly how we are going to fit a daily meditation practice into our lives. During the MBSR/MBCT courses, the group is asked to split into pairs and discuss how this might realistically be achieved and what might support and hinder it. Probably the more difficult step is, next, to consciously experiment with how to create a *sustainable* routine within a life that is likely already full of huge demands from family and work. To consciously experiment means to try things out and see how they work. Can I meditate at this time each day and in this place with a reasonable hope that I can keep it going and not be distracted? In my own experience, getting this perfect is just impossible—unexpected events always conspire to disrupt the routine. However, we can, without turning these disruptions into a big problem, more or less establish a "good enough" routine that will really support our practice to grow.

Ann describes a typical course of discovery in which she finds herself struggling with guilt, not knowing exactly what her meditation method is, and practicing (or not) depending on how she is feeling. Elizabeth also describes her experience of trying to find a place to sit in her home, and a position to sit in, working out what is possible and what is not:

> It has been a developing thing. I fiddled around for ages when I first started, trying to find a place, a position—a place in the house, but also a place in my body, to make it possible. Yes, I did try all sorts of things, like sort of sitting on the floor and cross-legged, but it's just so incredibly uncomfortable—I'm not

bendy enough. And I've also tried sitting and have sat on that sofa, which I occasionally still do.

This type of experimenting is time well spent. Fran tells the smiling group that her experiment of meditating lying in bed just before sleep has not been entirely successful, while John quickly discovers that his heroic intention to get up an hour earlier, when his schedule already requires an early start, lasts only three days.

Both of them have now learned something about their own limits and what is possible. Tess explains why her routine helps:

Because you don't have to plan. Once the routine's there, then that's one part of meditating taken care of. So without the routine, then your mind is beforehand thinking, "Now, when am I going to fit this in? Shall I do it now or shall I do it later?" So, yeah, the routine's definitely easier.

Sam, a painter who has the good fortune of being in charge of his day, talks about the supportive and pleasurable morning routine he has created:

I just get up and have breakfast, and then I get washed and changed and all that, and then I sit in my kitchen for thirty or forty minutes and it is pretty nice and quiet in there. The only possible disturbance is a very rare knock at the door or occasionally a phone call. It depends where I am in the meditation whether I answer the phone or not. In the middle I sometimes don't, but if I am near the start or the end, then I often do.

I try to keep a routine and finish by about ten. The routine is important because I find it a nice thing to do in the morning. I suppose there is some desire to settle my mind or empty my mind and feel fresh for the day. Perhaps that's an ulterior motive and I feel I do it best in the mornings really. I know it's suggested doing ten minutes before bedtime, but I am too tired and sleepy really to do that. So I am afraid I haven't. I just do the forty minutes after breakfast.

However, for many of us keeping a routine going is hard. Life has a way of continually bursting in and distracting us. Weekends, holidays, and overnight visitors are particularly challenging. Ben says of his meditation:

It needs to be just part of the routine, so it feels like a normal rhythm, and if I don't do it, I feel like I didn't take a shower or something like that. Where things go wrong, actually, is in holidays when my routines are disturbed. Then I find it very difficult to get myself to do practice, and then very often I don't. But once I get in my work routine, no problem.

Elizabeth also struggles with the disruptions:

It doesn't take much to completely throw it, like going away for the weekend . . . we're going away tomorrow, but I don't think I'll meditate. I'll be packing my little suitcase, making sure we've got the bottle of wine to give the people as a gift and that sort of thing. And I won't do it when I get there on the Sunday morning. Well, we'll see. It doesn't take much to throw me . . . holidays, wrong environment, other people wanting me to do something else. And there's a sadness about that; I'm sorry about that, you know.

Elizabeth's sadness and regret here perhaps work well for her; they tell her that her mindfulness practice is growing in value. However, in another situation this could easily slide into self-recrimination and guilt—beating up oneself for not meeting the standards one has set for oneself. While establishing a meditation routine does take discipline and commitment, mindfulness is best practiced within an atmosphere of kindness and acceptance. We learn and are inspired to continue through the pleasure of the experience, not by making ourselves bad and wrong. Therefore, creating a routine for ourselves works best when it combines the firm intention to do and maintain it with the kindly ability to accept the truth that we *will* sometimes fail and that this "failure" is simply an opportunity to start again. And again.

The Time

It is enormously helpful to meditate at the same time every day if our schedule will allow it. This cannot be emphasized enough: the secret to developing a good habit is to choose a time and stick to it. But what time? Listening to those who already meditate, it seems the favored times are on waking in the morning, on returning from work, and last thing before bed. Of these, on waking in the morning is generally felt to be the most supportive because one's minds is fresh and not full of the day's events, and one's body is rested so less likely to fall asleep. However, this is not always possible, and if not, we should not make it into something to feel bad about. Nicky, a nurse who works shifts, describes finding a time of day that suits her.

Well, when I was off sick I quite easily found time, but now I'm back at work, and I do shifts, and I haven't really got a pattern as such. On a late shift, I tend to meditate first and then walk the dogs. On an early shift, I sometimes fit it in in the afternoon. If I'm on an early shift, I always do a three-minute meditation, but I don't sit down for half an hour and do it. Then I normally do it when I come home from work.

I don't think I'm properly in a routine, 'cos the other day I was on a late shift and I thought, "Well, I'll do it now," and then the plumber came and so I didn't. I really need to do it before I do anything else. I need to get up early and do it when nothing's going to interfere with it.

Fitting in Around Family

For many of us, family competes for our meditation time. This is perhaps one of our greatest struggles: how can we find time for ourselves without taking it from them? To this there is no easy answer, but what is especially important, yet again, is the centrality of kindness. Hard-and-fast rules cannot be applied, but that need not be a problem as mindfulness is not about being perfect but about being *present*. Tess describes her experience of being drawn into her family life:

The biggest obstacle probably to me is my family. I have the time and the space, but quite often my time and my space will get eaten up by other people. I should be able to take myself out of that and say, "I'm going to have this space as mine now," but quite often that isn't the case. So when my children are at school every day during term time, I'm quite good. They'll go, they'll leave the house; I will go and sit and meditate. But the moment anything else happens, like they've got a school holiday or we have visitors coming, I find it very hard to say, "I'm going to go now and sit and do my meditation in my space."

Elizabeth describes how important it is to get family to support our practice and if that support is not entirely there to find it elsewhere.

George, my husband, is not even thinking remotely in this area, so then it became important to set up support for myself. It was around when I first started that I went back into therapy, and I very specifically chose a person who I knew did meditation. And then, subsequently, finding other people was hugely important, just to have the support.

Martin Wells describes being mindfully present with whatever is happening, even when a daily sitting practice is proving hard to establish:

We've had someone in this last training year who has got young children and he asks, "Where do I find the necessary space?" Without wanting to be too fixed about it, I do recommend people have a time and a place to practice, because I think both those things are helpful. However, they're not meditation; the time and the place are simply anchors and ways of us keeping a commitment, not something to get attached to. With situations like his, I think it's important to think about other ways to prac-tice being mindful. For instance, using the kids as his practice—realizing that the disturbance that they bring him doesn't disturb anything on the level of his fundamental stillness or the peace that is inherent in him. So in a way, practice can be heightened by those sorts of challenges and what appears as disturbance can serve as a reminder to the background stillness.

The issue of not striving for a perfect situation in which to practice is an important one. Finding a place that is per-fectly silent and entirely undisturbed is almost impossible, but more importantly—within limits—it is not even desirable, as it would not help us cultivate the ability to be mindfully pres-ent and accepting of *whatever* our situation and circumstances are. Good or bad. Martin talks about this in the context of a family, reminding us that silence is not so much a quality of our environment as a place in ourselves that is not in reaction to what is going on in our own minds or the place we physically inhabit:

There might be ways—practical ways, again—to deal with finding a time and place to practice: When do the kids get up? When are they in bed? Are those the times to more formally practice? Or put some headphones on and let your wife deal with bath time. There are ways round it usually! But one of the things that often comes up . . . is people assume that to medi-tate they need to have silence—they need to block out the world rather than embrace the world and its distractions and noises. But distractions and noises can be just like a bell ringing. Its

sound alerts us to the silence when it stops. And that's a useful
shift for people to make because sometimes people are caught
with that almost impossible struggle to create a space, or create
silence, and of course it doesn't need to be created—it's there
already. Unchanging.

The Place

Besides finding a time to meditate, we also need to find a place.
Finding a place to sit when we practice mindfulness is important, as the place itself will come to support our practice both by
association and by the special atmosphere that builds up where
we meditate. The Buddhist texts recommend that we take ourselves off to the forest and sit beneath a tree, on a cushion of
grass, to start meditating. Nowadays our largely urban existence
makes such a setting improbable, but we can still usually find a
corner in our home—or even our car—that can be the place we
routinely sit in. Ann sits on the sofa in her sitting room because
it has lots of light and space. Ben says that although he has a big
house where he could make a special meditation room, he pre-
fers his kitchen:

> *I'm sitting at the table there, and it works fine for me actually,*
> *so I don't really bother about it. But people talk about their*
> *meditation room and shrines and this and that, and I think,*
> *yeah, I don't have that. I could have that. But I live here alone.*
> *I'm in no one's way. I can sit anywhere, anytime, so that isn't a*
> *real problem. But on the other hand, yes, it would be good to*
> *have a special place; I think that would be good.*

Nicky describes making a special place—her Wendy house—and how it really helps her practice:

I go down to my shed to meditate—well, Wendy-house type of thing—so I have a lot of the time to think, "Oh my God, it's too cold," or "It's wet," or . . . you know, all these excuses. But it's quite nice, 'cos I go down and I look at the garden. I see the ducks, I see the chickens, and, you know, I just think, "Oh, I love it; it's lovely being out here." So I think it's the actual physical walking down to the garden . . . it shouldn't make a difference, but it really feels like it does.

Tess talks about her special place of refuge that has to double as a guest room and TV room for teenagers:

It's up in my attic, at the top of the house. It's quiet. I've got a sheepskin cushion and my blankets, and I go up there and I sit down. I've got a mobile phone, which has got a timer on it, and I pop that on for mostly twenty minutes. Then I'll do some yoga after that. So, yes, in that sort of routine way it's very easy. Now disruptions to that are that it's also the spare room for guests, of course. And in the evenings there is a television in there, so if I fancied meditating, then maybe one of my daughters might be watching telly, so I wouldn't be able to use it. But mostly it's for guests, and as my children get older it can sometimes be a bit of a teenage hole. And, of course, then I have to tidy up as well, so in my lovely haven, which a lot of the time is just this beautiful peaceful place with a skylight, sometimes it's full of crisp packets and Coke cans, and I have to clear all this debris, so . . . yeah, it's not kind of rock solid.

Making a Ritual

Ann, Ben, Nicky, and Tess all share the experience of discovering the necessity of finding their "spot." A spot that can be a sofa, a kitchen table, a playhouse, or an attic. Once we have our spot it may be possible to strengthen it further by making our going there something of a personal ritual. For those of us who are Buddhists, or practicing within another explicitly spiritual or contemplative tradition, we may already have a ritual that contains our meditation sessions—perhaps lighting a candle or a stick of incense and maybe having an image or an object that represents something important to us and is connected to our meditation. However, for those of us coming from a secular background, ritual need not be excluded. Caroline tells me she is not currently interested in images of the Buddha or anything like that but finds that a stone that "speaks to her," found on a beach, embodies the qualities of immovability and calm. Having this where she sits reminds her how to sit and why she does it. Nicky, not a Buddhist either, finds that along with her ritual of the walk through her garden she also has a special blanket:

> I go down and I put out my blanket. . . . I don't like spiders, you see, so I won't leave anything down there. I've got a big, beautiful colored blanket that I put over the chair, and I get my meditation bowl out and sometimes I light a bit of incense, and it certainly feels nice. But as I say, sometimes I will meditate in the car when my husband's driving if I haven't done it and I think, "Oh, I should meditate. This is a good half an hour to do

*it in, rather than not do it at all." It doesn't always work, but I
think, "Well, it's better than nothing."*

Nicky's willingness to be fluid about her ritual, and to try,
when necessary, to catch a space for her practice wherever one
offers itself, wisely reminds us that while ritual can be an invaluable support for practice it can also limits us by making it impossible to practice without it. Ritual, unless done mindfully, is not
practice and should be neither a substitute nor an alternative for
it. However, having our own special corner and making going
there a ritual event does signal, "This is my time and what I do
here is important for me."

How to Make
a Ritual for the Nonreligious

Whether we are religious or not, we all already have our
rituals—our morning cup of coffee, where we eat our
lunch, set conversations with our partner, the six o'clock
drink—and these create shape and form in our lives.
To make a ritual for your meditation, you might try the
following:

1. Create a set time and a set place as far as you
   are able.
2. Make the place special—maybe have something
   already there that represents mindfulness for you: a
   stone, a view, an image, a candle.

3. Have your seat waiting—if you have a blanket or cushion you use, let that be where it lives.

4. Start meditating then pause for several minutes, taking in where you are and what you intend to do. Go slow, let this experience consciously register, enjoy this quiet space, and let it support you.

5. Make a wish inspired by what motivates you. Perhaps, "May I experience some calm and acceptance," or "May this help everyone I know." And then practice with kindness.

6. At the end, pause again. Recognize what you have just done—whatever you experienced, it was good simply because you tried. Savor it, however it was, for what it was.

7. Share as a gift, with others and yourself, any good that may have come from your meditation. Make the wish that this will benefit all others as well as yourself.

Stand up slowly—the day will be there without rushing into it.

What Do We Sit On and for How Long?

Once we have established our routine—when and where we are going to sit—we then experience the hard physical fact of sitting still for an extended period of time. Whether we choose to take the sensible solution for those with long-term stiff legs and knees and sit on an upright chair or the more traditional variation of cross-legged on the floor, supported by custom- or homemade meditation cushions, the truth is that at some point it is going to become uncomfortable. Here another middle way is necessary. Though there are schools of mindfulness meditation that intentionally use the pain of not moving as their object of mindfulness, there are others that believe this to be unhelpful. My sense is that while it is important to be present with our experience, including any physical discomfort, there is no need to turn something that is a stretch into something so bad we are forever frightened to explore that edge again. As Lama Rabsang, from Palpung Changchub Dargyeling in Wales, suggests, it may be best to recognize that we are working with stiff legs and backs, and to slowly and gently extend the duration of our practice.

Because of this it is recommended that we get our seats comfortable and sit still for as long as we can, but without turning it into torture. Then, when the posture becomes too painful to continue, we intentionally and consciously move, rather than being unthinkingly driven to it. This way we find a balance between the overly self-protective meditator, who avoids all discomfort, and the overly ambitious, who injures herself in an attempt to maintain a cross-legged position too long. While it is natural to avoid physical discomfort, mindfulness invites us to turn with conscious curiosity toward what we are experiencing and to explore how the physical sensation is added to and made worse by emotional reactions in the mind.

Given, then, that taking our seats means meeting ourselves, how long exactly should we sit there? My feeling is to take the middle way. We must sit long enough to have an experience of our practice. This means beginning to learn how we can be present with a whole variety of experiences: feelings of deep pleasure, calm, comfort, and joy and also of boredom, restlessness, endless distraction, irritation, and the desire to stop—to name but a few. However, we must not sit so long that our practice becomes a battleground or a torture chamber. If our practice is solely self-punishment, we will very quickly come to associate it with pain and withdraw from it entirely. Likewise, if it becomes just a chore or a duty, we will find all sorts of reasons to put it off.

In the context of the MBSR/MBCT courses we teach, we have come round to asking those who participate to practice initially for thirty minutes. This is slightly shorter than the forty we started out with, but we have found that, this being a more manageable duration, the likelihood of continuing after the course is increased and so more people are able to make it a foundation to build on. This accords with the time initially specified by many meditation teachers. Interestingly, according to Alan Wallace, who has a special interest in teaching the calm-abiding aspect of mindfulness meditation, the traditional length of a session in Tibetan Buddhism is just twenty-four minutes. Then rest and then sit again. Clearly, the idea is to establish something we are going to be drawn to do, and as we do it more, because we are experiencing its value, we will want to do it for longer.

For those of us who have already become ambivalent about meditating—on one hand having a "meditation phobia," a feeling of deep antipathy to meditation, and on the other still wanting to practice—the answer might be to severely limit the time we sit. On several occasions I have been asked by someone who had come to dread meditation what could they do to restart it? One solution that has worked is to do it for just five minutes each day *but absolutely no more*; however tempting it might be to do it just a few minutes longer, we determinedly insist on stopping. We could even attach a penalty: if I do six minutes, I will do all the washing up. Of course, this becomes quickly ridiculous and evokes the rebel within us who is definitely going to do a lot more than just five minutes. If this happens, that is great—it means we are practicing again—but it is important to build on this wisely by only making small incremental increases from week to week and avoiding the way of practicing that caused the phobia in the first place. Again, the need for compassion and wisdom while working with our tricky psyches is clear.

The Perfect Seat: Get Comfortable

If you have gotten this far, you will most likely already know if you are more comfortable sitting on a chair or on cushions on the floor. However, if you are not sure about your chair, or are a chair person hankering for the cushion, here are some tips.

USING A CHAIR
The perfect chair is an upright one that supports you sitting straight and relaxed, allows you to place both feet flat on the ground, and leaves your arms unimpeded, so you can rest your hands on your lap.

USING A CUSHION FOR YOUR BOTTOM . . .

A meditation cushion should, when sat on, lift you at least three to six inches from the floor, so that it helps you to sit up straight and relaxed when your legs are folded in front of you. Experiment to find a suitable cushion; a feather cushion from the sofa probably will not do because once sat on it will go flat and not support you. A tall cube of foam or several ordinary cushions doubled over might work for you.

If when sitting on your cushion only your bottom and ankles touch the floor, then you will be unable to comfortably sustain this position for any length of time. Place folded blankets under each knee until they take your weight. This way your knees will gradually relax and eventually touch the floor. But do not force it.

AND A FLOOR MAT FOR YOUR LEGS AND FEET

The floor mat should be big enough to fit your sitting cushion and folded legs. It should also be thick and soft enough to protect your knees and ankles from the pressure of the floor. Using a single folded blanket or a yoga mat probably will not be enough, as these both become hard to the touch after a few minutes. Try a piece of foam a couple of inches thick, or if you use a blanket, try several thick ones doubled over several times. Experiment to make sure the cushion is comfortable enough that you can sit for some time before you need to move.

If you would like to use proper meditation cushions, the small one to sit on is called a *zafu*, and the floor mat for the legs a *zabuton*. Make sure to try before you buy, as they come in different heights and with different fillings. If you have no local shop, they may be found on the Internet.

USING A MEDITATION BENCH

A meditation bench is a little bench that you sit on while kneeling on the floor mat (so your legs go underneath it). If you are handy, it's simple to make one, but if you want to purchase one or see what they look like, try searching "meditation bench" on the Internet.

Most important is to get your seat as comfortable as possible. We all experience discomfort at some point in our practice; this we work with, but there is no need to add to it.

What Is Our Practice?

Recently a friend told me that she just could not stop her thoughts during her mindfulness meditation, unlike someone in her meditation group who could. I was very surprised by this: where did she get the idea that she was not meant to be thinking? As far as I knew, she had never received this instruction and the supposedly thought-free meditator had never been offered as someone to aspire to. The truth was that she had made this up and applied it to herself despite it being an idea that made her feel inadequate and unhappy. What this story shows us is that even when we have practiced meditation for some years it is still possible to not clearly understand what our meditation "technique," our method, is and how to usefully think about it. On "what am I meant to be doing when I meditate?" Lama Rabsang says:

> *Having many thoughts, some people think there is something wrong because they mistakenly think in meditation there is no thought. Other people know it's OK that there are some thoughts, but they can't be relaxed with this, with the just coming and going of thought. They are unable to just let the thoughts be there, so that there is no problem, no difficultly with the meditation. They are fighting inside against the thoughts: "I don't want to think about that; I don't want to feel that"—that's the mind being tight, which makes obstacles, makes difficulties.*

Ben illustrates just how busy it can get trying to achieve and adjust our meditation method so that it feels right:

> *When I close my eyes it enhances the racing of my thoughts. So there is this thing of being too much immersed in my own thoughts. Also, I like the idea of concentrating on breath, although I'm easily getting bored with that. So I like to expand that a little bit to include all sounds and everything my senses take in and that includes also visual, so I also like actually to have my eyes open. It is good to have my eyes open, even if things are moving and I also hear sounds, and I'm fine with that. I like that, in a way. So I want my eyes open, but sometimes I find it difficult to find a point to look at.*

Finding the balance between properly following the technique without adding anything else to it and unknowingly trying to arrange it so that it produces "good" experiences is hard. Our mindfulness meditation method (that is, rest the attention on the breath and bring it back when it wanders) is easily subverted by the intention to create desirable experiences rather than to be present with the experience we already have. Barry Magid, a psychoanalyst and Zen teacher, calls this "our secret practice"—the one that has the corrupting secret motivation to feel good instead of being present. The truth is, we all probably do this to some degree, and we may not even know it, as it can be extraordinarily subtle. Instead of just staying with what we are experiencing, we add something more to it, adjusting it to make it "better." But while it is an integral part of our mindfulness practice to monitor itself and make adjustments when we find ourselves particularly agitated or sleepy, these adjustments are best motivated by wanting to cultivate a clear, unwavering presence, not a comfortable place safe from all our "stuff." Stephen Batchelor, Buddhist writer and teacher, notices just how difficult it is to hear meditation instructions and follow them. He says:

> I find again and again that I bend over backwards to try to make it as simple as possible, and in fact the forms of meditation I teach are very simple. And yet it sometimes takes an awful long time for the student to actually realize how simple it is. To some extent, I think, because they've already come loaded with some preconceived ideas of what meditation is all about or, even worse, this dreadful idea, enlightenment. And it takes a while for them to let go of the idea that it's not as complicated or as difficult. The thing is, of course, that even when they realize it's simple, that doesn't mean that it's easy. It's very difficult, but it's very simple.

Stephen highlights a profound truth here. *All* of us come to our practice with preconceived ideas of what it is, and it is part of the practice that these ideas become conscious and, when incorrect, discarded. However, this goes deeper than simply mishearing. What we do hear is inevitably a reflection of who we already are. If we bring to our seat the desire to feel good during each session, we will only hear that this is a practice that cultivates calm and stillness. If we come believing we always get things wrong, we will feel the practice is impossible to succeed at. If we feel that we must control the world and that it is only through diligence and sustained effort that anything is achieved, we will try very hard. In each case, and many other similar ones, the practice is unknowingly colonized by the same distortions we bring to other areas in our lives. For this reason, Buddhist teachers repeatedly ask us to relax and not hang on so tightly to our ideas about meditation, our fantasies of what it is like when it "works"—not to clothe it in our personal stories.

Martin Wells talks about how we also bring unrecognized assumptions from our culture—expectations that are all about something more, rather than something less:

> There's a strong sense of learning something, about progress, about accumulation, or getting somewhere, achieving something, attaining something. I think for some people, the notion that there's nowhere to go and that it's more about relinquishing and surrendering than accumulating and progressing, is often a big transition.
>
> People turn up for one thing, and what they are faced with is something very different from what they expected, so they expect to be made to feel better by something that they grasp, or

*learn, or accumulate, or have more of, and what they run into
is that it's actually the opposite that liberates them: it's a letting
go that liberates, rather than a holding on or an accumulation.
Now, that's a huge thing for people to face. And initially it
doesn't get any easier because the more we let go, the more there
is to let go of, and ultimate liberation involves the ultimate letting go of everything.*

And this starts with simply taking our seat at a good time
and in a good place each day. Following the method of meditation we use, without adding anything to it, and noticing our
expectations as they arise and letting them go. We just sit.

A Meditation Journal

In MBSR and MBCT courses we are invited to keep a meditation journal because it both provides a real insight into
our practices and at the same time strengthens them. Daniel Coyle, who has explored how the brain acquires skills in
his book *The Talent Code*, describes this as "deep learning":
making our learning conscious, noticing where we struggle,
and intentionally returning to those edges, so that exploring them we can see clearly what the struggles are and what
helps. In this way we build particularly powerful and resilient neural pathways that dominate other pathways and so
have greater impact; in other words, we significantly
empower our meditation habit. While not turning our
meditation into an anxious chore, this focused work,

according to Coyle, is not an option: "It's a biological requirement," he says, because it is the way we best learn. So how do we do this?

At the end of each session, note, in a notebook kept where you meditate, how long you sat and when, and write just a few words that describe the general quality of your practice—maybe "sleepy, "agitated and full of thoughts," "very calm," or "first relaxed, then keen to get up and move."

Try to write what you notice—just that and nothing more. Be careful not to slide into judgments such as "Bad meditation today, slept throughout it." Be truthful and write down the days you miss.

After a month or so, read the journal and see what it has to say about your practice. This is not a criticism, but a mirror that reflects back to us where our learning edges are. Do we need to relax more because our practice is too uptight and results oriented? Do we need to crisp up our practice because we use it to happily snooze? Do we attack ourselves or too easily let our daily meditation become intruded upon? Whatever we find, we have now made it conscious and can bring this awareness back into our practice.

EXERCISE: CHECKING MY SEAT

Asking these simple questions (without fudging the truth) will tell us whether the practical foundation for our meditation is established or not. If we find that we have no routine, it is a valuable insight rather than cause for self-criticism.

When do I sit—what time of day? How regularly do I sit?

Where do I sit and what do I sit on? Is it comfortable? For how long do I sit?

What do I do when sitting—what is my meditation method? (Try writing this down, as if you are instructing someone else; it will show how clearly you understand what you are doing.)

Where do I go to find an answer for questions about my meditation?

Taking Our Seat: Key Points

- When we start meditating, our practice is enormously strengthened by creating a routine—if possible—whereby we meditate at the same time each day. Experimenting to find what will practically and sustainably work for us is worth the effort; just hoping it will fall into place is often unsuccessful.

- Working within our constraints—family, job—and the feelings we have about them can all become part of our practice. We are not trying to create the perfect situation but to be present with the one we have.

- Finding a place and making a ritual of being there can help to support our practice, but we should be cautious not to become obsessive in our need for it.

- When we sit, we find the balance between sitting for so short a time that we never get an experience of the practice and sitting for so long that we become phobic about our practice and stop. This is best gauged as a feeling rather than a rule.

- It is far, far better to do five minutes every day regularly than an hour every now and then.
- It is a good idea to ask ourselves whether we clearly know what we are meant to be doing when meditating. Many of us distort the instructions we are given, turning them into something that reflects our habitual way of seeing things.

CHAPTER 3

The Guardian
at the Gate

I will do anything rather than sit, in spite of the fact that I really want to.

RUTH

Of course, a lot of people want to meditate to avoid their pain; however, the practice creates just the opposite. It forms a relationship with our self that makes conscious those processes within us which generate suffering.

FRANKLYN SILLS

Finding the willingness to turn towards and to befriend . . . is the most radical transformation in a person's life.

CHRISTINA FELDMAN

So far we have looked at what motivates us to want to start and to continue meditating and, having "taken our seat," how we begin immediately to discover just how difficult it is to stay present during our practice of meditation. For some of us, our bodies quickly become uncomfortable and, struggling with feeling either dull or agitated, we want to move, while our minds seem to have a life of their own as they freely range through memories and fantasies, some useful but many having no more apparent significance than a bus ticket. For others, meditation brings painful emotions to the surface. Past events or fears for the future and parts of ourselves, usually repressed, become accessible to our consciousness. Our meditation becomes stressful and difficult, and the temptation to stop and bury again what we find painful is almost irresistible. Stephen Batchelor, talking about his experience working with meditators during retreats, says:

> In retreat situations, the problems include whether on a particular day of the retreat the student is sleepy—big problem—or they're compulsively distracted, or they're bored, or they find that the meditation brings up stuff that they find a bit difficult to deal with: emotional stuff, trauma . . . sometimes people get into very negative perceptions of themselves, a certain kind of self-loathing brings up anxieties and self-doubt.

None of these experiences need be a particularly big problem. It is simply what we find when we slow down and look at ourselves. With time and kindness, our relationship to what we find initially difficult to accept will slowly but radically change. However, there will also be times when we find that, for some unknown reason, we are cutting short, missing or have entirely stopped our meditation sessions. It is as if something unknown within us has simply decided to resist the whole meditation thing and shows itself by forgetting to do it or skipping days. Or if we are still limping along, it may manifest through continual distraction and an irresistible desire to sleep. When we realize this is happening, and this realization may take some time, it is necessary to discover why we are doing this and find a way to get back on track.

Resisting

At the end of the fifth week of the eight-week mindfulness course, Sarah looks worried. Asked how it is going, she replies that her experience of the practice was very good during the first couple of weeks, but now she has become scared of it. She has found that her ability to tolerate constant pain has changed for the better, but more problematically she has also noticed that she is defending herself against a traumatic period in her life that she will not allow herself to feel. And so she has stopped.

While Buddhism is extraordinarily insightful about the emotions that drive us, it does not have a concept of the unconscious and how this unknown part of ourselves can profoundly influence how we think, feel, and act. However, psychotherapists working along broadly psychoanalytic lines have begun to understand how unconscious processes work. Unsurprisingly, at the center of this is our universal experience of feeling endangered. Quite simply, to defend ourselves when we feel under threat, we resist what threatens us. Whether this threat is an external situation, perhaps aggression directed toward us, or something within our own psyches, the result is the same: by one means or another we do all we can to avoid the stressful emotions it engenders. Resistance, as a defense, is therefore natural and happens spontaneously without our even having to know we are doing it. When the perceived threat is meditation, or rather the way we feel when meditating, then our defenses are activated and we find ourselves resistant to practice. Ruth describes how difficult being mindfully present with oneself can be. Despite having an interest in meditation for many years, something inside her finds it almost impossible to just sit with herself and accept what she finds:

> *I will do anything rather than sit in spite of the fact that I really want to . . . but there's something that is just intolerable about it. A whole load of emotions about longing and at the same time fear, a lot of fear and I don't know fear about what, but . . . it's just much easier not to go there.*

Exactly what is so unbearable about the longing and fear Ruth finds when sitting with herself is unclear, but what is clear is that she does not want to experience them. Ellen has much the same experience. Panicking at the thought of sitting meditation, she has to duck and dodge continually so that she does not feel anything:

> *I just find it impossible. I become busy. I can't make a time in the day, and I think I'm going to and then I don't. I suppose it's a sort of panic. I want to fill up the space. I'm always doing something. I'm that sort of person. Very rarely sit down. I could spend the whole day standing. I hardly ever sit. I'm always on the go. So, the prospect of sitting down first thing in the morning is appalling.*

Ruth and Ellen are perhaps caught in their resistance, the desire not to go too near to themselves in case they have any thoughts, fantasies, emotions, or physical sensations that are upsetting or, worse still, leave them feeling in some way in danger. This is familiar. We all have resistance to going near what we dislike or fear in ourselves. When something happens to make us feel uncomfortable, we automatically employ defensive strategies that enable us to screen out the threat and thereby protect ourselves from the anticipated vulnerability. In extreme cases, our resistance is employed to protect our sense of psychological coherence, continuity, and physical survival. We feel like we are literally fighting for our lives.

Ellen: Discovering Layers of Resistance

Ellen, now in her late sixties, is the daughter of strict Calvinist parents. As we talk, it becomes apparent that she has several layers of defensive resistance operating that together have virtually brought her meditation at home, alone, to a stop. The more obvious resistance is against feeling guilty when she sits down and does "nothing," but as we continue, we find there is a second level of defense that is much cleverer and far darker. Of her meditation, she says:

> I just do the "watching your breathing" and when you find yourself thinking and distracted, naming it and coming back to the breath, and that feels guilty because I haven't got going—I haven't started getting the dogs organized to take for a walk—so I put bad feelings in it. They're dying to go out for a walk. They're more important. Maybe I'm quite firm on the first day, but after that panic sets in: I can't do this another day.

When Ellen tries to meditate, instead of resting in her breath and letting her thoughts come and go, she is almost immediately consumed with guilt because she is doing something just for herself and not others. The only way to avoid this bad feeling is to stop. However, as the conversation continues, it begins to emerge that there is a hidden gain from what begins to look like a willful determination not to hear all she has been taught about the kindness and simple presence of mindfulness meditation.

NIGEL: What did you practice on the eight-week mindfulness course?

ELLEN: Umm, I practiced the body scan. But that doesn't seem to me to be as hard as doing the listening one. And the breathing one.

NIGEL: That sounds like that discredits it in some way?

ELLEN: Yes, because you're thinking about the body. But when you come to doing the breathing meditation, that's really hard because that's emptying your mind of everything.

NIGEL: Except an awareness of your breathing?

ELLEN: Yes, but you quickly go off that, don't you, and that's a terrible failure.

NIGEL: A terrible failure?

ELLEN: Well, it is, isn't it? I feel there's a goal that would be you sit for an hour without thinking. And that's getting it right. That I'll get it right eventually if I can do that. There's a sort of perfection out there that's got to be attained.

NIGEL: Is that what the method is, or have you possibly made that up for yourself?

ELLEN: Well, I certainly feel that it's a failure if you think. I'm sure someone said that the idea is for the gaps to get longer between your mind thinking.

NIGEL: I know for a fact that that's not the meditation method you've been given, so is there something inside of you that has picked something else out—

ELLEN: And made it really punitive?

NIGEL: Really punitive.

ELLEN: No wonder it's hard.

NIGEL: It's impossible!

ELLEN: (Laughs.)

NIGEL: You can't actually stop the mind thinking.

ELLEN: But you will with practice, won't you?

NIGEL: Not the sort of practice you and I do.

ELLEN: Oh . . . well then, do you mean to say that the thinking is different? That instead of thinking about taking the dogs for a walk, or whatever I'm in a state about, I'll be thinking about angels or something? You know, something very good?

NIGEL: The method you've been given is that it doesn't matter how much you think. The important thing is that you recognize when you're carried away by thinking and remember to come back to the breath.

ELLEN: Hmm.

NIGEL: So that you have a way of disengaging yourself from being completely caught up with whatever is going on in your mind. That's the important bit. It's not to change the content of your mind—thinking about angels. Nor is it to stop thinking, because that isn't the goal, even if it were possible.

ELLEN: So, can you do that for hours? (Said doubtfully.)
NIGEL: You don't need to do it for hours. You only need
   to do it for a moment and then another one and
   another one.

Ellen's setting of an impossible goal for herself—not having any thoughts in her mind—rather than following the method she has been taught is, on one level, another expression of her internalized, punitive parents—an inner voice that is critical, perfectionist, and that leaves her feeling "a terrible failure." However, it is interesting that toward the end of the conversation, as I question and try to diminish the authority of this voice, she seems to feel deflated—as though she is losing something that, even though it made her feel bad, was valuable. As we continue, it becomes clear that being the victim of self-inflicted impossible goals—what will emerge as an aspect of her personality she calls Ellen 1—gives a raison d'être for the existence of a deeply hidden Ellen 2, whose purpose is to rebel against the tyranny of her background. Of course she feels deflated—were she to lose her victim, there would be no possibility of rebellion.

ELLEN: I panic I won't get everything done. There's always
   deadlines like picking up the grandchildren or walking
   with a friend. So not having the discipline to say, "No,
   I'm meditating first." Not having the discipline
   because it's about me. It just goes against everything
   that I've been brought up to do, really. My life is out
   there—it's not an internal world. I have a Scottish
   background, so that sort of working ethic and then the
   discipline of a dancer means every moment of your day

is mapped out. And I suppose the Christian thing about thinking about other people, that you mustn't be selfish—all those come together. And a poor self-image, I suppose. That I'm not worth it. I think that's another fear: that if I meditate alone there's the fear of annihilation. If you sink low enough, there is a sort of stripping away. There is also something that I was taught by a priestess at the Rudolf Steiner place, that the devil can get in, that evil can enter you if you become absent, so to speak. Meditation feels like being very vulnerable, very open so other things could rush in—evil spirits or something.

NIGEL: So there's two levels to this keeping busy. There's the busy because that's what a good person does, the Scottish work ethic, but there's also a deeper level that is if you don't keep busy you experience a fear of annihilation and a vulnerability to something invading you.

ELLEN: She used to call it Lucifer. Lucifer will get in. That you have to defend against Lucifer. That sounds a bit like the devil makes work for idle hands! (Laughs.) But it's a real feeling of vulnerability, terrifying. I mean, I feel tense thinking about it. Anticipating it, I am stopped in my tracks. I don't like the feeling of not trying to be good in some strange way, because I'll be punished for not being busy.

Ellen clearly identifies the roots of her anxiety in her background—the formative experiences that have taught her the truly dire consequences of just sitting still. However, perhaps because she is stepping back and reflecting on this, she is able to see it more clearly and laugh. This seems to wake up her Ellen 2, who has her own style of resistance.

> ELLEN: There is also something else. While I am compliant and easily scared by stories about Lucifer, my Ellen 1 personality, there's also another person inside, a more hidden person, but a strong and determined person, very stubborn, called Ellen 2, who finds devious ways of saying no. I'd find some complicated reason for Ellen 2 to say "I can't comply." For instance all the reasons for not meditating, the busy business, is also Ellen 2, isn't it? Finding the excuses for her own purposes. So it's not just simply Ellen 1 feeling that she's got to do something all the time, but there's an Ellen 2 in there who uses it also for her own purposes, her hidden "no" to authority. So, by not telling someone who is coming round to take the dogs out walking, that I am meditating, I manage not to do it, and it's also not my fault—they stopped me. It's sort of dishonest. Well, it's not quite dishonest, but it's . . . hmm, rebellious. Kind of "fuck off," but in a quiet, hidden way. I once had a horse who you had to keep kicking and kicking and kicking—terribly lazy—so it's not like that at all. It's not a mulish sort of stubbornness; it's a very active one. It's a sort of thoroughbred one. It's a highly strung one. It's a very flighty sort of horse.

This new voice is full of authority and clarity. The very structure of how she speaks changes: no longer tentative and vague but with an absolute certitude that does not pull back from naming honestly her own games. However, Ellen 2 works against Ellen's own wishes—her wish to meditate. While Ellen 2 is a dashing, life-saving figure—a thoroughbred able to express her "no" powerfully—she also has a dark side that is an internal saboteur. That is, her "no" can be unknowingly employed destructively against herself. Ellen 2 prevents her practicing by misreading meditation as an authority that leaves her extremely vulnerable and must therefore be secretly thwarted. However, it is no exaggeration to say that Ellen 2's existence has saved Ellen's sanity by giving her a sense of self that no one can overwhelm and destroy. As such, Ellen 2 is a defense against the fear of annihilation that Ellen first felt as a child and that remains a background terror for her as an adult. When Ellen sits to meditate and feels panic, it is not just that her parents and others have told her that the devil makes work for idle hands but that her body retains a memory of what it is to have your will broken if you do not do what you are told. While she continues to unconsciously associate her meditation with all this, her only way to survive is to say no. In the face of this far greater need for psychological survival, her meditation is just not as important and is therefore unlikely to really start.

Resistance and Defenses

We resist anything that threatens to put us into contact with emotional experiences we do not want to have. We may not even know what these experiences are, because as we approach them anxiety occurs, which causes us to defend ourselves in whatever way we usually use. For the meditator, this may be all manner of distraction—for instance, monkey mind or overwhelming sleepiness. Here are some of our principal defenses and how we may see them at work within and around our mindfulness practice.

SUPPRESSION AND REACTING

Unknowingly suppressing anxiety-provoking thoughts and emotions is called "unconscious repression." Examples of this cutting off are found throughout this book: situations where we find ourselves compelled not to meditate because there is something about it that is unbearable, although what this may be exactly, we are not entirely sure.

At the other end of the spectrum is reacting, which is to be impulsively caught up in our thoughts, emotions, or automatic behaviors. This is also called "acting out," which is different from helpful expression, or indeed from being mindfully present, because there is no management of the feelings. Acting out, at first sight, does not seem to be a defense, because it is identified with and being compelled by everything that is going on within us. However, what makes it a defense is that often these reactions are a means to avoid or obscure more difficult thoughts and feelings. Anger perhaps hides sadness, impotence, or despair. Distress perhaps hides aloneness, resignation, and fear. By allowing ourselves to be caught up in this way, we need never go near what more deeply scares us.

DENIAL AND DISPLACEMENT

We practice unconscious denial—a subset of repression—when we cannot bear something because it is too painful. Knowing secretly our meditation is in trouble, we deny it because facing up to this and doing something about it is more difficult. This is closely related to displacing negative emotions—about our meditation, what is taught, or our usually esteemed teacher—on to something safer, such as the organization or other students. Both defenses take emotions that are felt to be dangerous and destructive away from the place where they "belong."

PROJECTION AND INTROJECTION

Seeing in others, and the situation, emotions, beliefs, and purposes that we cannot acknowledge as our own is called "projection." This need not be a bad thing, as we often project onto others great qualities that we are unready to accept as our own. Putting a person on a pedestal is a good example of this. We invest them with attributes that are, in fact, our own waiting in the wings. However, we can also project parts of ourselves that we dislike or disown. For instance, when feeling self-critical, useless, and shamed, we mistakenly believe it is the course teachers or the others who do not like us, who think we are rubbish, or who wish to humiliate us.

Closely related to this is "introjection," our ability to take things into ourselves. Frequently, when first practicing mindfulness, we find we are full of self-criticisms that on reflection turn out to have been acquired during childhood from overly critical parents or schools. These introjections are, of course, destructive. However, the same mechanism can work for us if we take in beneficial qualities such as kindness, compassion, and mindfulness. As a defense, introjection is a good way to protect us from loss; valued qualities are now held inside us.

RATIONALIZATION AND INTELLECTUALIZATION

We all use rationalization and intellectualization all the time. To rationalize something is to put a good and reasonable face on the irrational behavior of ourselves and others, while intellectualization is a way to keep emotions at bay and under control. The excuses we tell ourselves about why we cannot practice are most likely examples of this. However, while these are very popular defenses, they are also famously inadequate. Anyone suffering from strong emotions will know that they are impossible to reason our way out of: whatever the explanation, they continue to hurt.

It is essential that we bring kindness to our understanding of defenses. Not only are they ingenious, but they have been or remain necessary for our survival. Discovering a defense in ourselves is not a cause for shame or self-criticism, but an insight to value. Once known, we can bring the defensive activity into our mindful awareness and perhaps, in time, no longer need to employ it.

The Guardian at the Gate: Knowing Our Defenses

Each of us has defenses similar to Ellen's that, in their own way, defend us against feeling emotional pain or, more subtly, our *imagining* that something will hurt us. As we see here, having defenses, including resistance, is not a bad thing. It is not an emotional weakness, a sign of psychological ill health, or a failure; it is simply something that is necessary for us to survive. Defenses help us remain in healthy control and functional in the face of sometimes intolerable circumstances. A person who can put "out of mind" something emotionally debilitating is in a better position than someone who, having post-traumatic stress, is unable to defend against flashbacks and finds themselves uncontrollably reliving what was unbearable. Defenses, when looked at in detail, are often ingenious, and they do their job in all sorts of ways. In fact, there is a very long list of identified defenses that is still being added to. This is because many of them are very similar to each other and the distinctions between them are not clear. However, one way or another, all defenses can be described as forms of repression. We repress anything we cannot bear to feel consciously. In this way we unknowingly put out of mind events, emotions, unacceptable thoughts and fantasies, parts of ourselves that are disavowed or as yet unacknowledged. These need not all be "bad" things; we are as disturbed by our repressed, aggressive instincts as we are—as with Ruth—by our repressed longing for a spiritual life. Either way, what is repressed causes anxiety when it approaches consciousness. Of course it does—why else would it be repressed?

Franklyn Sills, codirector of the Karuna Institute, a mindfulness-based psychotherapy training center, believes that the distraction we experience during meditation is, in fact, a defense attempting to protect us from becoming consciously aware of material—emotions, thoughts, sensations—that we find uncomfortable and perhaps have had to previously repress. Talking about teaching meditation, he says:

> *Part of the territory is about how we protect or defend our self from our suffering through distraction. So people, when they start to enter a meditative state, continually go into distraction. They start thinking about this or that or what they should be doing tomorrow.*

At first sight this may seem a bit of an exaggeration—surely not *all* my distraction is about wanting to avoid feeling something I am made anxious by. While it is certainly true that nearly all of us start our meditation practice with very low levels of concentration, it is also true that most of us are avoidant of any form of discomfort. Merely the experience of the hard work of cultivating sustained attention can bring to the surface thoughts and feelings about how useless we are: the self-criticism and self-doubt Stephen Batchelor mentioned above. Franklyn continues:

> *We get anxious as it's inevitable that when we start to pay attention and bring awareness to our self, one of the first things we're going to meet is our own pain and suffering. Of course, a lot of people want to meditate to avoid their pain; however, the practice creates just the opposite. It forms a relationship with*

our self that makes conscious those processes within us that generate suffering. But we have to actually hold these processes in awareness and for a lot of people that's very painful. And so the mind very quickly moves to distraction. That might be on a mental level with thoughts, memories, planning, or whatever, or it might be on an emotional level where feelings emerge— fear, annoyance. Impatience is a big one. The Buddha pointed out that impatience is an expression of a deep fear of meeting that which is painful within us. So then impatience with our practice comes up and moves us into distraction.

This is important to know. When we begin to practice mindfulness meditation, the first thing we discover is that our attention span is astonishingly short. Usually, after one or two breaths we have become distracted. Even when trying to be fully present through just a single breath, we may find we are some- where else by the end. We become acutely aware of distractions, that we are simply pulled along from one to the next. I sit down intending to meditate and spend half an hour thinking about problems at work or my next holiday. I catch myself and return to my breath, and next thing I know I have jumped up and am halfway to the fridge for breakfast or the computer for e-mails. Describing his own version of this, imagining distraction as a force that has its own intentions, Ben says: "I think that it is perhaps the same force that makes me take a drink or do day- dreaming or buy a lottery ticket!" When we begin to sit in medi- tation regularly, this addiction to distraction suddenly becomes conscious, and one of our first big insights is how we would rather be doing almost anything other than staying present—fully consciously aware—with ourselves in each successive moment.

Full of thoughts, distracted, aching, bored, wanting to space out, run off, have a different experience, read the manual—we'd rather do anything other than just sit with who we are.

It is week two of the MBSR/MBCT course. A group of us sit in a circle and talk about the group's first week of mindfulness meditation: what has it been like? Just about everyone has been struggling with sleepiness; keeping their attention on the sensations in their bodies has proven more difficult than anyone imagined. One man is particularly quiet and looks a little troubled. He has found that during his meditation many distressing memories have arisen from his years of frontline social work—memories, we discover, he usually does his best not to go near because he fears they will make him incapable of properly doing his job. Christina Feldman talks about why this may be so difficult:

> In the beginning, people have not yet built up the inner resources of calmness, of mindfulness, of attentiveness, of kindness, to be able to meet what is suddenly "on the table" without reservation, so initially it can feel quite overwhelming. But the practice is finding the confidence to develop and sustain within that initial chaos the inner resources of calm, of focus, of mindfulness, of compassion, so that which initially feels overwhelming becomes approachable. But those first days, and for some people it might be first weeks, are very challenging times . . . many people are just tempted to flee.
>
> The first challenge of the practice is actually just to begin to calm down. That sounds simple, but for most people that's really difficult because what many people realize when they

begin to stop and to pause and to look, is the degree of agitation in their life. The agitation of fixing, of avoiding, of getting, of becoming, of doing anything but meeting what is. This initial calming is the shift from aversion, the turning away from, to finding the willingness to turn towards and to befriend. It is the most radical transformation in a person's life.

Nicky: Welcoming In

As we calm down, it becomes clear that our defenses, however valuable, become out of date. As we grow older and leave the circumstances that made necessary their creation behind, some of our defenses also begin to work against us. Ellen gives us an example of this: while the spirited, defensive stubbornness represented by her Ellen 2 character (see page 92) has saved her as a child and teenager from being crushed by others, it now works to her detriment. Her Ellen 2 defense, perceiving meditation as a source of vulnerability, is misreading the situation. However bad trying to meditate may feel, it is not *actually* an annihilating authority. When defenses reach this place—when they become unnecessary and work against us—it is time to see them clearly and begin to let them go. Nicky, who has had many terrible things happen to her, begins to recognize that she is probably repressing memories and emotions that, until she had started practicing mindfulness, she had not been able to approach. Noticing that someone else in the group was describing their resistance, she reflects upon her own and discovers that it points toward painful events in her childhood and others that happened later, as an adult. In making this journey she is particularly courageous:

NICKY: He was saying he could feel the resistance in himself, and I couldn't feel the resistance. Nonetheless, I think that's what I was doing because I wasn't really aware of what was going on. I'd hear somebody say, "Oh, you were saying this or that" [as the meditation was being led], and I was thinking, "Did they? I don't remember that!" So I think there must have been a resistance to that meditation, and although it felt absolutely wonderful and I felt really blissed out, I just wonder whether I . . . I don't know how far it went in.

NIGEL: Because there were periods during it when you had no memory, so you felt that you were distracted and had not been present?

NICKY: Well, yes, maybe. I think that was very nice, but I don't think I was engaging. . . . I don't know if that is a resistance or not. I don't know.

NIGEL: You're suggesting that when we're sitting, we can experience resistance, and that resistance manifests as just simply drifting off, being distracted, not being there, spacing out.

NICKY: Yeah, I think I often go somewhere else, maybe. It's very nice; I don't dislike it at all. But I do think it's maybe a bit of resistance against actually seeing what's really occurring inside.

NIGEL: So why would you want to resist seeing what's really going on inside?

NICKY: Well, because it could be very painful.

NIGEL: You think it would be painful, or you know it'll be painful?

NICKY: I suppose I think it will be painful.

NIGEL: So it's an imagination about what it might feel
like inside?

NICKY: I suppose it is. Yeah.

NIGEL: Where does that imagination come from?

NICKY: I think it comes from probably blocking out a load
of childhood stuff.

NIGEL: So your way of defending yourself against difficult
experience?

NICKY: Yeah, it is, definitely. I know I didn't deal with
anything at the time. You know . . . my dad died
nearly four years ago, and I still haven't actually
grieved for him. I have been on antidepressants since
then, so I don't . . . I haven't . . . And certainly the
abuse—I haven't touched it, although since I've been
doing this, it's far more "in my face" than it was before.

NIGEL: The memories and the emotions around the abuse
have become much more accessible to you.

NICKY: Well, not all the memories, no, but I've actually
acknowledged it more than I have in the past, and I
did contact the police, although I didn't do anything
else. I just found out what you had to do and stuff, but,
you know, that's the first time that I've gone down
that route.

So on the face of it Nicky's meditation seemed to be blissful,
but she is suspicious because she realizes that she has not been
consciously present during parts of it. She wonders if those periods of distraction are her resisting going near memories of being
abused as a child and more recently her unmourned father's
death. Initially, what is happening is unclear. Our practice can

be blissful without this being a defense and not being a hundred percent present need not mean we are repressing something. However, after a little inquiry it seems to Nicky that this is what is actually going on. She then goes on to explore how this resistance affects her establishing a regular meditation practice and discovers that her not doing it mirrors self-abusive behaviors that she has struggled with throughout her life.

NICKY: Well if I have a day off, I sort of think, well sometimes I'm motivated and think, "Right, I'll do it first thing; well, not first thing in the morning, but as soon as I've taken Molly to school." But sometimes I just think, "Oh well, I'll do that in a minute. Or, you know, I'll fit that in somewhere or other." Instead of getting on and doing it, I'll think, "Right, I'll just put that load of washing on," or "I'll just . . ." I don't always make it my priority, I suppose. And I think, in a way, I should—"should"—it's good for me to make it my priority.

NIGEL: Why do you not make it your priority?

NICKY: Some kind of self-punishment? I don't know! I can only think it's some kind of neglect, I suppose.

NIGEL: Neglect of yourself? By yourself? Why would you do that?

NICKY: Hmm . . . Probably because I'm fairly fucked up emotionally! Or have been. You know, I've had years of never feeding myself properly. . . . I've never been bulimic or anything like that, but until I had my daughter I would never bother cooking meals—I'd just eat rubbish. It's years of neglecting myself; I think that's a trait.

NIGEL: And do you have a sense of what's at the root of that neglecting of yourself, the not feeding yourself and . . .

NICKY: I presume it's either the sexual abuse or losing my mum when I was young. One of those two things, I think it would have been.

NIGEL: So that's two really big traumas there.

NICKY: Hmm . . . I presume it's one of those that's triggered all the depressions and that's why I neglect myself.

NIGEL: So what you're saying is that because of those two really big traumatic experiences during your childhood, you think, you feel, that's led to not looking after yourself, neglecting yourself, and that even shows itself in the choice whether to practice or not—that sometimes you'll find yourself neglecting yourself even with that?

NICKY: I don't know, but that is my gut feeling that that's what's occurring.

Nicky has the ability to look clearly into herself. She sees how she is resisting her imagination of how painful it would be if she were to go closer to her history of sexual abuse and how the subsequent neglect of herself is a product of this, which then influences her meditation. This clarity bodes well for her practice. Using curiosity and kindness, Nicky is learning that she can gradually approach the unapproachable and survive.

Tough Love

Kindness and compassion are at the heart of mindfulness meditation. Together they create the atmosphere in which our mindfulness flourishes, protecting it, with their intrinsic warmth, from degenerating into cold observation. However, kindness and compassion also have teeth that prevent us from distorting them into something that we use to avoid unwanted experiences. Seeing things as they really are is an activity of kindness and compassion and, as such, these two challenge us to look carefully at what we are really doing. Here are several particularly unkind and unskillful things that we can do to ourselves while believing we are doing ourselves a favor:

TAKING THE EASY OPTION
We can let ourselves off the hook when we tell ourselves that we are being kind to ourselves by not practicing, or by bringing our practice to an early, unplanned end, or by just allowing ourselves to drift along in our thoughts. Often these decisions have very convincing rationalizations: we may believe that it is better not to force anything, that we are tired and need to rest (even though we have just got up), or that our thoughts are so fascinating and creative that we need to have them. All these, and many, many others, are ways we can dress up what ultimately is just a decision to avoid what we find more difficult. What makes such decisions so seductive is their apparent truth. It is

important not to force anything—we could be tired and certainly some thoughts are very productive—but with growing self-awareness we learn to distinguish what is true from what is merely an excuse we are choosing to hood-wink ourselves with.

WILLFUL CONTINUATION

Closely associated with taking the easy option is willful continuation. Here we may have already seen that what disrupts, cuts short, or aborts our mindfulness meditation is actually something we are choosing to do, something we are entirely responsible for. And yet, without admitting it to ourselves, we choose to continue in the ways that we know are unhelpful and will cause us pain. Many examples of these ways of behaving are found later in the book, particularly in chapter 5, on the hindrances to mindfulness. What is important here is the insight that we can choose to continue on autopilot even when we have already decided that it is time for a necessary change. There is just something inside that is resistant to letting go. Recognizing this with a fierce kindness and compassion, and clearly seeing it, will enable our practice to become established and grow.

When Meditation Becomes the Defense

Several weeks after she has completed the eight-week course, Jane tells me about going to the beach, when on holiday, with the intention to practice mindfulness. She says she imagined that the beautiful beach, quite empty and going on for miles with huge breakers, would be a perfect place to have a fantastic mindfulness experience. However, what happened was quite the opposite: she could not concentrate, and she felt her practice was rubbish—she considered it a "failure." While this is a sad tale, that this should happen ought not be a surprise. Jane's intention was not to be present with whatever she was experiencing but to have a certain type of predetermined fantastic meditative event: calm, chilled, serene—a bit like the consumerist expectations we build around buying an ice cream or going to a movie or, indeed, going to a beach on holiday. As such, she was practicing the opposite of mindfulness, not just being present with no particular expectations, but picking and choosing and being disappointed when she did not have the pleasurable experience she wanted. Jane demonstrates for us the desire to use our meditation to make ourselves feel good and not feel bad. While it is necessary to be attracted to our practice if we are to develop a strong motivation to do it, it is entirely destructive if that attraction is based on achieving, during the practice, a desired state of mind while excluding others. Treated in this way our mindfulness becomes a mere commodity that we use for distraction; it has become a defense.

Over forty years ago in his seminal book *Cutting Through*

Spiritual Materialism, the Buddhist teacher Chögyam Trungpa Rinpoche put his finger on how we can misuse our meditation—in fact, our whole spirituality—as a defense against what we do not want to feel. Using the word "ego" to mean that part of us that partitions experience, keeping what we do not like under control and out of awareness, he says:

> *Ego is constantly attempting to acquire and apply the teachings of spirituality for its own benefit. . . . We go through the motions, make the appropriate gestures, but we really do not want to sacrifice any part of our way of life. We become skillful actors, and while playing deaf and dumb to the real meaning of the teachings, we find some comfort in pretending to follow the path.*

Trungpa was not pointing the finger at just a few of his students. Rather, he identified this as a tendency in all of us. This shows in many ways. In meditation we may believe we are present with our breath, with physical sensations, emotions, and thoughts, but in reality we are only superficially applying the method. We have an occasional awareness of our breath, or whatever our object of mindfulness is, but most of the time we are content to drift in a diffuse state of consciousness that is not aware of being carried away in the stream of barely conscious thinking. When this becomes a partial trancelike state that is extremely pleasurable, without stress, rather like snoozing in a warm bath, but lacking any clarity and awareness, it is what Tsoknyi Rinpoche calls "stupid meditation." This is particularly seductive, because while giving the illusion to ourselves that we are practicing, we are entirely absent. Barry Magid, psychoanalyst and Zen teacher, comes close to the same idea. In his *Ending the Pursuit of Happiness* he calls this, as mentioned above, our "secret practice"; that is, we use our practice to get rid of parts of ourselves that we do not like or want. Like Trungpa, he is convinced this is something we all do:

> *Whatever method of meditation we adopt, we are inevitably going to try to enlist that practice in the service of one or more of our curative fantasies. A curative fantasy is a personal myth that we use to explain what we think is wrong with us and our lives and what we imagine is going to make it all better.*

When we approach our meditation in this way, our secret practice is not to be present but to be better. Feeling that we are deficient in some way, our practice becomes both a means for self-improvement and a defense against the emotions deficiency engenders—guilt, shame, anxiety, depression. Barry Magid says, "Whatever we are, we feel that we want or need something else. . . . Almost always we conclude that there is something wrong with us as we are." Our meditation becomes an exercise more in self-hatred than in presence and kindness:

> *Over and over again, I see students whose secret goal in practice is the extirpation of some hated part of themselves. Sometimes it is their anger, sometimes their sexuality, their emotional vulnerability, their bodies, or sometimes their minds that are blamed as the source of suffering. "If only I could get rid of . . ."*

Stephen Batchelor talks about meeting this in a student and his advice that we must embrace ourselves fully, our unwanted experiences and also our *not wanting* unwanted experiences. All of our experiences are included.

> *Someone who was very sincerely and almost desperately trying to be a good meditator was convinced that if they could just quieten their minds, then they'd be happy. And so they basically subverted their own process. They pushed themselves way too hard. They're impatient, they're frustrated. I think there is a deep inability to accept themselves as they are, and meditation, Buddhism, can easily be used as a form of self-avoidance, by positing some kind of higher or better or wiser or happier sense of who they are. There is a conviction that by mastering the nuts and bolts of meditation, they'll get to this state. And I have to point that out to them, "Look, you won't get anywhere unless you can actually say yes to what it is that's going on, right now, on the cushion. It's not your business to fantasize or expect some result down the road. You'll get nowhere unless you can really embrace your experience with all of its angst and its pain and its frustration right now. And that's the practice you should be doing."*

Finally, a third way we can use our meditation defensively is to use it to defend against life. Many of us who are attracted to meditation, and perhaps more so Buddhism, may be afraid of entering the world of emotional and material complexity. John Welwood, a psychologist and exponent of mindfulness-based psychotherapy, speaks of this in his essay "Between Heaven and Earth." He says those of us "who are having difficulty navigating life's developmental challenges . . . earning a living through dignified work, raising a family, keeping a marriage together, belonging to a meaningful community" may try to resolve the anxieties these tasks create by simply "transcending" them:

> There is often a tendency to use spiritual practice to try to rise above our emotional and personal issues—all those messy, unresolved matters that weigh us down. I call this tendency to avoid or prematurely transcend basic human needs, feelings, and developmental tasks spiritual bypassing.

Martin Wells confirms this, speaking of the demands of life:

> There's no bypass to what is being asked here; many people, me included, have been looking for a way for transcendence on the bypass of life, rather than facing head on what we need to face and relinquish, including some dark material from the unconscious.

Spiritual bypassing superficially mimics practicing our meditation, but it has the hidden intention to create a spiritual self-identity that is immune to pain. As such, it is both a secret practice and an expression of spiritual materialism. It is about resisting (which only continues our old dysfunctional behaviors) thoughts and emotions, all our unresolved psychological issues, rather than mindfully befriending them with kindness and acceptance. With this defense we cheat ourselves.

EXERCISE: WHO GUARDS OUR GATE?

How do we defend ourselves? It may be helpful to pause here and ask whether we have noticed experiences, sensations, emotions that we want to avoid and, if so, how do we do it?

*Remember, what we discover here is not bad or shameful. We
all have and need our defenses—all we are doing here is making
them conscious by applying curiosity with kindness.*

The Guardian at the Gate:
Key Points

- When we start meditation we immediately discover
  how hard it is not to be distracted.
- Distraction may come from simply being unused to paying sustained attention, but it may also be a way not to
  be present with ourselves.
- When distraction is this, it may be acting as a defense
  against the anxiety of having to go closer to previously
  and unconsciously repressed thoughts and emotions.
- There are many styles of defense, but they are all basically forms of repression—repressing what we do not
  want to consciously know.
- Defenses have a very valuable function, but some
  become unnecessary and when they do they may work
  against us. When this happens, it is time to let them go.
- Meditation itself may become a defense by being used to

  - *– achieve only pleasurable mind states;*
  - *– get rid of parts of ourselves we do not want;*
  - *– avoid ordinary life with all its challenges.*

CHAPTER 4

Meeting Ourselves

*Looking for something special creates lots of struggle. We have to learn to
let go of wanting special experiences. Everything's easy when you learn
that all the ordinary experiences in meditation are enough.*

LAMA RABSANG

Oh shit, still ten minutes.

BEN

*I think that's the greatest shift that people can make: no longer trying to
manipulate the conditions in our life to fit in with our image of how things
should be.*

CHRISTINA FELDMAN

After we have fed the dog, done the washing up, or checked
our e-mails, we may finally bring ourselves to sit and meditate. A group of people who have all completed the eight-week
mindfulness course talk about their mindfulness meditation:
what in themselves do they meet when they practice? Sophie
immediately says thoughts and emotions that she recognizes she
is scared of. She has noticed that when a particular emotion
arose she became anxious and "chose" to let herself drift off into
a diffuse state of consciousness. Kit says her thoughts were like
fleas jumping all over the place, but as she continued there came

a point where she could step back from being in the center of them and, letting them go, rest in her breath. Then, perhaps for only four or five breaths, she could be present with the sensation of breathing, until assailed by a new wave of thinking—this time about whether she was doing it right. Gwen had much the same experience: initially attacked by her inner critical voices, she was overwhelmed by thoughts, but after a while they settled and she found a very difficult-to-describe calm space located in her chest. This accorded with Julia's experience: why, she asked, did she do anything other than sit, even when she knew how good it was? Just sitting this evening it had felt like coming home to herself. Paul agreed—his practice was going through a period where he just felt a background pleasure. Each day he found he was looking forward to his meditation and the replenishing stillness he found there. Finally Caroline spoke. Who was it she met, she wondered? Someone who was watching perhaps; she was not entirely sure.

Expectations

There is a story about one of the Christian Desert Fathers called Abba Theodore. A young monk came to him complaining that he was unhappy practicing in solitude, and so the kindly old man advised him not to torture himself with too high expectations and to practice while living with others. Some time passed and the monk returned, saying he had found no peace with others either. At this the wise old man asked the young man how many years he had been a monk, and the young man said eight. The sage replied, "I have worn the habit for seventy years, and on no day have I found peace. Do you expect to find peace so soon?"

Meeting ourselves in the midst of our resistance and defenses may not be easy. Like the young monk who had unrealistic expectations and could not accept what he experienced, what we find may not be what we want. Christina Feldman says the person we find in our practice is exactly the same person we were before we started:

> *People discover that their life has followed them onto the cushion, and somehow people may have had an expectation that they were going to come into meditation and fall into a previously undiscovered land of bliss and rapture. Instead they find they're meeting their life, they're meeting their body, they're meeting everything that their life holds—all of their emotions and memories, their past experiences, their preoccupations with the present—and that's by far the greatest difficulty for people.*

There is often a gap between our fantasy of what practicing mindfulness will give us and the actual experience when we meet ourselves just as we are. Christina again:

> *There is that gap, but that discrepancy is no different from the discrepancy that has haunted many people through their lives. The gap between the way we think things should be or ought to be, the way we want them to be, and the way that they actually are. In many ways, that gap is what the Buddhist teaching is all about, that discrepancy is always going to get us into trouble. Much of the torment in people's lives is born of that gap between the way we want things to be and the way they actually are.*

Sitting with a body that really wants to move and a mind that will not sit still can challenge our faith in our ability to meditate and the value of meditation itself. We think, "I should be a different meditator from the one I am—I cannot believe that I still find it so hard, that having sat with myself for all this time I am still criticizing myself, my meditation experience, the value of the whole thing. And I can find no peace. Thoughts, emotions, memories, and fantasies continually break in upon me. I have no control, not even over the next thought." When our daily practice is like this, it is very easy to doubt the whole enterprise and want something different. Not able to include her thoughts and emotions as objects of mindfulness, Linda miserably describes the tedium of waiting for her meditation CD to end. She says, "Returning from a long daydream, the thing was *still* playing." Tsoknyi Rinpoche describes how failed expectations cause impatience and loss of confidence:

> *Students understand the meditation, the practice, but they expect their transformation to be very fast. Some have an immediate cognitive understanding, but to transform habitual patterns takes time. So they become impatient and think: I understand but I don't transform—I think it's not working.*

Jean reported that the moment she sat down her thoughts began to whiz unpleasantly around in her head until it felt like a band of pressure. Connor asked whether it was meant to be trancelike as he seemed to drop into a disconnected weird space when he practiced. Behind both descriptions was a shared feeling of disappointment: the experience of mindfulness was not as they had imagined or wanted. Both struggled to accept this as just their experience, not making it wrong, but as something they could choose to be present with. Lama Rabsang observes:

> *It's difficult to be satisfied with this precious moment and just let it be; instead we're looking for something. In meditation we want to see some kind of special light or to have some kind of special experience, some special openness when we think, "Wow, that's what we're looking for." Looking for something special creates lots of struggle. We have to learn to let go of wanting special experiences. Everything's easy when you learn that all the ordinary experiences in meditation are enough. Being aware and mindful in the present moment, then it is special already.*

For many of us, ordinary experience just does not seem enough. We are frustrated with being ourselves and we want something better, something different, or just something *more*. Barry Magid suggests asking a question to see if we are truly content to have the meditation experience we are having. Ask yourself whether you would continue meditating if all the sessions for the rest of your life were going to be like the one you had this morning. If the answer is no, this may mean that you are hoping, wanting, expecting, something other than how it is. Christina Feldman talks about how what we yearn for—perhaps finding some calm in our busy minds—can paradoxically only happen when we accept our minds as they currently are:

> *What the Buddha taught was the more we are aligned with the way things actually are, the more peace we will discover in our lives and the less conflict, the less tension. Mindfulness practice*

is taking steps, moment to moment, towards that alignment with the way things actually are, however they are, in this moment. I think that's the greatest shift that people can make: no longer trying to manipulate the conditions in our life to fit in with our image of how things should be. That gap is one of the primary breeders of conflict and suffering in people's lives, so with the practice, with mindfulness, we begin turning towards, rather than turning away.

On hearing this, many of us will ask: Is this not just accepting something that is not right, that feels bad, when we should be doing something to make it different? If we just accepted everything, then nothing would change. Surely the whole point of putting all this effort into meditation is to feel better? While it is true that mindfulness does have a destination—the ability to be present with whatever we find in ourselves, moment to moment, openhearted, unafraid, welcoming of ourselves—it is also true that this cannot start from a point of self-rejection. Nor does it mean that we should approach ourselves with a grudging acceptance, with a resigned acceptance of what we find that has no kindness and still harbors a secret wish that things should be different. Martin Wells differentiates between these two types of acceptance, making the point that resignation just creates resistance:

We have lots of conversations in the courses about the meaning of acceptance, you know, the difference between acceptance in a passive sense, in terms of resignation, and an active sense, the embracing of life and feelings and thoughts. Distinguishing these perspectives is very important for people—particularly people who've felt oppressed and invaded in any way, because they've learnt a system of resistance and fighting that has helped them survive and that is not easily let go of.

Sam speaks of stopping his practice. Thinking he may have used his meditation as a covert means to not feel things he would rather keep repressed, he eventually finds a level of real acceptance that includes the "nasty smell" of "unfinished business." He has made a journey that our young monk in the desert (see page 116) has yet to make. With his letting go of expectations and his acceptance of things as they really are have come self-trust and rest.

What stopped me doing it was increasing feelings of anxiety about my life, and I got into a state and I eventually had to come out to my parents about my sexuality and come out to myself really. Then I had counseling, and then I had some therapy for about six months. I came to realize that you can't just sit and meditate and achieve some state of wonderful silent calm and stillness if there was unfinished business burning away on your back burner and making a nasty smell in your mind or in your soul or wherever you like, and I realized that I had to accept myself hook, line, and sinker, sexuality and all. So that is what that bit of meditation taught me—that it brings up things about yourself that you have to acknowledge and deal with in therapy and in life really. . . . I learnt that it wasn't about achieving stillness; it was a lot to do with, or even mostly to do with, accepting yourself as you are and not wishing to be some different, amazing person.

Realistic Expectations

When we start meditating, we do not know what to expect. Why would we? We are just beginning. Here is a realistic picture of what we might expect of our ability to be present with our object of mindfulness, but with a word of caution: this is not a race or a challenge. If we are motivated by reaching a goal, we have created a situation that is the opposite of being mindfully present with where we currently are—here, now, in this moment:

1. Very simple, we all start here. We direct our attention to our object of mindfulness—our physical sensations, our breath—and it is almost immediately washed away in a flow of thoughts and completely forgotten. There is no staying with our object of mindfulness. This is not wrong; it is a successful first step when we notice it.

2. We develop the ability to stay with our object of mindfulness for a little longer, maybe a minute. Most of the time we are washed away in the flow of thinking and the object of mindfulness is completely forgotten.

3. As our practice develops, we return more quickly to our object of mindfulness. We still cannot stay present with it for an extended period, and there are still times where it is completely forgotten in the flow of thoughts.

4. We no longer completely forget our object of mindfulness. The flow of thoughts continues, but because our mindfulness is now strong, it is not distracting.

This takes a lot of practice.

Thoughts and Thinking

It is a common mistaken fantasy that mindfulness meditation aims to become thought-free. While it is true that sublime meditative states exist that are entirely without thought, these are only achieved through extremely rare feats of prolonged and uninterrupted superhuman concentration.

Mindfulness, as described here, does not have the goal of suppressing thought. Rather, its job is to simply notice when thoughts have carried us away from our object of mindfulness—our physical sensations, our breath—and to kindly and gently escort ourselves back. Mindfulness is not at war with thoughts; it is the awareness in which we come to know how our minds, our emotions, work.

As this process deepens, we become aware that there are different levels of thinking. The most obvious is the strong thoughts that carry us off, totally absorbing us in memories, fantasies, dialogues—the list is almost endless. These are the thoughts that cause us to forget our object of mindfulness. There are also much fainter thoughts, less strong, that continue while we remain mindfully present with our sensations or breath. These we need not worry about; they are peripherally present in our awareness without being a distraction. Finally, it may sometimes happen that the usually unnoticed tiny gaps between one thought and the next become longer and so we have a brief awareness of our minds being thought-free but still entirely conscious. This is not a goal to be achieved and is of no greater value than being mindfully present while our thoughts are active. We mindfully notice this and nothing more.

Emotions

Being emotional beings is complicated and yet it is intrinsic to our nature—to be a mammal is to have emotions. We could not form relationships or function without our emotions, but at the same time our emotions can cause us discomfort and sometimes unbearable suffering. Without our emotions we would not be inspired or motivated to continue meditating, but, on the other hand, it is our emotions that make us want to give up when it gets tough.

Buddhism has a great deal to say on emotion. It recognizes that our emotions can be either life enhancing or a source of great unhappiness—a truth that any of us who have experienced depression and anxiety and then been released from it will immediately understand. Among the many emotional qualities that Buddhism values are loving kindness, compassion, empathetic joy, and equanimity (which it calls the "four divine abodes") and also generosity, virtue, renunciation, vigor, patience, and finally wisdom (the "six perfections"). These complex emotional qualities are necessary for and engendered by the practice of Buddhism. However, we also have a very large selection of destructive emotional mental states that arise when we are confronted by circumstances that we do not like, that scare us in some way, perhaps hinting at our own annihilation. These evoke reactions to compulsively seek what feels pleasurable, aggressively avoid what is painful, and disregard that which is neither. These three reactions are called the "three root poisons." Seeking what is pleasurable includes grasping, unhealthy attachment, desire, and greed. Avoiding what is painful includes aversion, anger, aggression, and hatred. And indifference, being unconscious and disengaged, when considered as a fundamental state of ignorance, includes confusion, bewilderment, and delusion. These core reactions are behind an unlimited number of destructive and conflicted emotional states that can drive us unhappily along, searching for happiness but never really finding it. Buddhism believes they are one of the two principal causes of our pervasive feeling of things being unsatisfactory and that together with the second, not knowing how things really are, they leave us alienated from our awakened nature.

The Buddha also talked about this emotional conflict within ourselves as the "two arrows." He says the two arrows are sensation and our emotional reaction to it. When we experience unpleasant sensations, we add to these with "crying and lamenting until we become deranged." We are caught up in the poisons of grasping and aversion—wanting this, not wanting that—whereas of those who are able to be mindfully present, he says:

When they feel the pangs of unpleasant sensations, they are not sorrowful nor mournful; they do not wail, lament, nor beat their breasts crying, nor do they become deranged. They only feel physical sensations, not mental torment.

The unpleasant sensation remains, but there is no additional emotional reaction to it. Jim starts a discussion during his MBSR/MBCT class. Thinking about what he would wish for his children, he says that part of life is to make many mistakes and learn from the emotional turmoil this creates. For instance, getting a hangover—would not being mindful detract from this? Perhaps many of us would agree that we certainly do learn from our mistakes and emotions are a central part of this. We would not want to go through life like a robot or a zombie. Getting a hangover, a really bad one, is an invaluable "learning opportunity." However, this is to miss the point. The first arrow is all life throws at us—in this instance, including the biological reality of alcohol poisoning and the pain this causes. However, we have a choice over ways of being with this. Feeling the dry mouth and the throbbing head, we can make the hangover worse by becoming afraid of the pain and anxious that the aspirin will not work. Or we can berate ourselves for being stupid and drinking too much. Both emotional reactions—both second arrows—do not help in any way. In fact, we can exacerbate things by becoming afraid. Alternatively, feeling the same horrendous aftereffects of too much drinking, mindfully noticing the inclination to panic and blame, we could let the thoughts go and, returning to the sensations alone, get curious, be present with the experience, just as it is, not adding anything else. Plainly, this is a better solution. No longer resisting, the tight head relaxes and the moral implications are not impaired in any way—it still hurts, and we will still (probably) hesitate before doing it again. This has been one of life's enriching moments, and we have been fully present to receive it.

What this teaching gives us is the truth that we unnecessarily wound ourselves again with the second arrow when we resist what simply is. Being angry, I become ashamed of my anger; being vulnerable, I am afraid of my vulnerability; being anxious and depressed, I am resentful of my anxiety and depression. In all cases the second arrow only makes things worse. Anger, vulnerability, anxiety, and depression are never helped by shame, fear, and resentment. Learning to recognize when we are wounding ourselves with a lack of acceptance and to be comfortable with whatever emotion is arising within us is the practice and fruit of mindfulness. It takes the three poisons and turns them around. Less frequently driven by our desires, resisting what is and disengaging from ourselves and the world around us, our emotional conflict and distress diminish. In their place grow emotions that can be life enhancing and lead us toward the realization of our deepest potential. Emotions such as the four divine abodes we met above—loving kindness, compassion, empathetic joy, and equanimity—nourish us, reducing stress and creating happiness. On the other hand, emotions such as ill will, pride, shamelessness, greed, conceit, hatred, envy, and miserliness, to name but a few from the many lists of destructive mind states derived from the three poisons, do the opposite. This is where our practice begins to extend into our lives: meeting our emotions, becoming mindfully aware of what we are feeling, we can cultivate those that support well-being and do something other than be compelled into reactivity by those that do not.

Emotions, Moods, and Temperament

Emotions, moods, and our overall temperament—whether positive or negative—can all be felt in our bodies, but some are easier to notice than others.

EMOTIONS

A strong emotion is typically felt as intense and fleeting. One emotion can quickly give way to the next, seemingly leaving little trace. It is difficult to experience two very different emotions at once, and emotions are usually triggered by noticeable events that lead to reactions. Emotions are also easily identified—anger, fear, sadness, disgust, etc.— and they give birth to others, which can turn into a cascade of emotions all firing each other up. Once this has happened, it takes time for our systems to calm down and for the reverberations of the emotions to recede.

MOODS

Moods are persistent background emotions that may last between an hour to several days or even longer. Though not acute, they can color our whole experience, perhaps infecting it with sadness and depression or happiness and joy. They may be triggered by events that are happening in the present—being invited out by a friend, for example—or something physical, such as tiredness or low blood sugar, or by unconscious associations that create a mood without our being aware it has happened or even exactly what it is.

TEMPERAMENT

It seems that each of us has a basic emotional disposition: we may be optimistic or more gloomy or anxious. Whatever our more fleeting emotions are, our temperament remains much the same and can persist throughout life. It is possible that our temperament may be partially something we come with and partially something that is a result of our infancy and early childhood. As such, it may be accompanied by beliefs and ways of behaving that reaffirm and perpetuate it, often becoming more apparent as we get older.

Lists of Emotions

Attempts to list emotions and divide them into different categories or types have so far failed to arrive at a consensus. One way of thinking about them is to split them into basic, secondary, and tertiary emotions. A basic six might be love (or happiness), disgust, surprise, anger, sadness, and fear. Each of these may then be subdivided. So, for example, love contains affection, lust, and longing, all of which, in turn, open into further emotions still—so lust contains desire, passion, and infatuation. What is surprising about such lists is just how many emotions we can have: one list contains just under 150 separate, distinguishable emotions, with joy, anger, and sadness being the biggest groups. Buddhism's list is somewhat longer, identifying, as the sum of what we can experience, 84,000 conflicted emotions.

EXERCISE: HOW LONG DOES AN EMOTION LAST?

Opinion differs on the question of how long an emotion lasts—perhaps only ninety seconds, perhaps several minutes. Certainly, a really intense burst of emotion is short-lived—feeling suddenly angry, afraid, or moved to love and wonder. We can do an experiment for ourselves, asking questions like these:

How long does a burst of strong emotion last for me?

Does this emotion just come and then go, or does it cause further emotions? What happens next?

What do I do with my strong emotions? Do I try to contain or smother them or let them out and be swept up in them? Do I find myself prolonging them?

Being in Two Minds

Once we begin to meet ourselves more consciously, the realization dawns that inside we have different and sometimes warring parts of our personalities. Rick Hanson, in his book *Buddha's*

Brain, describes the neural functions that are concerned with creating relationship and those that are about aggression as the "wolf of love" and the "wolf of hate"—images borrowed from Native Americans. Quite simply, we have evolved to make strong affectional bonds with those we consider our group, particularly our family, while being aggressive and dangerous toward those we consider other. On the whole, the ability to love is far stronger, but for it to be so it has required the existence of our aggressive side, and this, unchecked, can—and does—create all the horrors our world seems so full of. The good news is that we can build on our innate ability to love by encouraging empathy and compassion to grow while restraining fear and aggression.

As we meditate mindfully, it is possible to see the "two wolves" within us. Emotions that are kind, compassionate, and accepting further our practice, but all too often we turn our aggression on ourselves, castigating ourselves for some part of us we do not want to accept. Talking about her practice, Molly, someone who seems bruised by her life, says she starts out quite well, but when she realizes she has been distracted for a long while is angry with herself, which starts a cascade of ferocious self-hatred. Her "first arrow" wound of simply having a distracted mind that is slow in learning to concentrate is joined by the "second arrow" of vicious self-recrimination. Her wolf of hate has decided that the part of her that gets distracted is other and a threat, and closes in for the kill.

Molly's experience is not unusual. One of the things just about all of us realize during the eight-week mindfulness course is how critical and unaccepting we are of ourselves. Meeting our inability to remain present, finding how hard it is to sit still and be awake, it feels as if there are parts of ourselves that are quite independent, doing their own thing, unrelated to each other and, frequently, openly hostile. There are varying schools of thought within psychology and psychotherapy regarding the mechanics of this idea of different parts of ourselves. Personally, I think of each of us as a bus full of people, many unknown to each other. Generally only one person drives, but occasionally someone with a quite different character and intentions will jump up and, seizing the wheel, drive off in a completely novel direction. What is especially disruptive is when someone from the backseat—the place where the most anarchic and disturbed always sit—grabs the wheel, and then we find ourselves feeling and doing things that seem almost alien and not "us." As you read on, this idea will begin to show its value: why am I in two minds over my meditation practice, wanting to do it yet somehow never finding the time? Why am I so horrible to myself when my meditation does not go "well"? The answers are that at least two people are driving our meditation bus in different directions. Sam describes his experience of this:

> The negative part me says, "God, I have got to go to the supermarket later and pay that bill and get money out of the bank. What a bore. I would rather sit here and listen to Stravinsky and read a bit of something and ponder the mysteries of life. Sit on my arse and dream of Dante's Paradiso." I think it is probably just the "sod it" part of me that wants to sit and be grumpy and think, "Oh, fuck the world, what do they know? I am doing all right anyway. I am quite a good painter, although a lot of people don't realize it. I am this deeply sensitive, musical person really, and the world can go fuck itself." That sort of feeling. There is this grumpy little child who gets a bit bored and

snappish about things: "I don't want to just sit here on my own,
in the kitchen, meditating. Where's the fun in life? Give me a
treat. I want something nice to happen, Mummy, Daddy!" It is
quite interesting, isn't it, to think about that grumpy and cross
little inner child: "I am going to treat myself to a CD later, so
there! Sod this meditation." So it is good to laugh about it, and
I try just to go into it with an emptyish sort of mind and not
prejudge it all and just sit there and go with the flow, really.

So the person who comes forward wanting to drive Sam's
bus is a grumpy little child who feels essentially hard done by
and resentful. For most of us, our official bus driver will usually
try to ignore or deny the set of feelings such a child symbolizes,
not wanting to admit that this character is there within us.
However, when the driver is ousted from their seat, we may discover ourselves run by a different story and, on autopilot, find we
are driven by emotional reactivity. What Sam does is something
quite different: acknowledging these emotions exist, he neither
pushes them away (represses them by saying something to himself like "Don't be silly; stop it"), nor does he identify with them,
jumping up from his meditation and stomping off to buy the CD
that represents his parents' love. Rather, he takes the middle
way of mindfulness: he remains present with his emotions—he
feels them and sees them clearly, but he does not become them.
He has his emotions, rather than they having him. Of course,
this is easy to say, but much more difficult to do. Much in ourselves wants to go along the well-trodden ways and change nothing, and when this happens the person we meet on our bus is
called resistance. Speaking of his meditation, Ben shows us a
version of this:

It seems like my organism sometimes wants to get away from it, rather than embrace it. There are sessions where I just long for the time, and it's very helpful to realize that doing sitting meditation, securing that time, is actually a gift that you may give yourself, which is really a very nice thought. But there's also a force that tries to pull me away from it all the time, and sometimes I think, "Oh shit, still ten minutes." But that's a very strange thought, isn't it? It's like making it a duty. So there is a force that wants me to get away from it, and maybe that is also a very strong force in general that takes us away from being aware of here and now. It's like a wild horse that wants to break away all the time rather than sit down here and be quiet and face the music!

Ben has discovered a collection of figures on his bus. In addition to his principal driver, who likes the idea of meditating because it is giving himself much-appreciated time, he also finds a part of himself that, when it is driving, feels the meditation as a repressive imposition—a duty that he is not enjoying fulfilling. This then alerts him to the person who is like a wild horse who, when driving, is resistant to being present and a strong force of distraction. This is a particularly interesting collection of figures because they suggest an arrangement Sigmund Freud noticed and one that was later taken up by transactional analysis as the tension between the "inner child," "parent," and "adult." The idea is that when we look into ourselves, we may find there is a part of us that is largely driven by wanting to do just what we want, without any constraints or consequences. This has the benefits of spontaneity and feeling intensely alive, but, like a child, it can be shortsighted in its goals and lacking the wisdom to see a wider picture. In opposition to this is another part that is big on duty, on doing what has to be done and finishing it, regardless of how we may be feeling emotionally. This parental voice has the benefits of achievement, continuity, and seeing the bigger picture, but it can also be individually stifling and repressive—following the letter of the law and not the spirit. Finding a way to balance these two is the place of the adult, who can moderate and regulate the "wild horse"—or the child—without entirely killing off its life force through too much of the parent's discipline.

This way of seeing the characters on our bus can be very useful. When we are practicing our meditation because we feel we ought or should, it is fairly likely that the parent is driving, while if we meditate only when we feel like it, then it is the child who has the wheel. Neither of these is a good driver because while the positive side of the parent helps us to be disciplined in our practice, the negative side can make us insensitive to what is actually happening from moment to moment, turning the whole thing into a chore we gradually come to resent. Likewise, the child: the positive child is excitement and engagement with the practice, but on the negative side, when these emotions change—as all emotions do—there then seems no reason to continue. The adult, on the other hand, is a very good driver because she or he can balance the practice by mixing the right amounts of intention with relaxation. Mindfully aware in each moment, we assess what our practice needs, and if we find we are drifting, we crisp up our attention to the details of the method, or, finding we are too tight, we relax and loosen up. Having our bus driven by our adult means it stays on the road. It means that the driver knows who is on the bus, and, seeing them through the mirror of mindfulness as they approach along the aisle, knows what to do: accept with kindness that they are there but remain firmly at the wheel. And when the adult driver loses it? Well, like Ben, accept with kindness that this happens too and then, taking the wheel again, get back on track.

EXERCISE: GETTING THE BALANCE RIGHT

Using the idea of the child, parent, and adult, think about your own practice:

Do I run my practice mostly on emotional reactions, only doing it when I feel like it or judging each session upon whether it felt good or not?

Do I run my practice mostly based upon my ideas about what I should be doing, how a good meditator ought to organize daily meditation sessions, according to the teacher or the book I have read?

If we can identify a definite bias one way or the other, what would it be like to introduce something of the other into the way we practice? So if our practice is based predominantly upon the emotions we feel, we could explore being more disciplined and diligent; if we find we are doing it all in a rather fixed but unconscious way, we might pause to see how we are really feeling and relax.

And lastly, if we have a bias, is it always the same way, in meditation and other areas in our lives? Might this be something to be more mindful of?

EXERCISE: CHARACTERS ON THE BUS

Who are the characters on your bus? Here is an exercise adapted from transpersonal psychology:

1. When you have an uninterrupted hour find a quiet space and either sit with your eyes closed or lie down comfortably but not so you immediately go to sleep.

2. In your imagination find yourself somewhere calm and safe outdoors. This could be a lovely hillside among the grass—sunny and with good smells.

3. As you sit there, notice a bus parked nearby in a small pull-off. What sort of bus is it? Describe it to yourself.

4. Now get up and—if it feels comfortable—walk over to the bus with the intention of looking more closely. Notice how this feels. If you feel uneasy, stop now and just enjoy the grass and breathe. This is enough.

5. If you have continued, then, arriving at the bus, have a good look at it: walk around it, notice where the driver sits and the seats around him. Is there anyone sitting in the seats? Describe them to yourself.

6. Next, walk away a short distance and sit down facing the bus door and seeing the whole vehicle. Get comfortable, become curious, breathe.

7. Now, as you sit in the sunshine, the characters on your bus get off one by one and join you, sitting on the grass in a circle. There may be one or two characters or

more. Is there anyone in the backseat who has not yet come out?

Notice each one. What do they look like? What is their feeling? Do they have names? How do they seem as a group? Do they all get on? Are some complete strangers? Whoever gets off, meet them with kindness and acceptance. Welcome them all equally and breathe.

8. Finally it is time for them to return. See each character in turn climb aboard the bus and the door close behind them. You now walk away, returning to the sunny, safe place you started from and, when ready, open your eyes, back in your quiet space.

When you have completed this exercise, record it with words or, better still, drawings, however amateur. Many characters may be known to you, but pay special attention to those that are not. These are the ones who, when they drive, take you to places you would rather not go.

The value of this exercise is that we begin to know all the different thoughts and emotions that together make us up. Making these conscious, perhaps finding a name for them, being present and breathing, makes them all into objects of mindfulness. Once identified, we can recognize when they are about to start driving, and we can stay at the wheel of our bus.

Elizabeth and the Elephant in the Room

On the face of it, Elizabeth's meditation displays none of the divisions and tensions we have just described. In fact, it is so harmonious that she becomes anxious that she is doing something wrong by not being aware of any difficult emotions when meditating. However, with the arrival of this anxiety we begin to see that her bus is being driven by someone unexpected. She says:

> *What comes up for me is quite a strong feeling of "this is the bit that I can't do." I'm not aware of any big emotion that wants to be expressed, that I'm suppressing or resisting. Yet reading or hearing about other people's experience, I'm thinking, "Oh, I'm clearly a bad case! There's something I'm not getting."*

Elizabeth's anxiety may be baseless. There is no rule that says our meditation should involve being present with big emotions that want to be expressed. Mindfulness means being present with everything, happy and sad. However, given that even simply sitting and breathing brings its challenges, it is unlikely that Elizabeth has *no* emotional reactivity whatsoever. She goes on:

> I notice I've got a hierarchy of thoughts and that I am judging them. I've noticed that before I get to the point of saying "thinking" and escorting myself back to the object of mindfulness, I will often have judged the thought that I've just had as being somewhere on

the hierarchy. So if it was planning supper, it would get nought out of ten, but if I was thinking a deep and meaningful thought, it might get nearer ten out of ten.

NIGEL: So it's a hierarchy of use?

ELIZABETH: More legitimate thought. So I notice that in me there's a judgment. You know, to think that's better than something else, and as I say that now, I'm thinking, "Right, how often do I notice that?" And then I can perhaps hear the person leading the meditation saying, "Just be open to that. Just notice that. That's what you're doing; that's what's happening now."

NIGEL: When we've spoken previously, you've mentioned that throughout your life you've been persecuted by feelings of whether you're "good enough," and then here you are, in your meditation, judging your thoughts in terms of how "good enough" are they.

ELIZABETH: Yes.

NIGEL: So the preoccupation with "good enough" sounds like the presence of quite a deep wound in the meditation, and as you say, how often do you take a sufficiently big enough step backwards to incorporate that preoccupation as the object of mindfulness itself?

ELIZABETH: Yeah. And you know, the answer is I don't. What I'm aware of now is that I haven't exposed myself enough or understood enough about what else I can do beyond staying with the breath and coming back when distracted. So I feel as if there's a bit in my understanding that I haven't yet got, about how

I could use as an object of mindfulness my pattern
of putting something in a hierarchy. I haven't tried
to step back and use that thought as an object
of mindfulness because I feel as if I don't quite
know how.

NIGEL: Would it be possible, when you notice you are
doing that, to ask yourself what is the emotion felt in
your body, what your felt sense is, and to be present
with this as the object of mindfulness—"what does it
feel like in my body when I'm doing this?"

ELIZABETH: Yes, so when I think that thought can I,
instead of thinking the thought, notice there's a felt
sense that goes with that? Yes, that seems like a
possibility. . . . You know, I couldn't have said that a
couple of years ago; I couldn't have had any
confidence that I could ever notice a felt sense. I'd
think, "What do you mean—I don't get it; I don't feel
anything," or "Whatever I feel is so ordinary that it's
not worth commenting on." I was going to say
"making a fuss about."

NIGEL: So feeling "I'm not good enough."

ELIZABETH: Yeah!

NIGEL: OK, so when I asked the question, "Now that
you've started practicing, what resistance to practicing
have you noticed and what, if any, strong emotional
experiences have you had?" you answered me: "No,
nothing much comes up, but it does feel nice and
peaceful a lot of the time, and that's what motivates
me to do it." And then we looked a little bit deeper and

we found that when you're thinking you are judging
yourself—what's valuable and what isn't valuable.
And this reflects a core belief, a core wound
originating in childhood, concerning feelings of you
being judged and being not good enough. And here,
right in your meditation, you are doing it to yourself. Is
that right?

ELIZABETH: That's a wonderful insight! It's the elephant
in the room. Yeah.

Elizabeth's elephant is so all-pervading she does not see it. As
is the case with our deepest wounds, they are so continuously
present they become invisible. Here the child who feels she is
falling below what she believes are her parents' expectations, as
an adult applies similar expectations to her meditation practice.
Not seeing that she is judging herself and repeatedly failing, her
experience of childhood continues to play itself out. As she
rightly grasps, what is necessary is that she take a sufficiently
large step back, to disidentify with this pattern and make the
thoughts and the emotions it generates, as a felt sense, the object
of her meditation—to incorporate it into her ring of mindful
awareness with a great deal of acceptance and kindness. The
anxiety that she was not doing it right alerted us to a criticizing
character that was standing right next to the driver all the time,
but entirely unseen.

Working with the Felt Sense

Being able to recognize our emotions, what we are feeling, as a sensation somewhere in our body is probably the most important and useful skill in this book. For some of us, the observation that emotions are felt as physical sensations—for example a full heart, butterflies in the stomach, a tight throat—will come as no surprise, while for others it will be a revelation and something that is not immediately easy to notice. Wherever we are in this spectrum of sensibility, becoming consciously aware of our felt sense gives us access to a deeper knowledge of ourselves and also enables us to intentionally respond rather than automatically and unconsciously react. In this way recognizing what we are feeling in our body, resting our attention on what we find, in a non-judgmental and kindly way, and staying with what we find until it changes of its own accord is to lift the recognition of our felt sense to the level of a mindfulness practice. Here is a simple way to do it:

FINDING THE FELT SENSE IN OUR BODY

Giving yourself a minute to slow down and pay attention to the feeling within your body, ask yourself, "What's going on for me right now? How are things going?" Alternatively, there may already be a noticeable emotion occurring, so you need only pause and recognize its presence.

Sensing inside, notice where in your body you are feeling something—at this point it may not be clear what the emotion is. Let this awareness come slowly, and when something is felt make sure to keep a little distance from it. It's like saying, for example, "Ah, there's something—I can feel it in my stomach," or "Yes, there's something going on up here in my chest."

It may be that you find more than one felt sense—that's OK, just notice whatever you find, with curiosity and acceptance.

BEING PRESENT WITH THE FELT SENSE

Having identified where in your body you have a felt sense, simply continue to rest your attention lightly on this place, allowing yourself to fully feel it but without going right into it so that you are overwhelmed. You are not thinking about it from a distance, nor are you trying to change it or do anything with it in any way. You are simply feeling it and nothing more.

Typically, we may do this for only a moment, but here we prolong this experience, and when we find ourselves disconnecting or becoming distracted, we just bring ourselves back, asking. "Where am I feeling this in my body?" Stay present with this.

If we have several felt senses, we choose first the one that is strongest. Also remember that we can have a felt sense of every type of emotion—happy, sad, or mad.

NAMING THE FELT SENSE

This stage is optional; just staying present with the felt sense is already enough.

Still present with the felt sense, see if you can find a word, phrase, or image that really captures it. The trick here is to let the felt sense do the work. What comes forward from the felt sense that perfectly expresses what is going on? What fits it just right? This could be absolutely anything—try to accept what immediately suggests itself without editing it in any way.

CHECKING

Still using your body, go back and forth between your felt sense and the word, phrase, or image (or a combination), making sure that it really fits. Here it is important that you do not lose contact with the felt sense and turn it into a purely mental event.

The felt sense is surprisingly robust. Try out your word, phrase, or image. Does it fit with the felt sense? Is it right? If anything changes—the felt sense, its location in your body, or what describes it—go with those changes until it feels just right: "Yes, that's it. That's exactly what's going on."

TAKING IT ALL IN

And then just stay. Rest your attention on the felt sense, feeling it fully and with an awareness of the word, phrase, or image that really captures what it is about.

At this point several things might happen. Quite often

the felt sense simply fades away after having been acknowledged. For instance, consciously resting our awareness on a felt sense of anger and frustration we may feel it slowly melt away without our doing anything. However, sometimes the felt sense changes into something else, perhaps another emotion beneath the one we were feeling—for instance, sadness beneath anger or rage beneath guilt and shame. When this happens, we just repeat the process. Ask, "Where am I feeling this in my body?" Stay present. Breathe.

Getting the Right Distance: Too Far or Too Near?

When we begin to practice mindfulness of our emotions through the felt sense, it sometimes takes time to find our way into the right relationship to what we are feeling. If in our minds we position ourselves too far away from our felt sense, we can easily slide into a subtle (or not so subtle) way of cutting off. We view ourselves with a distant, cool objectivity that has no felt relationship to our emotions. At the other extreme, we can go so close to our felt sense that we entirely lose our ability to witness ourselves and, identifying with the emotion, become soaked in it, so it has us rather than our having it. Here all mindfulness is lost.

It may help if we think of the best distance between ourselves and our emotions as being like a relationship between two people. To be with another person we must be close enough to really feel who they are and hear what they say but not so close that their proximity makes any relationship impossible. Just imagine trying to communicate with someone who is standing a hundred yards away, or with someone who insists on sitting on your lap and touching noses! For the relationship to work, you have to be near and in touch but still just a little separate. Just so for the felt sense—right up close but not overwhelmed.

Our Deepest Wounds

It is session six of the eight-week mindfulness course, and we are discussing what stresses us. Before us, all over the floor, are pieces of paper on which we have written the things we do when we can no longer cope: get angry, drink, forget things, zone out, cry, make it our own fault. There are dozens of them, many of them "second arrow" reactions colored by our wolf of self-hate. But what becomes increasingly apparent as we talk is that these self-destructive ways of survival all have their roots in early childhood.

From the moment we are born, not coping, becoming emotionally stressed, and learning how to manage this are central to our psychological development. How this unfolds has been minutely mapped in a variety of ways by different schools of psychotherapy and developmental psychology. However, the broad consensus is that once we are born we enter into a journey of relationship with our world and those in it. The first leg of the journey is the experience of gaining confidence in giving and receiving love. The second is becoming aware of our growing separateness—much evidenced in the two-year-old's self-assertive "no." And the third is more fully entering into the complicated world of multiple relationships with mother, father, siblings, and the others we meet. This is never a smooth ride, and the problems we have along the way are important opportunities to learn how to manage our emotions. However, when problems are particularly difficult or unremitting, they do leave their mark. Then, depending on their severity, we are left with a coloration of our experience that influences how we perceive and interact with the world and ourselves. When we begin to practice mindfulness, these colorations become more apparent, as do the circumstances that created them. As we have seen, Elizabeth, the child of demanding parents, takes their pervasive assessment into herself and unknowingly applies it to her own meditation. Finding her practice falling below a standard she has unconsciously set, she attacks herself for her failure.

Identifying these wounds, our patterns of hurt and how we defend ourselves, is valuable. Knowing what we do when we feel threatened, we can begin to recognize whether we unconsciously perceive our meditation as a threat and defended ourselves against it with a resistance that prevents us from doing it. However, our patterns of hurt are not necessarily easy to recognize. As we saw with Elizabeth, the repeated, self-inflicted judgment that she was not good enough was entirely unconscious. Likewise Nicky (from the previous chapter): the abusive and neglectful treatment she received as a child, and then continued herself as an adult, manifests in neglecting her practice and only becomes conscious when she begins to suspect her rather disengaged, perhaps dissociated, meditative experience. And there is Ellen (see chapter 3), the beaten-down child who first discovers that she is made anxious by an inner parent who tells her it is life-threateningly bad to sit still and then, at a deeper level, reveals a very powerful resistance that uses cunning to avoid what she perceives as the hated and dangerous discipline of her practice.

These three examples do not represent the full spectrum of our defense mechanisms, which are varied, complex, and, in their detail, quite individual. However, as long as we avoid being prescriptive, there are some very general patterns of hurt that help illuminate what might be going on beneath the surface. None of us has just one of these—we are invariably a mixture.

- For those of us who find the world and relationships frightening and overwhelming, going near our emotions will be particularly challenging. Jerry, a committed meditator, correctly diagnosed that his emotionally flat experience of mindfulness was connected to his generally disconnected relationship to life. If inclined to dissociation, we will prefer to sit and calmly space out.

- For those of us who feel not "good enough," like Elizabeth, we will, with our wolf of hate, judge our practice harshly and believe others are better. Pema Chödrön speaks of the many letters she receives from the self-titled "worst person in the world," each of whom feels that he or she is uniquely and exceptionally bad.

- For those of us who find being a separate and autonomous person confusing, feeling suffocated in groups yet uneasy when alone, it may be difficult to choose and settle with just one practice or group. This is not the entirely legitimate initial search for a qualified teacher and a meditation that "fits" but something that could prevent us from ever feeling at home, and growing, within a community of practitioners.

- For those of us who have a rather inflated sense of our own value and who feel easily used, meeting our hidden and vulnerable underbelly will be hard. Felix says nothing throughout the first weeks of the eight-week mindfulness course, but by the end it becomes clear he is subtly signaling his superiority. Doing everything just a bit more mindfully than everyone else, he finally speaks, disclosing that he has learned mindfulness many years before but now applies it in his own way. Being part of the group, being ordinary and getting things wrong, is simply unbearable. Being vulnerable to vulnerability, Felix has what some Buddhist meditation teachers call the "I know" problem.

- Those of us who, like Ellen, have been suppressed by excess discipline will resist external influence, feeling our lives depend upon it. To change is to lose. This is a particularly tough one because we are fighting against ourselves. If we begin to allow change, we immediately must prevent it. Like Eeyore in *Winnie-the-Pooh*, we are powerful in our immovability.

- For those of us who feel unheard and unseen, and who

may have been sexually exploited, having particularly expressive and quickly changing emotions will make it hard for us to settle. Christie, having been such a child, full of thoughts and emotions, found it extremely difficult to slow down and be in her body, to feel the physical sensations of her breathing.

- Lastly, those of us who are rather uptight and rigid, who come from emotionally cool and controlling backgrounds, will find the single most important instruction for meditation the most difficult: just relax. And that is not all. Life continues to be extremely exacting after childhood. As the Buddha witnessed, together with the personal stuff, birth, old age, sickness, and death visit us all and leave their marks. Meeting this in our practice with an ocean of kindness, patience, and equanimity is the practice—our practice is not somewhere else.

EXERCISE: RECOGNIZING CORE BELIEFS

How might we identify our core beliefs about ourselves? There are a variety of ways.

This one is cognitive and is called "laddering" or the "downward arrow" technique.

1. Take a negative thought. Let's use, for example, "I'm bad / wrong / not good enough."
2. Write the thought down and then ask yourself, "If this thought is true, why would it be upsetting to me?" Then draw a downward arrow to the next thought that

comes into your head. That might be, "Because I've got to be on my own or be what everybody else wants me to be."

3. Write this down, draw another downward arrow, and ask yourself the same question: "If this thought is true, why would it be upsetting to me?" The next thought might be, "Because I don't have a right to be me."

4. Do the same again, but now ask. "If this thought were true, what would it mean about me?" And the answer to this might be: "That would mean I have no validity in myself." This is a core belief.

Another way is to remember situations that are emotionally difficult and particularly fraught. Typically, these may involve conflict and loss. Ask yourself what emotions usually accompany these times, how such experiences leave you feeling about yourself, others, and the world. Try to put this simply into words: "It leaves me feeling . . ." It may be that you have already recognized a repeating pattern of hurt, and when it happens yet again you struggle with being in the same old place.

We can have core beliefs about ourselves that involve our life, others around us, and the world. For example, beliefs that say, "I am worthless." "I don't exist." "Others are there to please and make happy." "Life is a burden." When colored by such beliefs, meditation may feel like a place where we are trying to self-improve, because our basic belief about ourselves is that there is something fundamentally wrong—plainly a belief that is deeply at odds with the kindness, curiosity, and acceptance of mindfulness.

Core Beliefs

Here is a selection of core beliefs. Remember, what is important is the feel of them rather than the exact words, and also that we can have combinations of them. Each and all of them is capable of becoming an obstacle in our meditation if not recognized and the feeling, the felt sense, made into an object of mindfulness.

I'm on the wrong planet. I can't trust anybody. It's dangerous here. I'm not welcome.

There's nobody here for me. I'm on my own. I am judged and found wanting. I am never good enough.

Don't get too close to me. You can't hurt me. I don't need anybody. I will never show my hurt.

I'm a hopeless person. I do everything wrong. I'm miserable—please love me. I must obey others if I am to be loved. It's not OK to have fun.

I have to work to be OK. I have to be on guard to keep safe. I can't relax. I have to perform.

No one hears or understands me. My emotions are unacceptable. Love is dangerous. I can't get the attention I need.

Fear of Death

By now it is apparent that while our meditation can bring into our lives a place to pause and replenish ourselves, it can also bring a meeting with parts of our personalities, with emotions, with experiences, that we are resistant to feeling and that we defend ourselves against. Martin Wells sums up:

> When we sit and open ourselves to everything, we do not dis-
> criminate thoughts and feelings as good and bad. They simply
> arise. But the things that arise are often repressed material from
> the unconscious mind. So, of course, particularly for beginning
> meditators, the stuff that's been repressed emerges in a way that
> feels very uncomfortable. It doesn't feel like what they signed up
> for. And of course a lot of people drop out and back off and
> stop, for those very reasons.

There is perhaps at some point a barely conscious but growing intuition of fear: that this thing, this accepting, kindly meditation that we are doing, is going to dismantle who we feel we are; that we cannot do it in the way we take a relaxing bath or have a drink because our involvement with it will not only change our state of mind but also, eventually, who we believe we are; that patterns of unconscious behavior, thoughts, and emotions will become transparently obvious and no longer tenable; that the world we have created in our own imaginations, to make ourselves feel safe, is not at all like we thought. All that is frightening, really frightening! Our stories are going to unravel. Willem Kuyken speaks of his own growing intuition of this as he drives to a retreat:

This is going to be a bridge too far; this is going to be too much. . . . I've experienced that going on a retreat, you know. I'll go on a retreat after a busy time, like just now, and I will be driving there and I'll be thinking my mind is full, my mind is busy. I wonder what I'm going to find, and I'm not sure I want to find what I'm going to find . . .

Stephen Batchelor describes in detail why this may feel like a bridge too far:

For many people, meditation exposes them to the fact that it's very easy to entertain the idea of "everything is impermanent," but to actually experience that, when you're doing awareness meditation, is something else. When you're paying attention to your breath and your heartbeat and the pulses in your body, you may suddenly realize how incredibly fragile these are and how they could stop at any moment. Meditation sounds sort of nice and peaceful, but once you take impermanence on board in a real way, it's terrifying; it's absolutely terrifying. You know, everything is going to come to an end. I think what that does in people's lives, outside meditation, is that they become increasingly sensitized to that dimension of life—that our society is in the business of basically covering up and pretending it doesn't happen. But once you take on board these rather innocuous ideas like "all conditioned phenomena are impermanent," when that begins to really hit home, and when you start thinking in those terms, then your sense of your world begins to change, and features of your daily experience start to stand out that previously you'd either not noticed or deliberately ignored. Then your sense of life as a whole starts to be transformed.

*And at a certain point you go beyond a point of no return.
Once you've had those experiences, it's difficult to forget about
them. You can't "unremember." That's the scary thing. Once
you get so far into Buddhist practice, you can't turn back.
Because you've had experiences that you know are much truer
than anything else you've ever had. And you can't just put the
lid back on. It starts to become something really rather serious,
and rather unsettling. It provokes a turmoil of inner anxieties
that are sometimes very difficult to deal with.*

Martin Wells, first quoting Cynthia Bourgeault, modern-day
mystic and director of the Contemplative Society, takes this a
step further, spelling out what all contemplative traditions have
always known. When we embark upon the path *deeply*, we begin
a journey to a place where we will eventually be unrecognizable
to ourselves. Having previously hidden from so much of what we
are, this defensive story of an essentially fearful self gradually,
through acceptance, dissolves and transforms:

*"The practice of meditation is indeed an authentic experience
of dying to self, not at the level of the will, however, but at the
level of something even more fundamental, our core sense of
identity and the egoic processing methods that keep it in place."
Now, of course there's a wonderful paradox in there because by
letting go, we do have everything that we've ever needed and
wanted, but we don't get it by grasping, or progressing, or
achieving, or feeding the ego in any way. It's a form of death
that of course the ego is likely to resist, tooth and nail.*

*And, I guess, as teachers we can only say, though it will be
tough, and will involve the sort of surrender and relinquishing*

that you maybe never experienced before, hang on in there—
it's worth it.

EXERCISE: TAKING STOCK

We have looked at a lot of ideas in this chapter, and you may
have taken the time to explore the various ways of understand-
ing what is going on below awareness and possibly affecting
your meditation practice. This is a lot, so perhaps pause here,
take a rest, and let the material digest. The slower the absorp-
tion, the deeper in it goes.

Meeting Ourselves: Key Points

- Expectations of meditation are frequently not confirmed by experience. This can cause disappointment
  that may make us want to stop. We need to let go of our
  expectations and accept our experience just as it is.
- We are emotional beings and our emotions can be
  healthy or dysfunctional.
- When confronted with threatening experiences, either
  outside or within us, we meet them with the strategies
  of grasping, aversion, or disengagement; these Buddhism calls the "three root poisons."
- These poisons are an attempt to resist things as they
  really are—in each successive moment. Resisting puts
  us in conflict with our own experience.
- This conflict may be conceived as the "two arrows."

The first arrow is sensation; the second is unnecessary and harmful emotional reactivity to it. We have no control over the first—life—but we do over the second.

- The conflict may also be thought of as two wolves, one of love and one of hate. The wolf of love evolved from our drive to relate, empathize, and care; the wolf of hate from our drive to be aggressive toward others whom we perceive as a threat. We can cultivate the first and restrain the second.

- Various schools of psychotherapy have observed that we are many persons within one skin. I call this "the people on our bus." These people may not know each other or be in accord.

- There are a variety of ways to categorize the people on our bus, including as the inner child, adult, and parent.

- Both the bus and the family analogy help us understand more deeply the emotions that we meet in meditation.

- Together, these may point to patterns of hurt that developed in early childhood. These affect every aspect of our lives, including our meditation. Identifying them is valuable, as it makes more conscious what we find when we sit.

- At the back of all this may be the existential anxiety that there is something about meditation that, if taken to its limit, would dismantle our sense of self. This is correct—though not immediately likely—and may be at the root of our resistance and defensiveness.

CHAPTER 5

Grabby, Grumpy, Sleepy, Jumpy, and Maybe

The traditional explanation is we didn't get the right antidote to move. We want dharma, but we kind of failed. So when we connect to this basic well-being I call essence love, and some calm and clarity and with a warm heart, then I think we'll start.

TSOKNYI RINPOCHE

The meditation orientation is not about fixing pain or making it better. It's about looking deeply into the nature of pain—making use of it in certain ways that might allow us to grow. In that growing, things will change, and we have the potential to make choices that will move us toward greater wisdom and compassion, including self-compassion, and thus toward freedom from suffering.

JON KABAT-ZINN, "AT HOME IN OUR BODIES"

My mind still goes blah, blah, blah!   TESS

Polly started her eight-week mindfulness course convinced that she would be able to find time for the daily meditation. During the initial individual meeting, to discuss whether it was the right course for her at the right time, she was certain that it was exactly what she was looking for: now that her small children were going to school she at last would have a little space for herself. However, by the middle of week three her practice had faltered and then stopped. As she had slept through the body scan, moving to mindfulness of breathing was a nightmare—she thought and thought and was seldom present. Becoming conscious of how chaotic her mind was, she just felt defeated. David had been interested in Buddhism for years and had recently attended several weekends and a six-day meditation retreat that he had enjoyed. However, once back in his own home, despite all his good intentions, he found he could not meditate alone. Whenever he thought about it, many tasks to complete suddenly presented themselves before he could begin, and if he did manage to lower himself onto his seat, he was overwhelmed by pressing reasons to get up and attend to something more urgent. Although he realized his distraction was a problem, he simply could not stop his behavior. It was deeply troubling and confusing—why did he do it?

Whatever the reasons, when we find ourselves in similar positions to Polly and David our meditation practice has become vulnerable, and there is a strong possibility that it will either stop altogether or continue to limp on indefinitely. What might help Polly and David—and all of us who struggle in the same way—would be to step back and look at what is *actually* happening in the meditation, to ask ourselves what obstacles are hindering us in establishing a practice and what we can do to clear them.

Polishing the Mirror

Traditionally in Buddhism, problems with meditation are described as meeting obstacles or hindrances to establishing calm abiding and insight. Essentially, this boils down to one thing: simply to be present with ourselves is very difficult because the habits of distraction are so deep. In our meditation this shows itself as an inability to create the circumstances that support our practice, high levels of distraction, or, more fundamentally, a loss of heart in the whole project—one interpretation of outer, inner, and secret obstacles. More precisely, we are struggling with the "five hindrances": desire, aversion, sleepiness, restlessness, and doubt. Or, perhaps more memorably: grabby, grumpy, sleepy, jumpy, and maybe. There are many such classifications, among them "the seven dispositions to negative patterns of mind," "the ten fetters," "the ten defilements of insight," "the ten impediments," and "the fourteen unwholesome mental factors." We quickly get the point: there is a great deal that goes on in our thinking and emotions that makes practicing hard. However, the good news is that to practice meditation we are not expected to be saints or yogis, and all the qualities found in these lists— worries, concerns, preoccupations, afflictions, and conceits—are what we work with in our practice by recognizing their presence and applying the "antidote": embracing them with mindfulness. Christina Feldman describes her growing awareness, over the years, of just how central it is to work at being present with what hinders us:

When I first began, I used to be very dismissive of the hin-drances. You know, sloth and torpor, agitation, doubt, craving, and aversion. Thinking that these were things people would experience in the beginning of their practice and that they should get over them. Not really understanding how the hindrances are the five manifestations of greed, hatred, and delusion and that to really be free of the hindrances is to be awakened.

We usually think of an obstacle hindering us as something to get past. If we are driving and a road is closed, we immediately find another way, or if we want to buy something that is out of stock, we quickly look elsewhere. The obstacle itself is not something we notice once we have recognized its obstruction, because our minds go around it while still focused on the goal. However, in mindfulness meditation we approach things differently. Discovering an obstacle or a hindrance, we turn toward it rather than look beyond it. When we find we want one sort of experience and not another, when we constantly zone out and fall asleep, when we are restless and worried, and when we doubt the value of what we are doing, we turn toward these experiences, and rather than see them as problems to be immediately surmounted, we include them in our mindfulness. What this amounts to is that being present with hindrances and obstacles is an essential part of the practice of mindfulness. There is not some other, better, sort of meditation that lies beyond it. The practice is not something that only starts once the hindrances are removed; working with hindrances *is* the practice. As the classical metaphor says: the awakened mind is like the sky; it is already perfectly clear—once the clouds that obscure it are blown away, it is instantly revealed. The clouds are our hindrances; that is what we work on. The sky is fine.

Desire: Grabby

Every moment, every second we have changing experiences, but we're not satisfied with these experiences; we are looking for something else. It's like somebody has one day a meditation and they feel nice and relaxed and then the next day they don't feel comfortable because the body's uncomfortable or the mind's a little bit tight or there are many thoughts. Then people think, "Oh, yesterday I had few thoughts and nice experiences; why is it that I can't get that experience today?"

LAMA RABSANG

Almost without exception, every one of us will have been drawn to meditation because we desired something. Attraction can give us important information about where we need to go on the next part of our journey, and yet we all know what it is to be plagued and driven by wanting, craving, clinging, grasping, unhealthy attachment and hanging on, all of which can come in a variety of strengths, from addiction to recurrent fantasies to just a passing whim. As a feeling, this is experienced as a contraction within our bodies. Desire often shows itself as a hindrance in our meditation in the following ways:

- Becoming seduced by our own distractions, we find our thoughts more absorbing than our practice, letting ourselves float along in our internal dramas. For those of us who are intensely interested in ourselves, this can be a significant problem. Some psychologists believe it is why we in the West find it more difficult to meditate than people in Asia and the Far East do—we have more of the cult of the individual.

- We become attached to and want more of a meditation experience that we like or think we should have—we want to have "good" meditations. This is an understandable hindrance, particularly when we first start, but it is destructive nonetheless.

- We make comparisons to meditations we have had and create expectations of what might yet come. This can be cloaked as making an effort in our practice, but it obscures being present with what already is.

Christina Feldman takes this further and suggests that our desire for "good" meditations reveals a deeper unhappiness:

Think about craving, the emotion of craving for sensual pleasure, the mental state that's underneath that is discontent. We don't crave when we feel deeply contented in ourselves, we don't feel that sense of lack, so craving for sensual pleasure's really pointing to a much deeper underlying state of being discontented.

Pinpointing this deeper layer of discontent returns us to what motivates us. Most of us start meditating because we feel dissatisfied and unhappy. As we have seen, this is a very good place to start from, but if we take this entirely legitimate need into our meditation, as a desire for a meditative experience that makes us feel better, then it becomes counterproductive. On our meditation seat or cushion, we try to practice equanimity and acceptance, content with whatever is.

Aversion: Grumpy

I find sitting alone a bit difficult. If I'm going through a difficult patch, I find it's more difficult. And if I'm not going through a difficult patch, I don't feel the need to do it, so, um. . . . But I have no excuse really, now I'm not working every day, to not to be able to do it. When I was working every day, I had to be up in the morning early, busy all day, and then I'd be knackered in the evening, so there was an excuse, and now there is no excuse, so, yeah.

ANN

Directed outwardly, aversion shows as avoidance, procrastination, not wanting, irritation, annoyance, anger, and rage. Directed against ourselves, these emotions and behaviors can be joined by fear, depression, self-pity, self-recrimination, guilt, and self-hate. Aversion also includes frustration, discouragement, and bargaining with ourselves to achieve a more desired outcome. As a feeling, it is again sensed as a contraction and a pushing away. That there are so many expressions of aversion tells us how big a part of our psychology it is. We discover aversion in our meditation when we do the following:

- We shut our meditation out of our minds, passively resisting it by repeatedly forgetting to do it or finding endless reasons for "not now, later."

- We resist and reject our meditative experience as it is, especially difficult physical sensations and painful emotions, such as unworthiness, despair, hopelessness, and anger; we want it to be different from how it is.
- Or, more subtly, we practice mindfulness with the *intention to change*. John Welwood, psychologist and exponent of mindfulness-based psychotherapy, says this attitude is a subtle form of self-abuse: we reject ourselves as we have felt rejected in our past.

Christina Feldman believes that aversion originates in our fear and, as such, is extremely strong and compulsive:

Aversion generally has a strong behavioral aspect—what I avoid, what I push away, what I hide from. Aversion is a manifestation of a mental state of fear. Fear of injury, fear of not having enough, fear of being overwhelmed.

Finding a way to work with this group of emotions must be one of the most difficult and yet most necessary things we can do. As we saw in the previous chapter, the wolf of hate (see page 131) is hard-wired into us and cannot simply be repressed and ignored. Given, then, that we are who we are, we must acknowledge these emotions as they happen, neither beating ourselves up for having them, nor acting them out, but learning to be mindfully present as we witness them arise, stay for a while, and then fade—meeting them with acceptance and kindness.

Sleepiness: Sleepy

My biggest obstacle is extreme laziness, where I just think, "I can't be bothered, really."

TESS

Kay devotedly attended her weekly Buddhist meditation group, but within minutes the others in the group noticed that her head had sunk onto her chest and she was gently snoring. It seemed an agony for her to be there. Periodically she would wake with the shock that she was asleep yet again and struggle ineffectually to remain awake. At first, not noticing the emerging pattern, and then not taking it seriously, she only gradually began to wonder if what she had heard about sleeping being a way to avoid being present with ourselves might apply to her. Falling asleep is one of our most powerful distractions, and perhaps the most difficult hindrance, we will ever have to face in meditation. There is just something about the uncontrollable, relentless slide into unconsciousness that is virtually impossible to resist. If we are not simply exhausted and need to sleep, why does this happen?

- Given that practicing all forms of meditation requires getting the balance right between relaxation and stable, focused attention, sleepiness may be the result of too much relaxation and not enough detailed attention. Tsoknyi Rinpoche calls this "stupid meditation"— a drowsy, unfocused, but pleasurable half sleep.

- It may be that our objects of mindfulness—sound, breath, body sensations—are simply not interesting to a mind that is used to being highly stimulated by fast-changing distractions. We are bored and fall asleep waiting for something more interesting to happen.

- Or, as we have been exploring, sleepiness may be a means to not be awake to our present moment—a shrinking away from uncomfortable or painful emotional experiences. Christina Feldman describes this last reason for sleepiness in meditation and its limitations:

I think on a meditation cushion, the desire not to feel what is going on, or the fear of it even, manifests as sloth and torpor—sinking into a kind of sleepiness. It's a layer; it's a veil. When the Buddha talked about the "hindrances," a more accurate translation of this is "veils"—what veils experience, what covers experience over so it's not seen, not experienced or not found. Sloth and torpor are particularly effective at doing this for a time. But only for a time. Very few people actually sustain sloth and torpor over long periods, because the mind, the body, the heart start to creep through the veil.

So what is sleepiness veiling? Christina says that often we know about the "great bubbling cauldrons of distress" we have on our back burners, but there are frequently also unconscious elements. Talking about the difficult initial period of arriving in a meditation retreat and the "cold turkey" we may experience from no longer having distractions, she says:

Suddenly we are in this environment where we're not in control of almost anything. Food appears at certain times, bells ring, distractions are removed. I think on some level the mind perceives that as deeply threatening. You know, I'm just sitting here, and I don't have the ability to order my world or conditions in ways that I feel will protect me. So it's more of a fear of the unknown, of what might emerge. It is a vague, unnamed level of resistance that, I think, is ultimately the fear of not being.

This idea that it is ultimately our fear of not being that hinders us is confirmed for many of us when we really ask ourselves, what *is* so seductive about being distracted when we meditate? What is it in us that just does not want to be bothered? Kate wonders why she does not meditate more. I tell her that many mindfulness teachers suspect that mindfulness fundamentally threatens our sense of who we are. Immediately she agrees—she says it takes her to a place where everything that she feels she is becomes transparent and leaves her feeling personally unimportant. She finds it very unsettling.

Restlessness: Jumpy

My mind won't shut up. I haven't got anywhere in the four or five years, whatever, that I've been doing it for. I'm in exactly the same place as I began! My mind still goes blah, blah, blah!

TESS

When we feel we cannot sit still or remain seated, when we are powerfully distracted by obsessive and cascading thoughts, we are being hindered by restlessness and worry. Why does this happen?

- As sleepiness is an imbalance of relaxation over focused attention, so restlessness may be an imbalance of attention over relaxation. Our practice has become too tight or too pushy.

- Restlessness can also be created by having too much on our minds: pressing concerns, worries, and plans. For this reason, practicing after waking is a good thing, as we are more likely to start out with a fresh mind, not one that is full of the day's events. It is also why taking an occasional retreat from daily life can be so valuable.

- It is common when meditating that we find ourselves thinking back over past events and doing a "moral inventory" that may induce shame and guilt. In Buddhism remorse for bad things we have done is considered good—we look our actions in the face and, being sorry, we resolve not to repeat them and then move on. However, the lacerating self-hatred of guilt and the refusal to let it go mixes the hindrance of restlessness with the aggression of aversion. Christina Feldman adds:

Restlessness and worry is part of the agitation spectrum. There's a core level of agitation, of just not feeling at ease or at home anywhere. There's a whole psychological emotional aspect of agitation that is the proliferation of thinking, the waterfall of

thinking, and there's also a worry aspect, trying to guarantee
what the next moment, the next day, the next week is going to
bring by obsessing about it, rehearsing it and planning it.

She adds that this is particularly difficult because it emerges as the sleepiness of sloth and torpor recedes: having at last stopped falling unconscious the moment we meditate, we wake up to a mind we have little control over—a mind that compulsively worries in a hopeless attempt to keep things under control.

Doubt: Maybe

I have sat here for thirty to forty minutes, and there's not a lot
going on really, and the rain's falling and it's a February morn-
ing or something, and I don't feel very inspired, and here I am
meditating, but I don't really know quite why sometimes. Well,
I do, but parts of me perhaps protest and think, "Well, this is
boring. What are you doing this for?"

IAN

When we cannot decide what is valuable or important for our practice, and are unable to commit ourselves, we may be experiencing the hindrance of doubt. This is different from the intelligent testing Buddhism recommends we use on our teachers and their teaching before we decide to fully engage. It is something that is fundamentally fearful and self-protective and is felt as a withdrawal and a contraction. This shows itself in the following ways:

- Holding back and being skeptical or distrusting: this makes it impossible to hear what is being taught or offered, as we do not trust enough to let anything in, to grow and mature, giving it time to prove itself and to experience it personally.
- Doubting ourselves: we anxiously question whether we are doing our practice right or whether it is working or is the right practice for us. This is very common when we first start and is extremely corrosive. Speaking of her own doubt, Tess says:
  - *The thing that comes to mind is feeling like I'm not good enough. I'm not going to be good enough. Or there's something wrong. Everyone else can do it, but not me. I can't do it. There's that sort of obstacle, of doubting myself or almost wondering if there's some sort of quality that you need that maybe is absent in me—because it just felt that there were certain people that got it and then there would be me, whose thoughts would probably not ever still.*
- Intellectual conceit: we pile on more and more questions as a means to avoid personal engagement. The Buddha described this as a man who, having been shot with an arrow, wanted to know everything about archery before it was withdrawn.

Christina Feldman suggests that doubt finally penetrates down into the roots of our identity, asking questions that may be impossible to answer:

Doubt generally arises when all the strategies of the other hindrances have failed. You know, I haven't managed to rearrange conditions, I haven't managed to avoid everything, then there's doubt: "I can't do this. It's hopeless. I'm not getting anywhere." And that then opens much larger doubts: "Who am I?" "What is meaningful?" "Where am I going?" "How do I even know who I am?"

One more thing is when we doubt fundamentally the value of mindfulness or, if we are Buddhists or practitioners from another contemplative tradition, the value of our path. Rectifying our doubt, restoring ourselves to the path, from the perspective of Buddhism, does not happen by reestablishing belief or faith but by clarity and understanding derived through our practice. The message is clear: personal experience is the only real antidote to doubt.

A Tangled Knot

Of course, when we look at our own meditation, identifying what hinders us may not be obvious. While we easily know if we are asleep or overwhelmed by thoughts, recognizing when we are grasping at or trying to get rid of something, and when we are wavering or holding back, is not so clear. The complexity of our emotions takes each and all of the hindrances and weaves them into confusing patterns of thoughts, emotions, and behaviors. Willem Kuyken talks about his own observation of the obstacles we can face when meditating. We see that the categories he highlights—overthinking, anxiety, and ill will—are each a combination of several hindrances:

> *I think there's a class of quite intellectualizing, ruminating men who think they're meditating, but what is happening is just churning in their minds, rather than settling in their bodies or settling in some other kind of anchor like the breath.*
>
> *There's another group of people who are at the hypochondriac end of things, where there's severe anxiety. It is very hard to create the space for the oxygen of awareness to get in because any invitation to come up close to sensations, to the body, is met with, "I'm having a heart attack," "I'm having a panic attack," "This means I have cancer," blocking the awareness to mindfully see the process unfolding. Those folks can be really tough.*
>
> *And there is a person who experiences a lot of ill will and skepticism, so that their mind is closed. Quite how they get into the class, I'm not quite sure, but you can see their mind is so closed and full of ill will that it's difficult to find a way in.*

Plainly, we experience more than one hindrance simultaneously. Christina Feldman:

> *All the hindrances are interwoven, and of course they trigger each other. I can have sloth and torpor and I can have aversion to the sloth and torpor because I don't want to be that way. When I have aversion and feel uncomfortable with what's going on, I'll get hungry and try to find something that makes me feel good. So craving for sensual pleasure will arise, prowling the world for something to make me feel good, and I'll get very*

agitated with that. And when it doesn't work, I'll get doubt. The hindrances are constantly triggering each other and reinforcing each other. None of them can be divorced from the others, because they are all part of the tangle of conflicting emotions, all cooperating with each other to constantly re-create distress and confusion.

Finally, it is important to remember that our hindrances come in different strengths. They may simply be our disinclination to sit with aching knees and backs and tolerate our monkey minds. Or they may be manifestations of resistance to the anxiety generated by the emergence of previously buried memories or worries about the future we usually avoid. However, deeper still, they may also be expressions of our unacknowledged darkest concerns, our core wounds. As we have seen, desire reveals discontent. Aversion and sleepiness reveal anxiety. Restlessness reveals the need for control, as does doubt. Perhaps collectively what they all reveal are different facets of a fear of our own annihilation, so that, at bottom, what hinders us all, always, is our fear of death. Annie, an experienced meditator and a teacher of MBSR, describes how particularly anxious her mind was on going to bed:

I went up to bed knowing my mind was alert, not relaxed. Then in the night I woke in a complete panic that I had no distance from. My thoughts had activated my body; it felt like it was crawling with nerve sensations. I felt as if I was in a small, dark room with no air, and somehow I knew this was connected to my childhood because during the day the word "disgusting" had been used for a member of my family and this was now attached to me. I felt helpless in the face of my thoughts and emotions and all the instances in the present where I felt I had done something wrong—where I felt shame and where I would be caught out and punished. I could notice all this but not find any distance, so I just used distraction and got up and went downstairs for a bit.

Later I returned to bed and followed the rhythm of the breath, and my body atmosphere changed and I began letting go. Then I dreamt that I had come from a cold place and there was the Dalai Lama and another Tibetan monk. The Dalai Lama took both my hands in his, really grasping them in his, and I had the thought that they were not as cold as I had believed.

Then I woke again and did some more breathing and then came the realization that all my suffering was connected to this small, dark room of fear and towards all those I felt threatened by and wanted to keep out. I felt warmth—not love, but more open and accepting. There was no need to keep them out: we were all connected. And this was something I had known since being a tiny child but had become gripped by the fear everyone else lived in. Yes, a bigger place.

Annie's ability to open to the cold fear of her core wound and hold it in loving kindness turns it from being a hindrance that stops her from practicing and into the path itself. Struggling at first, and then succeeding in bringing mindfulness to the small, dark room of childhood fear, she has an important insight into the nature of how things really are. She glimpses the joy, tranquility, and happiness that mindfulness can bring and the interconnectedness that joins us all. When we become present with our obstacles, we see the original luminous awareness of the mind. Christina Feldman concludes:

> *There's a huge amount of insight and understanding born of turning the hindrances into objects of meditation, to see how suffering and distress are caused. How, in many ways, understanding the hindrances is the whole of the teaching of awakening. Turning them into objects of mindfulness enables us to see the many, many layers of the hindrances and how they all come down to the three core drives of greed, hatred, and delusion. And, underneath that, the ignorance of not seeing things as they actually are.*

Finding a Remedy

To recap: Observation makes us aware that when we operate on automatic pilot we are pushed and pulled around by our thoughts and emotions or we cut off from parts of our self that we cannot bear to feel because they are too uncomfortable or painful. These are the two options nature gives us: to identify and react, or to repress. When we meditate it is like our lives in microcosm. There are some pleasant experiences and some unpleasant: the pleasant ones we generally have no problem with, but the unpleasant ones—like a leg that hurts when meditating—may create more unpleasant ones, such as fearing the physical pain. And so it snowballs. In Buddhism it is said that these types of mental and emotional conflicts are endless, that they are 84,000 in number. However, they can all be reduced down to a basic group of three: grasping, aversion, and ignorance; or even to just one—ignorance of how things really are; i.e., how things really are in our experience, right now, in this moment. The selfsame emotions appear as we meditate, and in this context the basic group of three, now called desire, aversion, and sleepiness, are joined by two more, restlessness and doubt. Together they form the hindrances. However, the idea remains the same. We have emotions that veil the way things really are, and mindfulness is the means by which to realize this and see things more clearly.

Whether we approach our meditation from the MBSR or MBCT perspective or through one of the Buddhist contemplative traditions, we try to embrace all our experience mindfully. The instruction to recognize what is happening and stay present with it could not be simpler. In a single moment it takes physical, emotional, and mental obstacles and turns them into our object of mindfulness—the thing we rest our conscious awareness on. It takes what was a common, everyday hindrance and makes it an invaluable part of the path. Annie's ability to recognize her shame and fear and, assisted by her breath, hold it in awareness with kindness, shows us how this may be done. Whether it is sound, breath, thoughts, physical sensations, or emotions, each is an object that we can be mindfully present with, taking what veils our experience and allowing it to become a means to further wake up. Once our hindrance has become our path, we can even be mindful of its absence. Traditionally, this is seen as the starting point of a causal sequence of experiences that lead, via delight, joy, tranquility, and happiness, to deeper levels of concentration and insight. This absence of hindrances, even for a short while, reveals how things really are: a mind that beneath all its blather and chatter is spacious, clear, luminous, and dynamically still; an experience that is not something we need fabricate because once what obscures it is cleared away, we find it is already there, perfect.

Giving Our Practice a Helping Hand

So how do we take our obstacles and turn them into the path? Both MBSR/MBCT and the Buddhist traditions offer many ways to support our mindfulness and cultivate further insight, recognizing just how difficult it is to begin introducing mindfulness into our lives.

Supporting Insight

The most important helping hand is concentration. During the eight-week mindfulness course, we discover that unless we have at least some established ability to know we have wandered into our thoughts and come back to presence, then everything that follows suffers from a shaky foundation. This is no surprise— traditionally, concentration has been used to create a platform of calm and equanimity from which to gain a profound insight into how things really are. From the MBCT perspective, this insight is into the unconscious thinking patterns that contribute to depression. Insight here reveals not just that some thoughts are obviously destructive but that thought itself should not necessarily be followed. From the Buddhist perspective, insight finally reveals that what we feel is a solid world made up of individual and unchanging entities—you, me, all the things around us—is, more accurately, an entirely interconnected universe in perpetual flux, where nothing is separate or unchanging, the experiential realization of which creates unimaginable freedom and ease. Concentration then is indispensable, and although this is outside the scope of this book, which is for those of us making the first step of our meditation journey, there exists much information on how we can develop our concentration through a succession of stages: from it wandering off after just a few moments—our usual experience—to inconceivable states of sustained tranquility and absorption.

Perhaps the single most important thing to remember about concentration is that it is like a flashlight beam: the closer the beam is to the surface it is pointed at, the sharper and more focused it gets. Some years ago I spent two weeks on a lozenge-shaped island off the British coast that took fifteen minutes to walk across at its widest point and twenty-five minutes at its longest. I found that in such a confined space I began to slow down and really look at the minute details of my environment. I came to know intimately stones and small plants I would never normally have noticed, and out of this grew the deepest relaxation and contentment I have ever experienced during a holiday. The message was clear: having no choice, I was compelled, like the flashlight, to focus close up and to concentrate on where I was, and from this came my calm state of mind. Likewise, when we find our minds sleepy or scattered, what helps—apart from practice, practice, practice—is increasing the magnification of our concentration: not just resting our attention on breathing but paying acute attention to just one breath, and then acute attention to just the out breath, and then acute attention to just the beginning, middle, and end of the out breath. In this way we focus the beam of concentration to a fine, bright point, sharpening the steady tool of focused attention that enables us to remain present. One of the ways we may do this is by naming and counting the breath.

Naming and Counting the Breath

We need to be calm to gain insight into the nature of our minds. Early Buddhism values the breath for gaining both calm and insight. Well-known Buddhist teaching on this subject includes the Teaching on In and Out Breathing (the Ānāpānasati Sutta) and the Four Foundations of Mindfulness (the Satipatthāna Sutta). What is clear is that by repeatedly bringing our conscious awareness, our attention, to the breath, a calm state of mind that enables the sustained, mindful presence of the body, emotions, and mind is made possible. There are many methods to achieve this—here are some of them.

METHOD 1
Taking your seat in a relaxed yet upright position, close your eyes and rest your attention on the nostrils, feeling the breath as it enters and leaves. To increase concentration and diminish distractions, name the in breath "in" or "rising," and the out breath "out" or "falling." Make sure the sensation of the breath remains foremost; you are not concentrating on the words, just using them to concentrate on your breath.

Thoughts and emotions will naturally arise while doing this. These are not focused on, or followed, but allowed to naturally dissolve as you continue to rest your attention on naming the breath. Thoughts and emotions that are sufficiently powerful to distract you to the point that you forget what you are doing are named "thinking," in a calm, kind voice in the back of the mind, and then you return to naming the breath.

METHOD 2

As above, but instead of naming the breath, count the out breath from one to ten, and then, on reaching ten, begin again. If you lose count through distraction, go back to the start, counting one.

This is a very powerful concentration practice that quickly delivers a calm state if rigorously applied. Its strong intentionality may create some potential problems, which, if they occur, must be noticed and worked with. This means that the application of its precise technique must not get stressful and the hindrance of grasping at succeeding in counting ten breaths or the calm this induces must, like any other thought or emotion, be let go of. I have found that thirty minutes of this produces a deep calm that acts as a platform, supporting any subsequent practice of insight. Furthermore, it is also an insight practice in itself because it enables being present with thoughts and emotions without identifying with them, thus revealing their nature as ephemeral and transitory.

METHOD 3

As above, but counting on the in breath.

METHOD 4

As above, but replacing the counting with the breath poem "I have arrived" on the in breath and "I am home" on the out breath. Or an abbreviated version: "arrived" on the in breath and "home" on the out breath.

This is a beautiful practice given by the Vietnamese Zen teacher Thich Nhat Hanh. It is softer in feeling than counting and can induce emotion with its language. Another variant is to split the word "Buddha" between the in and out breaths (Bud–dha). I have found this softer still.

METHOD 5

As above, but the concentration is placed upon the belly as it rises and falls. Naming or counting may be done on breathing either in or out, or not at all, making the sensation of the breath in the belly the point of concentration.

This may give a more profoundly embodied experience by causing the attention to lower and deepen. However, if it produces a less intense concentration and a more relaxed, diffuse meditation with low clarity, it is not desirable.

METHOD 6

Any of the above with eyes open. Having our eyes open, and particularly looking above the horizon line, decreases the tendency to drift off to sleep.

Supporting Mindfulness

Along with improving our concentration, we can also improve our ability to work with our emotions through supportive attitudes and behaviors, taking what was an obstacle or a hindrance and turning it into the path. However, we must be careful here. The attitude that we bring with our mindfulness is acceptance of whatever we are feeling in each moment. *Obstacles and hindrances are not turned into our path by trying to banish them but rather by accepting them and then using them as our objects of mindfulness.* Likewise, when we get a helping hand from supporting attitudes and behaviors that are associated with clearing the obstacles and hindrances, we are not using them to make feelings go away but to help establish our mindfulness more fully. We could think of these supports as ways to sharpen a knife, so it may cut, or to soften a brush, so it may paint. Both actions do something that makes the tool more effective, so it may then be used. A helping hand helps our mindfulness become more continuously present.

Let's return to sleepy Kay (see page 167), who suspects that her falling asleep is a way of veiling, of not being present with, emotions she does not want to feel. Were she to support her mindfulness by opening her eyes and perhaps looking up, then she is using this method, not to fight off sleep, but to help herself be more mindful. Fighting off sleep would mean that she was entering into a battle with herself, an expression of aversion, while using it to be mindful means increasing her ability to accept and be present with those things she has not wanted to feel. The key point here is motivation. We all automatically try to make things into what we want them to be or think they should be, and this also applies to our ideas about our meditation. It is second nature to think, "I am sleepy; I will do something to wake myself up," but for this to truly reflect the acceptance associated with mindfulness, it must change to "I am sleepy; I will do something to support my mindfulness." The first thought is motivated by wanting to change, the second by moving toward and accepting what is.

This may seem to be making a mountain out of a molehill. Surely we can just do some breathing to relax and then feel better, without having to turn our thinking inside out. This may be true if our goal is relaxation, but here we are going for something different and possibly more valuable. When we come to an eight-week mindfulness course, what we are being offered is more than a way to unwind. The course is geared toward creating a new relationship to our thoughts and emotions that is not about keeping old ways creaking on but doing something radically different. This change of attitude is also at the heart of Buddhist teaching. We do not practice simply to make our lives a little smoother but, as Jon Kabat-Zinn says, by seeing deeply into the sources of unhappiness, pain, and suffering we find freedom from them. MBSR, MBCT, and Buddhism are unanimous in the belief that their purpose is achieved primarily through a change of heart, a change in how we treat ourselves (and others), and that the meditation practices are means to make this possible. The kind acceptance of who we already are is paradoxically at the heart of this change.

In practice, this means we begin to make wiser choices about how we think and feel, so that stress, anxiety, and depression, and the conditions that lead to them, are no longer encouraged in our lives. Perhaps recognizing, for example, that if we are thinking in a catastrophic and generalized way that creates feelings of helplessness and fear, we can notice this with our mindfulness and choose to do something different. Buddhism speaks of making such wise and compassionate choices as using skillful means to combat the unskillful behaviors, emotions, and thoughts that contribute to making our lives difficult. Again, once we are aware of what is happening in our minds, in our emotions, we can give ourselves the choice of fostering kindness, calm abiding, and a deeper insight into how things really are. Buddhism loves lists, and there are many lists of "mental qualities," cultivated by skillful means, that nourish and strengthen a more enlightened way of being. These include the "factors of awakening": mindfulness, investigation, energy, joy, tranquility, concentration, and equanimity; and the already mentioned "six perfections": generosity, virtue, patience, diligence, concentration, and their fruit, wisdom. This tells us that there are many means that we can draw on to help us be present from moment to moment with our experience, just as it is. A selection of these is given in the "recipes" below.

Recipes for Supporting Mindfulness

These recipes provide a selection of skillful means—behaviors, qualities, and ways of thinking, each related to the five hindrances—that can support our mindfulness when it wavers.

DESIRE

- We can try looking more deeply into the things we desire, past their surface, into their interior or what they really are. A classic practice is contemplation of the human body—what lies below the skin: imagine the flesh laid open or dead for some time. What do we feel then?

- Closely linked to this is not flooding our senses with stimuli or overindulging our appetites. It is not for no reason that advertisers target us with images—they know we want what we see. Plainly, the Buddha recognized just how powerfully seductive desire can be and, realizing its consequences, was mindfully cautious. Ramping up desire in our lives generally will mean it is equally more present during our meditation.

- Practicing generosity and cultivating gratitude takes our natural narcissism and transforms it into something less fearful and more open. Generosity, paradoxically, makes us happier than grasping. Gratitude links us to the world around us and banishes isolation. Doing our meditation for everyone else, as well as ourselves, is the greatest heart-opening motivator.

- Simplify and let go. Meditation helps to answer the question, "What makes me truly happy?" And this may mean letting go of attitudes and beliefs, old stories and futile struggles—all baggage that we need no longer carry. One part of mindfulness is to not add anything more.

AVERSION

- Given that aversion is so linked to hatred, cultivating and practicing loving kindness is its antidote. Having a heart that is open and vulnerable makes it very much harder for all the small, bitter qualities of aversion to find a place in which to contract. Such a heart is where we find the acceptance necessary for our practice.

- Actions driven by aversion—hatred, anger, guilt, disappointment—have consequences, and so careful consideration is required before we act. As such, once turned into the path, aversion contributes to discovering our wisdom.

- The great lesson the Dalai Lama has taught us all is to try shifting our focus from anger about a situation to the suffering. Instead of being angry with the Chinese, he has taught himself to see the thick web of suffering that all—Tibetans and Chinese alike— are caught in. Feeling the suffering of others opens the angry, fearful heart. It is an act of courage and strength.

- And one that leads to forgiveness. Yes, this is a tricky one, but it is true that to forgive is to be free. So, not a sickly taking of higher moral ground out of fear of our own anger, but a practical move to help us become unencumbered. When restless in meditation, our thoughts may revolve around situations where vendettas, grudges, and vengeance are alive. Finding a way to forgive, or even just let go, can clear these from our minds.

SLEEPINESS

- The antidotes to sleepiness are those things that literally wake us up, like not eating too much and not being too warm, because our bodies go to sleep when we feed and warm them. Look at babies, children, and pets: eat, relax, and sleep. An alcoholic drink before meditation is generally not wise either.

- Changing posture, sitting up, opening our eyes, looking up above the line of the eyes' horizon, shaking, standing, walking—these all help with sleepiness. Particularly taking some deep breaths to reoxygenate the system. I have noticed that those of us most persecuted by sleepiness are the most resistant to using these measures. I am unsure whether this is because the state of sleepiness resists being woken or because the need to be unconscious is so compelling. Perhaps both.

- Sharpening our attention increases our clarity. This may be done by using the naming and counting methods described above (see page 181). There are also yoga exercises and breathing techniques that will do this surprisingly quickly.

- Finally, we can also increase the level of light and air.

RESTLESSNESS

Restlessness seems to have physical, emotional, and intellectual expressions:

- Physically, restlessness may be an imbalance of energy—a need to let off steam or relax. We all know the feeling of needing to get out and move when cooped up; our practice must not become like a pressure cooker.

- As with emotional restlessness and worry, it is important not to enter into a fight. We can increase the focus of our concentration, but if the motivation is to crush or smother our restlessness, rather than to accept and be curious, this may make things worse. Try to allow it to be as restless or worried as it wants, but notice it at the same time. Our practice must not become repressive.

- With intellectual restlessness, the traditional antidote is to have a better understanding of what we are doing and access to those who can answer our questions and wisely guide us; then we can settle in our understanding. This seems to link it to doubt.

- Fundamentally, restlessness is founded on agitation;

that is, a discomfort within ourselves and with our circumstances. For this reason, its antidote is happiness, a basic being at ease that is deeply nourishing. A practice that tries too hard, that is harsh and ascetic, that focuses too much on suffering and not enough on joy, can easily exclude this.

DOUBT

- Doubt corresponds closely to intellectual restlessness. It too benefits from our having a firm and clear understanding of what we are doing and access to those who can answer questions and guide us. This includes knowing what to read—the amount of literature on mindfulness can be confusing, particularly when we start out. Finding the right balance between reading that confuses and reading that deepens our understanding requires skillful choices.

- Doubt undermines our confidence in what we are doing, and when we look into it, we may find that it conceals fear or/and anger. This may be a fear of commitment for any number of reasons or an anger from perhaps an entirely different time and circumstance. Identifying the backstory may be useful.

- Doubt undermines our confidence in our ability to

be able to practice or benefit from our practice.
Having faith in ourselves and what we are doing may
be an additional resource when we feel confused and
uncertain—a certainty the heart can hold while the
thoughts wobble.

However we approach our obstacles, it is important that we realize they are only our enemies as long as we resist them. Noticing we are getting caught up in something and then resting our attention on the feeling of it in our bodies, and breathing around it, immediately turns it into a friend we are learning to be with.

It is also important to remember that not all obstacles appear as something troublesome or uncomfortable. Jamie had his meditation seat next to a shelf of his favorite books on Buddhism and mindfulness. Whenever he felt his meditation was not going so well, he would stop and look up a solution in one of his books or read something inspirational to make himself feel better. This habit of turning to his otherwise helpful books when struggling to be present with himself was an obstacle, but it took Jamie some time to realize this. Similarly, if we are within a Buddhist group, putting all our energy into serving community projects, group organization, and devotion without meditation practice may all become obstacles without our realizing it. Even developing our concentration, practicing calm abiding to the exclusion of insight, may become an obstacle if persisted with. Each can become a means to avoid simply being present with ourselves.

A Light Touch

Perhaps the greatest obstacle of all is to take obstacles too seriously. Lama Rabsang talks about this as not making our emotional and practice problems solid—that when we start to grasp at our emotions or want them to go away we are effectively adding hindrance to hindrance.

> *Some students talk about their problems, their obstacles, with doing meditation, and I say, "This is not truly existing; it's not real. You don't need to make it solid; just accept, let it be—that's all you have to do and then rest in awareness." Sadness, hurts are just mind habits that happen. Because of ignorance, grasping, aversion, and attachment they arise, but they are not really solid. And then, people say, "Oh, talk's easy. He's always talking about compassion and letting go, but I can't. It is really solid, really painful—my life's full of suffering." I say, "You know, we have no choice about being sad; we have to accept this and get over it. We say, 'Thank you, my suffering,' and there is no big deal. But if you say, 'Oh man, I'm suffering so badly,' and you can't accept it, then it's really a big deal." Some people understand this and they get over it. Some people, not. These people get fed up with the Buddhist teachings. But some people understand, and it really opens the heart, creates real changes. Their whole life changes.*

What may help us not to take our obstacles too seriously, and to address them with a light touch, is to remember that the hindrances we personally experience are just like everyone else's.

There is nothing uniquely special about what we have to deal with—sadness, hurt, pain, and suffering are all universal and oddly impersonal. Christina Feldman believes that recognizing the universality of our hindrances begins the process of swapping from being one who suffers from them to one who can be mindfully present with them. She says:

> *I continue to be surprised about the reluctance to make the hindrances more explicit, to actually name them, simply because it does bring a sense of relief to people to know that this is just not my issue. This is what the mind, the heart, does in reaction to not seeing things as they are. This is what the mind and heart do, defending against the unknown. This is the mechanism of creating and recreating struggle and suffering. Developing emotional literacy around the hindrances makes them into something approachable as part of the practice, as part of who we believe ourselves to be. In fact, in many ways, when you unpack your sense of identity, it's just a tangled knot of hindrances.*

Finally, the hindrance itself, like everything else, is already in a constant state of change. It is not solid. As soon as it comes into being it is already moving toward its end. We need not struggle to change it, for it will change itself. We need only be present as it does so. And as we breathe with what we find difficult, it may be that we feel a sense of quiet well-being that tells us everything is basically OK: A well-being that is not dependent on our emotions. A well-being that is present even when we feel afraid, unhappy, and agitated. A background silence. The spacious, clear, and compassionate awakened nature we all already share.

There is a lovely Buddhist verse that exactly captures this lightness of touch by linking it to the ephemeral quality of everything. The Buddha says:

I came in my dreamlike form,
to dreamlike beings,
to show the dreamlike path,
to the dreamlike enlightenment.

Most fundamentally, all our obstacles, all our hindrances, are dreams.

EXERCISE: MAKING OUR HINDRANCES CONSCIOUS

The thing with obstacles and hindrances is that they slip out of awareness almost instantly, so that we cannot see them while they continue to adversely affect our practice. We can help this by asking ourselves:

What precisely do I notice in my meditation?
When I find myself distracted, what sort of distraction is it?
Is there a pattern to my practice? Do I go round the same circuit day after day? What is that pattern?
Do I have the same thoughts about my practice? What are they?
The same feelings? What are they?

This is a good place to use our meditation log. Writing down what we carefully notice—nonjudgmentally—will help lift our hindrances to consciousness, so that we may experiment with them, finding out which antidotes work best for us. There are no final outcomes here—it is an endless work in progress. Approaching it as an experiment, an inquiry, and not as something to fix, is an act of patience and kindness.

Grabby, Grumpy, Sleepy, Jumpy, and Maybe: Key Points

- When we find something is getting in the way of our meditation, turning it into a struggle, we might pause and ask what is actually happening.
- There are various classifications of obstacles to meditation. One is the "five hindrances": desire, aversion, sleepiness, restlessness, and doubt (or grabby, grumpy, sleepy, jumpy, and maybe).
- Obstacles and hindrances are not something we overcome in the early stages of meditation practice; they are something we will always have to be aware of and work with.
- Most often the hindrances appear mixed together and so are not necessarily easily identified. Because they are ways we defend ourselves from waking up, we may circulate around them, trying to use each in turn when we feel uncomfortable with something we do not want to be present with.
- Obstacles and hindrances work at different levels. They may be just a passing experience, but they also can originate from unconscious core wounds. At this level

they are more difficult to recognize because they are pervasive.

- The primary way to work with all hindrances is to turn toward them mindfully.
- We can support our insight into how things really are by stabilizing and deepening our concentration. There are various methods for this, such as naming and counting the breath.
- We can support our mindfulness by using skillful means—working with a variety of attitudes, behaviors, and techniques that, together, help us to be more mindfully present.
- Finally, we need a light touch when working with what hinders us. Like everything else, our hindrances are always changing. We need not struggle against them but only be present as they change themselves.

CHAPTER 6

A Deeper Insight

Whatever experience arises, good and bad, just be with it. The mind is like the ocean with waves moving across it. If we get caught up in thinking one wave good, one wave bad, picking and choosing, we do not recognize that all thoughts, all experiences come from the same ocean. They arise in the mind and dissolve into the mind. If we just be with whatever arises it naturally dissolves.

LAMA RABSANG

What the teaching is pointing out is the potential turning point of every moment, of walking a different pathway.

CHRISTINA FELDMAN

Acknowledging when our meditation practice is in deep trouble and nothing seems to help is difficult because it is not something we recognize until it has become a real issue. Typically, we do not notice that we are cutting our sessions short, missing them altogether, or are still sitting but have become emotionally disengaged from our practice. We may lose interest and no longer remember why we do it, replacing the pleasure of the practice with empty habit or, worse still, duty. Most of us can do all these things for an astonishingly long time. Days quickly turn into weeks, months, and then even years before we look at what we are doing—or not doing—and see it is not working. We are surprisingly willing to bear the discrepancy between what we believe can be experienced in meditation and what we accept for ourselves, rarely asking how we feel—*really feel*—about our meditation and seeing if there is something happening during our practice, perhaps rooted in our personal history, that is acting as an unconscious block against it. As we have seen in previous chapters, resistance to meditation, while being annoying and perplexing, may have its own hidden intention and intelligence. Discovering this deeper level of hindrance, what its purpose is and how it functions, is an essential part of our path—a piece of self-inquiry that may be helped by understanding more of our personal story.

Our Personal Story

Traditionally in Buddhism, our personal history—the story—has been given little value and has instead been seen as the arena in which conflicting thoughts and emotions are played out, causing distress. Christina Feldman speaks of her own Burmese teachers having no interest in her personal feelings, and I have had similar experiences with my Tibetan teachers, whereby my worries and concerns have been met with kindness but with no sense of the seriousness and urgency with which I viewed them. Likewise in MBSR and MBCT: although these approaches are seated in Western psychology, which does value our personal history, there is, nonetheless, a sense that we are primarily there to learn mindfulness and not to give greater weight to the events of our childhood. This attitude finds its origins in the Buddha's observation that our suffering comes from grasping on to things that inevitably change. In more contemporary terms, human beings have evolved for their survival by dividing things up, trying to control unwanted change, and wanting opportunities while avoiding threats. When any of these strategies fail, we experience suffering. Yet the universe in which we live is entirely interconnected, transitory, and uncontrollable. As such, it is a recipe for pain, unless we can happily adjust to the reality of how things really are and roll with it. When this insight is applied to our personal history, it suggests that while having a history—a sequence of changes—is not a problem, trying to freeze-frame any part of it is. And yet trying to freeze-frame is exactly what we do when we hang on to and defend our idea of who we believe we are.

Eva gives us a particularly poignant example of this. Entering therapy, she told me of her intense hatred of her mother, which she demonstrated with nightmarish pictures and terrifyingly violent poems. Slowly, very slowly, the hatred began to abate and give way a little to more vulnerable feelings of loss and sadness. Then one day she came in again raging and furious; she seemed to have suddenly gone backward. Gradually it became apparent that she was now no longer allowing her rage to dissipate but was trying to keep it going. When we at last found words for this, she told me that she felt she would have no idea who she was if she let her hatred go. It had become a source of identity, which she was now clinging to. Letting go of her lifelong story of being an abandoned child meant she would not know who she was—a truly alarming prospect. In this, Eva is not fundamentally different from the rest of us. We all have identities, likes and dislikes, beliefs, positions, goals that we try to maintain, even as we can see them being challenged, eroded and melted away. With this in mind, Tsoknyi Rinpoche talks about how important it is to see where we place our sense of identity:

> I think psychoanalysis also says that if you have some problem and you hold on to that for many years, it becomes like your thing, and you don't see it as a problem. And then, when you try to let it go, fear comes, so you hold back—you won't let it go; you cannot let it go. You don't know you are holding on, that the ego is fixated on the problems. Then if you hold on to the sadness, the sadness becomes part of your nature and you build up some happiness around that. But it's not really happiness; it's a fake happiness.

Eva's "happiness" is fake in that it is defensive. Having to maintain our pain because we are afraid of being different is a tragic and futile choice. Eva confirms the Buddhist, and perhaps to some extent the MBSR and MBCT, fear that we can become trapped in our stories—that we do this by giving undue weight and attention to destructive mind states, cementing them in more deeply and making it harder to do something different. Martin Wells shares this view when he speaks from his own experience as a psychotherapist. He feels it is vital to not become *overidentified* with "the story of me and my problems":

> What I hear is people identifying with something that they're not. So, for example, in the Health Service, people identify with their diagnosis, as though that says something about who they

*essentially are: people overidentifying with their ego, with mind,
with thought, with personality, with a scripted story, with their
narrative.*

However, with this caution clearly in mind, it remains unde-
niable that understanding our personal history can be very helpful. We all need to feel that our personal lives are valuable and
have meaning. Whether we live in a culture that encourages
individualism or not, we quickly descend into depression and
anxiety when who we are and what we do seems to be of no
significance and going nowhere—when we have no meaningful
story about ourselves that gives us a place and a direction. Stephen Batchelor picks up this idea:

> *Meditation practice, in and of itself, is meaningless unless there
> is a framework of values that give it a reason. I think that's true.
> If you do a very simple thought experiment, if you just grab a
> bunch of people at random off the street and bring them into a
> meditation hall and tell them to watch their breath, it's a totally
> meaningless thing to do. Anyone who meditates and values it,
> and thinks it's a good thing, will have an answer to the question,
> "Why do you do this?" And it's the "why"—the rationale, the
> reason, the goal—that actually renders the exercise or the prac-
> tice meaningful. The practice per se is meaningless. It's just an
> exercise.*

This observation opens the door to how important our personal relationship to our meditation is. We are not machines
meditating but people who are the sum of a complex emotional

history. Our emotions are important: on one side they provide the inspiration and motivation to start meditating, and on the other they are what we take and make into the path. However we may feel about them, the one thing we cannot do is entirely ignore them. In getting our meditation back on track, it will be our emotions that play the biggest part. We do not meditate simply because we think it is a good idea, but also because it feels good. Christina Feldman takes this a step further and says that it is important to understand our personal history—what made us the way we are—because by recognizing how little control we have had over much of it we may no longer take it so personally:

> I feel that it is very important on the spiritual path to include the psychological dimension—that is, understanding our emotional life—because they're both part of the same path. I think what contributes to developing an insight is clear comprehension, so it's very important to understand the conditions that have led to us to being where we are and who we believe ourselves to be in this moment.
>
> I think it's important to clearly comprehend that in this present moment experience doesn't arise out of a vacuum, that it arises out of the many conditions in our life that have come together in ways that we were never in control of. If I view myself to be an enraged person, where is the beginning of that story? I may have to go back through generations to know the context for it, but it can be helpful to know, to have that understanding, because it can help me to take it all a little bit less personally.

Christina goes even further and suggests that there are occasions when, along with our practice, it may be helpful to enter psychotherapy:

> *There have been times when I have encouraged students to go into therapy because they don't have enough clear comprehension about how their story has actually led them to be where and who they are in this moment. Sometimes people need to find that understanding in therapeutic situations; they may not be finding it on the cushion. Some do, many do, but I think there's a place here for therapy.*

By combining the "cushion" with the "couch," mindfulness meditation with what psychotherapeutic understanding can reveal, we can create a powerful tool to comprehend and unlock difficult and recurring experiences during our meditation and even complete blocks we seem to have neither insight into nor any control over.

Finding the Hot Spots

We usually get an inkling that there is something in our history that is causing a problem when we find ourselves reacting in a way that is out of proportion to the situation and that leaves us, afterward, wondering what possessed us. Once we start looking for such occasions, we begin to find that they are sprinkled throughout our daily life and that they tend to cluster around similar situations. We may also find that there are some things that we just handle badly—quite often big things, like being in a relationship or dealing with or holding authority—large areas of our lives that never seem to go right and keep presenting the same conflicts. If we begin to look back, we may find that these problems have a long history, that they reflect, or are connected to, experiences and periods of our lives that may have started as far back as infancy. Without blaming our parents for our discontent, it is extremely useful to be able to identify where we are especially sensitive, where we quickly end up feeling like a child, where we flare up in aggression, where we lose all rationality and are overwhelmed by emotions we really do not understand. This, of course, is usually the stuff of therapy, reconstructing our past and seeing what parts of it remain active in the present. However, we can do much of this ourselves by constructing a timeline of our lives and seeing what jumps out as either particularly difficult or missing.

EXERCISE: CONSTRUCTING A TIME LINE

Get a roll of plain paper and at the top write, "Stories about my birth." Then write (or draw) everything you know about what it was like for you to be born, what kind of emotional environment you were born into, who was there to receive you, how they felt—really anything at all. If you know no stories, ask your parents or those who were around at the time.

When complete, move on to the next stage by writing an age at the side—this may involve stories about being a baby and a toddler, but it could also be a big jump into childhood. Remember, it is all in the detail. When did your siblings arrive? When did that hospital stay happen? When did your parents begin to argue and separate? When did you go to school?

Generally, we begin to remember properly by about the age of three or four. It is not necessary to make a long list of facts; focus more on what was emotionally important. Events form emotional memories that have lasting consequences, so go through each age you remember—do not skip parts to get to the end or because you believe you do not remember. You probably do.

When you have a whole history—and there may be yards of it—stand back and see if you can notice any patterns in it. A trusted friend or partner might be of help here, as being outside of your history they may see it more clearly. Look for repeating instances of emotional difficulty; these places probably connect to the situations you find difficult today. And remember that things/people that were absent may be just as influential as what was present.

Once we have an understanding of what has gone into making us, we may find this influences our meditation in several ways:

- It may be that as we sit we experience emotions that were first experienced in our past—powerful emotions we are finding it difficult to stay present with now.
- It may be that we experience reactions to meditation itself, finding something deeply unpleasant or unsettling just in the sitting down and doing of it.
- Or it may be that even though we think our meditation is a good idea and we want to do it, we find there is something about it that is so unbearable we cannot even start. Linking these reactions to the emotions behind them is the next step.

What Happens Inside?

When we find ourselves reacting disproportionately, what is happening? Psychotherapists have for a long time recognized that there are "hot spots"—complexes—in us that, when feeling threatened by external events or our own physical sensations, mean our thoughts and emotions instantly react with little to no involvement from the more considered and wiser parts of our nature. More recently, neuroscience has acquired the ability to scan the brain and "see" emotion as activity within it. This has revealed that the hot spots are connected to an almond-shaped area in the center of the brain called the amygdala, which is part of a wider brain network situated within the limbic system. This is a part of the brain we share with all creatures and one that is primarily emotional and reactive. When alarmed by experiences that we unconsciously associate with threat, the amygdala instantly sets off chemical processes that trigger fight, flight, or freeze reactions that are, more or less, unmoderated by any rational and reflective consideration of whether there is a threat or not: walking in the twilight, we catch sight of something in the corner of our eye and veer away; only seconds later do we realize that what has frightened us is only a shadow. This is because in evolutionary terms the amygdala, and the brain networks that contain our emotional memories, are far quicker in their self-protective reactions than the more balanced and inhibiting capacities of the evolutionarily later cortex. To put it very simply, something comes along that feels dangerous and instantly we become aggressive, want to run away, or freeze like a rabbit caught in headlights. Any attempt to test reality—to question the truth of what we are feeling—does not get a chance until later, when we calm down and can think clearly again.

Furthermore, because the amygdala's key activity is to scan what is happening in each moment and be particularly alert to danger, it creates anxiety-laden, unconscious memories and is connected to others that have been generated during earlier periods in our lives. When the amygdala is made active by a perceived threat, these emotional memories flood in as body sensations, so that as well as being unable to properly reflect on what is happening we can also end up feeling and behaving like a traumatized child, teenager, or adult.

One more twist: the amygdala can become oversensitized by being fired too often. When this happens, the jumpy, wired-up amygdala can even become scared by its own emotions, particularly those emanating from our core wounds—we can scare the life out of ourselves with our felt but unremembered past. When we put this together with resistance to our meditation, we can see that experiences during meditation, or the whole thing of meditation itself, may be triggering an amygdala meltdown. And when this happens, we feel that our practice is in some inconceivable way a danger that we need to get away from. At this moment the more balanced view that this is not so is simply not strong enough to counter the unconscious sense that we must resist to keep ourselves safe. We are up and off before we can say "mindfulness." It is therefore no surprise that sometimes meditation feels life threatening. From the point of view of our misinformed, jittery, alarm-bell amygdala, it is.

Head and Heart

Neuroscience gives us a new (and more balanced) perspective on the perennial discussion about the best relationship between the head and the heart. No longer is it about which one should rule, but rather about their being simultaneously interdependent—each deeply relying on the other.

We could say the brain has been evolving for 600 million years, if we go back to its earliest biological origins. This evolution is seen in the brain's structure—like a Russian doll, it unfolds from the bottom up and the inside out, along what is called the "neural axis." The most recent stage of evolution, the outermost "doll," is the cortex, and beneath and within this is the limbic system, and deeper still the hard wiring of the diencephalon and brain stem.

The cortex is active in the areas of language, abstract reasoning, values, planning, self-monitoring, and impulse control. Its central hub, which is in direct relationship to the limbic system, gathers information, makes decisions, guides actions, and reviews the outcome of its intentions. Plainly, this is what is commonly called our thinking "head."

The limbic system is primarily, though not exclusively, emotional. Its central hub is the amygdala, which reacts to sense stimuli, spotting what is pleasant, unpleasant, or simply neutral, looking out for opportunities and threats. In this way it receives and shapes our perceptions, creating passionate motivations that are then communicated to other areas of the brain, including the cortex. This, of course, is what is commonly called our emotional "heart."

These two areas of our brain, "head and heart," continuously work together, informing each other, up and down the neural axis. To simplify, the "warm" amygdala, more immediate and connected to the body, emotionally excites the "cool" cortex, which responds by slowing these reactions down by thinking. The benefit of this alliance is that the nonrational limbic system provides our emotional reactions to the different areas of the cortex, which, slower and more reflective, then has a chance to make more informed and responsive choices. The amygdala pumps the petrol, while the cortex chooses the route.

The cortex and limbic system can be more or less in accord. One can be more dominant than the other, and they can communicate well or be out of step. When having an "amygdala meltdown," the more powerful and immediate limbic system easily overwhelms the fractionally slower and more ponderous cortex, disabling its ability to think rationally until things stabilize again. It is also possible for the cortex to appear to overinhibit the raw energy of the limbic system, smothering emotional spontaneity. The good news here is that with our minds we can literally create our brains: by intentionally keeping engaged with the more spaciously reflective parts of the brain during the presence of strong emotions, the connection between the two is strengthened and integrated. This is achieved through the practice of mindfulness, so we can say that our hearts and heads, reacting and responding, are brought into better relationship through being present mindfully.

Finally, those who come from a Buddhist background will have noticed the surprising similarity to the Buddhist description of what is continuously occurring in us in each split second. Receiving sense stimuli we instantly register them as pleasant, unpleasant, or neutral. This triggers a vast network of more complex associations that recognize and name what has just been perceived. This then triggers a variety of actions that, in turn, are known within consciousness. This psychophysical process—the five *skandhas*—seems to bear an astonishing likeness to the combined activity up and down the neural axis of the diencephalon (receiving sensory information), limbic system, and cortex.

Clara: The Hidden Hindrances

Clara tells me she has been meditating for thirteen years, with many gaps. During this time, she has tried mindfulness and a variety of more complex and structured tantric meditations taught to her by the Tibetan Buddhist meditation teacher she is studying with, but she never persists with any of them. She starts by describing a situation many of us will have met with: having been in a MBSR/MBCT course, or meditating with a Buddhist group, we return home to find we are not sure how we are meant to be practicing and doubt whether we are doing it right:

> CLARA: Well, a part of me is feeling, "God, this is really annoying"—lots of agitation. And then another part,

"I don't know what to do with that." Am I supposed to
just stay with it? Am I supposed to let it go?
NIGEL: So, not certain about the meditation instruction?
CLARA: Yes, and it's the same thing with physical pain.
When it becomes almost unbearable, the instruction
is "stay with it." But this just starts a battle in myself—
I think, "Oh God, so do I just let this go on even
though it isn't actually serving any purpose at all?" But
if I stop, I feel a failure. Then that sets up a
competition with myself. Other people stay with the
pain, with all the feelings, so why aren't I doing that,
then? Why do I just give up at a certain point?

Christina Feldman talks about how we approach feeling
pain (or pleasure) in our bodies. Averse to discomfort, we resist
the pain by pushing it away and telling ourselves stories about
what is OK to feel and what is not, what we can bear and what
is too much until, eventually, we open with kindness toward it:

> Then we find the willingness to begin to turn toward that land-
> scape of physical sensation and to explore. Beginning to dis-
> cover the reaction in the mind is not the same as what's
> happening in the body. That is the "befriending" I'm talking
> about; it's just a willingness to meet what's actually going on
> without the addition of all the layers of "this shouldn't be hap-
> pening." That is why in Buddhist training there is so much
> emphasis on mindfulness of the body—because, in a way, the
> body, the life of the body and all of our reactions to it, is a
> microcosm of how we respond to the difficult and the painful
> everywhere else in our life. You know, whether it's the difficult

people, or the disappointment of a loss, or a failure, or whether it's a painful emotion, really it's no different from our reactions to difficult body sensations or experience. So in many ways, mindfulness of the body, which is a starting point for insight meditation, for mindfulness practice, is really the training ground for skills that are then brought to bear upon difficult emotions, difficult mental states, and difficult life experience.

Clara begins to glimpse this as she meditates. Struggling to be present with what appears as a pain in her leg, she begins to see that it is her lack of control during sitting with a group that is really bothering her. I ask what stops her staying with the pain and being curious for just a bit longer.

> CLARA: I think it becomes unbearable . . . if I imagine myself sitting there and then I become aware of the pain, say in my leg. I can feel myself getting tight and kind of "aagh!" and then sometimes I can just let it go and it goes. But then when it comes back, I start becoming aware of time and I'm thinking, "Well, what time is it now? How long have I done? Is it ten minutes? Is it twenty minutes?" If I knew what time it was, I could last that bit longer, but because I don't know what time it is—because I'm not leading the meditation—so all that goes on then!

Clara is confronting a much deeper issue, brought to the surface by the pain in her body. As the hindrance of aversion unfolds, it becomes clear that the hindrance of restlessness and worry, with its underlying concerns of agitation and the need for control, is also present. Christina recognizes in this need for control the issue of identity: who am I when my practice does not confirm my sense of self?

> We imagine all our bugbears from the past are going to arise, or somehow we don't have all the information coming to us from other people that tells us who we are or that we're all right or that we're loved or that we're acceptable. We don't have that identity level of information coming in to soothe us, and I think that creates a deep level of uncertainty and anxiety about the reality of our identity that people find is really quite threatening.

Clara's growing anxiety when she is not in control during group meditations is also present when she tries to meditate alone at home and is confronted by her thoughts. Rather than recognizing them as just thoughts and letting them go, she partially identifies with them and then enters into an argument with herself:

CLARA: Yeah, so if I've got lots of things to do in the day, there's a bit of me that thinks, "Well, am I being selfish? I'm sitting here for half an hour, whereas there's lots and lots of other things I need to be doing." But then I think, "Well, today could be the day where I die, and actually I probably should do half an hour today, at least, if not an hour!" What could possibly be more important than that?

NIGEL: I know that you're a really busy mum with two kids and have to earn your own living. But do you ever get a sense that your busy life can be used as an excuse to not practice?

CLARA: Definitely. Yeah, it's like I can find excuses.

NIGEL: Why would you need to find an excuse?

CLARA: I think it's very difficult just staying with whatever's there, with all the agitation, the struggle of my busy mind, all that kind of stuff. So it's sitting there and looking at it all and thinking, "Ugh!" That can be quite hard.

NIGEL: It's an excuse to avoid having to sit with yourself just as you are?

CLARA: It is, yeah. Although sometimes when I do that, sometimes I can just acknowledge it and say, "Oh well, that's what's going on right now, at the moment— that's fine." Other times it's like "Ugh! That's just too difficult." Yeah.

Clara sometimes finds being mindful of the agitation in her mind just too hard and difficult. Her doubts about what she should be doing when meditating, her body pains, the problem with not having control of the time, the thought that she may be selfish, and the need to do jobs may all be means not to be mindfully present with herself. However, from previous conversations with Clara, I know there is also a more intransigent issue of not having settled with a meditation method that really "fits." She has tried and rejected many different practices, including the eight-week mindfulness course, but now has gone back to a practice she was taught years ago. I wonder whether she has confidence that this is now the practice she will stay with.

CLARA: I do feel comfortable with the practice I'm in at
the moment. It does feel right . . . although, having
said that, I am having some doubts about having given
up my previous practice! I was thinking, "Hmm, what
was that about!" Is it something about seeing
something through, that once it becomes difficult, I
think, "Errrgh! What am I doing this for? How
difficult should it be?" I think a thing I'm becoming
more aware of is that there's a bit of me that's trying to
find something, trying to get to something . . .

NIGEL: "Something" being a certain type of experience?

CLARA: Yeah, I think so. Even though in my head I know
that's not how it ought to be, there is definitely a part
of me that wants to get something rather than just
being able to watch it all. And another obstacle for me
is how to let go, how to relax . . .

NIGEL: Relax and not try to get something? Relax in
whatever is there and be happy with it?

CLARA: Yeah. And I do think that I set myself up with
this time thing, that although it's very useful to think,
"Right, OK, half an hour," there also comes with that
a pressure to have achieved something within the half
an hour.

NIGEL: That by the end of half an hour you want to have
a meditative experience that you like. And then, when
you do the practice and it doesn't produce that result,
you change practice?

CLARA: Yeah. Rather than just trying to just be with it
all. I can feel it now as you are talking about needing

to get somewhere, and I think that's quite an obstacle. That's my feeling about it.

Clara has identified her desire for what she considers a "good meditation" as a hindrance, and she also knows that being able to include this desire in her mindfulness—being able to notice when the desire creeps in, stays, and then begins to fade—is the way forward. Yet there is a part of her that seems deeply resistant to this—hearing it, but then ignoring it, continuing to grasp after an elusive experience that she fruitlessly pursues through a variety of meditation techniques never fully used. Why is this?

CLARA: It's as if doing something that's really good is so much more difficult than doing something that isn't good. I don't know why, but . . . One of the things that Lama has said about this is that there are all kinds of spirits and forces and they don't want you to do good things. They don't want you to be enlightened . . . but if I put that to one side . . . I don't know why it's so difficult to do something good.

NIGEL: Could we take that explanation psychologically? That there is something outside of our immediate awareness, something unconscious, that gets in the way of doing something that does us good, that nourishes us. Does that get us any further?

CLARA: Well, I suppose it's something about effort, then, isn't it? If I think about going for a run or doing exercise, I know that after I've done it I'm going to feel really good and I can use that knowledge. I can think,

"OK, it's wet and I really don't want to go, but I know that after it I'll feel good." But I'm not sure that I can see the same path to feeling good with meditation—perhaps because it takes longer, whereas if I go for a run, I know that after fifteen or twenty minutes, I'll feel good. But to sit down and meditate, although there may be something good after quite a long time, there's no immediate sense of something.

NIGEL: The good feeling isn't quick enough, isn't certain?

CLARA: Yes, perhaps that's what it is. Do I know, do I really know, that it's going to be worth the effort? Part of me does because I can see it. I see it with Lama. One of the things that he says is that when you live in Tibet you see amazing yogis and that gives you motivation. But over here we have to take it much more on faith or trust.

NIGEL: Sustaining confidence in our practice is more difficult when we have to do it on trust alone.

CLARA: I think so. As you're saying it now, I'm thinking, yes, if I imagine myself meditating and it becomes uncomfortable and difficult, then I start thinking, "Well, you know, I do have to make that phone call, and I do need to do the washing, and I do need to do this, that, and the other," and I think there is a gratification that comes from doing those things because I've done them; I'm doing something and I can feel, "Ooh, that's another thing ticked off my list!" Even though, actually, that's not really going to go anywhere, because for aeons there's going to be washing, and there's going to be phone calls . . .

NIGEL: So what is the gratification of ticking things off the list?

CLARA: Partly, I feel I've achieved something. It's a bit like an advert that holds out an idea of happiness. You can have this happiness, but actually you never really quite get there. Something like that. There's a feeling of something familiar like, "Ooh, well, if I can do the washing and iron it and put it out, that's great." Even though that's endless!

NIGEL: So there is an immediate if transitory gratification in doing the washing, making the dinner, walking the dog, because it gets one more thing ticked off the list and that feels good. But what is it in us that wants to tick all those things off? What's being satisfied?

CLARA: I suppose there's a sense of something being achieved and that creates happiness. But actually that's a distortion. It's going in the wrong direction. But it's an easy way of getting happiness, something like an instant gratification as opposed to a delayed one. But it gives you a hint of happiness, even if you've gone off on the wrong path.

NIGEL: The experience of pleasure is available in the tasks, but it's only available in short amounts, and it's never . . .

CLARA: Sustaining or satisfying.

NIGEL: Because we can't do anything that keeps the pleasure coming in. But because that pleasure is more immediate than the pleasure that meditation promises, that is supposedly sustainable, the temptation is to

keep on going to the easy access—to what is
immediately pleasurable.

CLARA: That's it. Yeah. I hadn't thought about that as
the reason for going off and doing things. . . . Yes, it's
almost about having some faith in sitting with
something, isn't it? Not quite knowing where you're
going with it.

NIGEL: Having faith in something that feels difficult to
do against something that feels immediately satisfying.

CLARA: Yeah, and I'm in control of it. So I can take the
dog for a walk and know where we go and what it's
going to be like. But I can't if I'm just sitting with
whatever I am feeling—who knows where it'll go?

Clara's realization reveals just how complex our hindrances
can be. She has discovered within her distraction the desire for
a "feel-good" meditative experience—an aversion to sitting with
what is happening in her thoughts, emotions, and body; an anxiety about having control; and doubts about the value of her
practice and her ability to fruitfully benefit from it. She also
wounds herself with many "second arrows": recognizing the existence of these obstacles, she does not want to feel them and
struggles with her hindrances rather than including them as
objects of mindfulness within her practice. It is this refusal, not
having the hindrances, that is the main cause of her problems. I
also wonder whether we have gotten to the bottom of what the
real obstacle is. Her habit of giving up on a meditation method
when it feels uncomfortable and difficult and does not give a good
feeling has effectively stalled her practice, and consequently after

thirteen years it has still never properly started. This is serious, yet the question remains unanswered as to why it is that she continues to go from one practice method to another, looking for happiness, even when she knows this is self-defeating. Perhaps what we are meeting here is a deeper level of resistance, emanating from Clara's core wound that makes meditating feel like an unconscious threat that evokes defensive flight reactions.

If we briefly look at Clara's history, we can begin to see some of the deeper influences that may be at the back of her obstacles. Clara was prematurely born and placed within the isolation of an incubator. While this need not necessarily have detrimental consequences, in Clara's situation it was compounded by an experience of being mothered that did not feel like being held within an emotional environment that was safe and nourishing. If anything, Clara's mother was felt as absent and distantly dangerous. In the language of psychology, Clara developed an "avoidant attachment style"—feeling bad about herself, being poor at making relationships, and not knowing where or how to fit in. Clara's schooling continued this pattern. While still very young, she was sent to a boarding school and then, later, unexpectedly moved several times to new schools and so repeatedly lost the tentative relationships she had managed to build. At university, now much more self-sufficient, Clara experienced the pleasure of being clever but was unable to find the confidence to exploit her abilities and realize the reward of her studies. As an adult her first relationships seemed to mirror her earliest relationship with her mother: they left her feeling isolated and alone and with a tendency toward depression and chronic low self-esteem. Things that went wrong were always her fault—a belief reinforced by years of unjustified persecution by an estranged partner. When we first met, her discomfort was so great that she found it difficult to comfortably relate and, when particularly anxious, would seem to emotionally "leave the room"—the last-ditch defense of dissociation. Establishing a relationship that was felt as mostly safe, warm, mutually concerned, and finally equal was a long time coming and testament to all the hard work she had put in to make this possible.

If we listen carefully to what Clara is saying about her meditation, I believe we can hear her history peeping through. Essentially, how it felt to be an infant and then a child is the same as it feels when she tries to meditate. Her core wound is the hurt of isolation, abandonment, and fear, and from this arises the feeling that there must be something wrong with her if she feels this way. Furthermore, in the same way that Clara felt the abandonment of her mother, so too does she now abandon herself. She feels that she is never good enough and criticizes herself for how she is, mirroring the rejection and lack of acceptance she was met with at birth. In going from one meditative source of nourishment to another without finding satisfaction, she mirrors her early experience of emotional deprivation. She simply cannot recognize the unknown and alien experience of being held in a safe place and receiving something good. As she approaches what may emotionally and spiritually feed her, it is difficult to form the stable relationship that will give sufficient time for an emotionally nourishing experience to be received. Many times when she sits to meditate, the feeling that she is returning to something that feels good is absent. Having never received openhearted acceptance, she lacks the resource to accept herself just as she is. For her it becomes a struggle of self-rejection and the longing for something—anything—to make her feel better.

Little surprise then that she will abandon her uncomfortable and sometimes disturbing meditation for the instant gratification but ultimate dissatisfaction of completed housework.

Interestingly, she has identified something important when she recognizes that meditating in a group helps her practice. Even though the group, by holding her, does cause some anxiety stemming from her loss of control, it also gives her a positive experience she has not previously had. Held in a group, her emotional tendency to quickly run away, without letting anything in, is prevented. And the same goes for her warm and emotionally available Tibetan teacher who provides a stable and consistent relationship that is affectionate, affirming, and uncritical. In these two choices, Clara's basic healthy intelligence and her innate movement toward wholeness shows. What remains to be done—Clara's next step—is to learn how to be present on her meditation cushion with all the feelings stemming from her emotional history and include them in her mindfulness; learning not to be unknowingly driven along, looking for something she finds hard to get, but instead to notice what she is feeling as she is feeling it and remain present with it, whatever it is, holding herself in the loving kindness and acceptance of her awareness.

Unlike Clara, many of us will not have pieced together our own history and the unconsciously remembered threats still held in our bodies—particularly those of our formative first five years. However, many of us will have our suspicions about ourselves and may have partially assembled an explanation of why we are as we are. Living in a culture that routinely thinks of the influence of childhood on being an adult, we quickly wonder what happened when we come up against messy patterns of relationships, pervasive anxiety, or repeating periods of depression.

Some of us will have had some counseling, psychotherapy, or analysis before learning to meditate, particularly if we are approaching it through the MBSR and MBCT routes. This therapeutic experience may have uncovered the creation of patterns based on unconscious ways of thinking, feeling, and behaving, like those found in Clara and others in this book. If this is the case, this understanding can be particularly valuable because it alerts us to the places of blindness in ourselves and where we need to be most conscious—insights that do not come so easily without some help. In the eight-week mindfulness course this consciousness is encouraged through logging our positive and negative experiences and the questioning of how accurately our thinking reveals our own state of mind and what is happening around us—effectively, how our amygdala colors accurate perception. For many, including myself, this part of the course can be a revelation—suddenly seeing how deeply we distort how things really are. However, whatever our level of understanding, we are all in the same position in this present moment. We can either be driven on by automatic pilot, emotionally reacting rather than responding, or wake up to ourselves and be present with what we find happening in our bodies, emotions, and minds.

Acknowledge, Do Something Different, Do It Again

Tsoknyi Rinpoche talks about how his teaching has evolved over the years, realizing that if we are to truly change, we must start from being present with what we feel in our bodies in the present moment:

> *I changed the emphasis from cognitive understanding towards feeling-oriented teaching, like transforming through our love, compassion, letting go in the body. A little bit of body teaching, not so much the head.*

This realization has also come to Western psychology. Previously, it was believed that talking about our difficult emotions and behaviors, our core wounds and beliefs, would give us an understanding that would then change them. Now we know that for these to truly, more lastingly, change it is necessary that we do not believe them nor be swept up and carried away by them *while they are active*. This is because the way our brain has evolved, as we saw above, our emotions, when aroused, are not susceptible to reason—which is hardly a surprise to anyone who has tried to talk themselves out of what they are feeling. If we are to deeply influence our emotional selves and help old patterns of dysfunction change, resolve, and heal, it is necessary to feel the emotions in our bodies, their felt sense, and remain consciously and kindly present as they change of their own accord and in their own time. In the language of very simplified neurobiology, this is to encourage and strengthen the link between the cortex with its thinking powers and the limbic system's emotions. This way of being present with ourselves in the body is sometimes called by trauma therapies, such as EMDR (eyemovement desensitization and reprocessing), working from the "bottom up" (as opposed to "top down," where we rely on working things out with our thoughts). Fortunately, this comes to us at a time when neuroscience can tell us approximately why this is effective and, simultaneously, mindfulness has been discovered as a way to put this into practice—a practice that has been used and perfected for almost two and a half thousand years in Buddhism. It is a happy alliance of psychotherapy, science, and meditation. Pema Chödrön, the American Buddhist nun we met in the introduction, makes this accessible by using the memory prompt, "acknowledge, do something different, do it again."

Acknowledge

To acknowledge means to be consciously aware of what is happening in the present moment—to simply notice what is happening now. If our experience is of being hindered as we practice, in one or more of the ways described here, then that is what we notice. For Polly and David (whom we met at the start of the previous chapter), this means they notice feelings of discouragement and the impulse to jump up and do something urgent. In Kay's case it means noticing the first tiny sign of sleepiness. For Clara it means she notices her panic when feeling trapped in a group practice and when sitting alone—feelings of wanting to get away, of wanting to feel good or be valuable. Of course, this is not easy. Just having that moment of noticing is probably one of the most difficult things we can require of ourselves, because the habit to not notice (but to act) has been deeply established through countless repetitions each day of our lives. But it is possible, with practice.

Do Something Different (Go to the Body)

Having noticed what is happening in us in the present moment, we then do something different from our habitual reaction, our automatic pilot. Nature gives us two "built-in" ways to be with ourselves and our world. The first is simply to react, and this, most often, is more or less automatic and involves little to no thinking. While this is good for many situations—for instance, immediately reacting to a distressed child—because it is unreflective it can also be unskillful: driven by emotions based in fear that fuel actions that may hurt ourselves and others. The second is to repress what we feel—to either intentionally or unconsciously put "out of mind" what we do not want or cannot bear to experience. One simplified way of thinking of this is the balance between the expressive emotionality of the limbic system and the inhibiting rationality of the cortex. All of us use both of these options, but if we pause and think about ourselves, we may see that each of us uses one option more than the other. Nature also gives a third possibility; that is, to develop mindfulness. Unlike the first two, this does not come fully functioning but must be cultivated through practice. To be mindful is the middle way between reaction and repression: it allows us to be fully consciously aware of what we are feeling—physically and emotionally—but not so we are entirely swept away and the emotions have us rather than our having them. To do something different is to choose this third mindful option and, as is now widely recognized, the best way to do this is to consciously feel what we are experiencing in our bodies. This not only strengthens the bridge between the reflective and emotional parts of our nature; it also helps us be mindful by giving us a place to focus on. Polly feels her discouragement as a collapse in her chest; David as his limbs tensing up; Kay as a draining of energy and the leaden eyelids; Clara, when panicking in a group, as palpitations, shortness of breath, constrictions, and erratic and racing thoughts—body sensations that she also feels sometimes when sitting on her own. Feeling into our bodies and noticing with kindness and curiosity the small, continuous changes occurring, not adding anything more, is the way to befriend ourselves with mindfulness. It is a truly healing path of change that starts, paradoxically, with the acceptance of ourselves as we already are. The box below gives you ways to do this.

Recognizing Our Felt Sense

There are some thoughts (memories, dialogues, grudges, pleasures, fantasies), and the emotions that accompany them, that incessantly return, to the point that we feel persecuted by them. We can also find ourselves sitting down to meditate but somehow either not starting or wanting to sit but not getting that far. When this happens, we bring mindfulness to the felt sense of these experiences, asking, "What does it feel like in my body right now to have these emotions?" This is how:

1. Noticing an emotionally charged resistance, we ask, "Where do I feel this in my body?" Let's imagine we do not really want to meditate. Resting

attention on the body, we can feel the resistance perhaps around the solar plexus.

2. Having located the place (or places) and resting our attention on it (or them), ask what words or images completely capture this felt sense. Anything may come up. Try to accept it, however unexpected. We need not understand it or judge it. It could even be a sound or a noise. So, for example, let's say the words "churning," "squirmy," "trapped" come up.

3. Having found these words, we continue to feel the felt sense, and while continuing to breathe, we name the felt sense to make sure the words really fit, and then we stay with it. So we try "churning," "squirmy," and "trapped," and, yes, "trapped" really fits, so we stay with that and breathe, keeping contact with the feeling in the solar plexus, the felt sense. Trapped.

4. Continuing to stay present with the felt sense, we may find that it changes in some way and that new words or images now fit it better. If this happens, let it. If not, that is OK too. So, let's say, for example, the felt sense suddenly has some new words: "I've got to get out." This accompanies a more intense feeling of claustrophobia and panic felt in the solar plexus and throat. So we stay with this felt sense, breathe, name it: "I've got to get out."

5. Still continuing to stay present with the felt sense—breathing, naming it, allowing it to change or stay as it is—suddenly a small insight occurs: this feels like all the other situations we feel trapped in: our meditation is being felt by something inside of us as a trap, not spacious and calm.

6. Back to the breath. Allow the insight to support the practice.

We can continue to be present with ourselves like this for as long as the process continues. Once we drift off or feel that it is complete, we simply return to our breath. Feeling deeply into ourselves in this way can release emotions we did not know we had. (My example was taken from my own resistance. I was very surprised that it linked to a feeling familiar to me, one with a very long history. Here it was again in my practice.) Feeling anger and staying with it may reveal sadness. Criticism may reveal shame. Fear may reveal courage. We can only know by being present with curiosity, acceptance, and kindness. Having found this way to be with ourselves, we can use it again and again, making this the central and most important means to be mindfully present with what we are really feeling.

LETTING IN NOURISHMENT

Rick Hanson, a neuroscientist, has a saying: "Our minds are like Velcro for bad things and Teflon for good." Behind this is the evolutionary advantage of vigilance—we get eaten less—but also the disadvantage that always scanning for threat creates pervasive feelings of paranoia. When this is added to a system that is hyperalert to threat, has a jittery amygdala, and stores up bad memories, it may help to intentionally redress the imbalance by mindfully stressing the good. This is how we do it when meditating feels bad or scary:

1. Intentionally look for something good about your meditation. You may sit for just one minute. You may sigh as you sit down. You may even feel quite concentrated and experience the calm that comes with this. During the eight-week mindfulness course, we repeatedly point out good things about people's budding practice which they have not noticed: "You did it twice this week for five minutes and noticed your resistance on several other days. Great—this is much more mindful than before!"

2. Now let it in and really savor it. Many of us habitually shut out or move off to something else when something good comes to us. This time do something different and really let what is good about your meditation in. Get a felt sense for this and prolong the experience of feeling what is good about what you have done within your body. You cannot do this long enough or often enough because every occasion heals what has been hurt

and builds a fresh perception of what you experience.

3. And do it again and again. One of the good things about keeping the meditation log we suggest in the MBSR/MBCT courses is that it creates an opportunity to notice and celebrate what goes well. This is not to mindlessly stress the positive but to make sure you are not forgetting to water the tiny green shoots that are present within your practice from the start.

SOOTHING THE WATERS

When we pour good associations onto our difficult experiences, the two will become associated in our memory as connected. We can use this to help phobic reactions to our meditation. This is how:

- When feeling a resistant feeling, a difficult emotion, around your practice, you can intentionally add to this a good association that focuses on an aspect that you like, have an attraction to, or that has been a success. For instance, when feeling anxious about sitting, you may recall the friendly faces of those you first learned meditation with, thinking of everyone sitting together and the warmth of mutual support, or perhaps remember occasions when something of your mindfulness has had a good influence on your life and you have noticed it and been pleased.

This may connect, for those of us involved in Buddhism or another contemplative path, to the experience of being inspired by a teacher or the history of all those who have practiced within a lineage of meditators. Our positive association with what they represent pushes into the background our new and stumbling efforts while at the same time inspiring us to go on. However, we need not be Buddhists to benefit from this—if research is our thing, we might remember all the good things that have been found out about practicing mindfulness. They are truly inspiring.

PUTTING OUT OF MIND

Sometimes the middle way of being mindfully present is not possible. When this is the case, we can use skillful versions of the two ways nature automatically equips us to be with our experience: putting out of mind and expression.

- When becoming aware of negative thoughts or emotions around your meditation that threaten to swallow you up, you can firmly say to yourself, "Let this go." I have found this particularly useful in the middle of the night when I can wake and have horrible, critical thoughts about myself. Noticing that I am being vicious and catastrophizing, I tell myself to stop and place my attention firmly elsewhere—like on my breath. A word of caution though: this is a skillful use of repression, but to be skillful it must not be driven by aversion. If it is, it is a hindrance. To be skillful we must know what is happening and choose to abandon it. It is the difference between a rout and a retreat. The first is driven by fear; the second is a considered move. Differentiating between the two is not initially easy.

- A variation of this is to put something aside until you are able to be with it. "Yes, I do need to properly have a look at my practice, but it would be better not to do this in the middle of the night when I know I do not think straight." Or when plagued by a thought while meditating, "Not now. I will do this later." Likewise, pressing emotions: for some things we need to be in the right space before we can address them, and we can consciously choose when that time comes.

FINDING EXPRESSION

On the other side, here are three ways to skillfully work with the expression of thoughts and emotions so they are not unconscious and reactive episodes of acting out.

- The first way is to transform or sublimate the energy of what you are feeling. My wife provides an example. As a little girl she could easily get caught up in her worries and concerns. Learning to do gymnastics and other sports took her anxious energy and transformed it into something positive. Similarly, when you feel pent up with feelings, noticing this,

you can skillfully choose to do something physical.
This is particularly helpful for depression and
anxiety. However hard it is to make yourself move,
moving can dramatically lighten your mood. This is
essential.

• The next way is to take a strong emotion you are
feeling—like throwing your meditation cushion at
your meditation teacher and screaming—and act it
out in your imagination, intentionally going through
the entire event, allowing yourself to feel it fully.
Given such license, you may also notice resistance as
you approach behaviors and feelings you usually
censor in yourself. Hold all of this, the imaginary
acting out and the emotions it evokes, within your
awareness. This means not just throwing yourself
mindlessly and indulgently into whatever you are
imagining but being consciously present at the same
time. This is a good method for imagining your way
into new possibilities—what do you meet in yourself
when you do something different? A word of caution
though: desires and aversions often start as fantasies;
keeping them in the imagination is as hard as it is
necessary.

• Lastly, you can take a behavior and just let yourself
do it but do it mindfully. Do not sit today. Be as
distracted as you can be. Say mindfulness is rubbish
and a pain—really anything, as long as it harms
neither you nor others. In many ways this is both the

easiest and most difficult thing to do. We all act on
impulse, all the time, so this requires no effort, but
bringing mindfulness to our actions addresses our
deepest habit: to remain asleep.

Do It Again

Having done something different once, having been mindful, it
is then necessary to repeat it many, many times until the new
pattern is established. This is why we practice. We are not practicing for some future event but to cement repeatedly in this
present moment a new way of being. A metaphor I frequently
use is that all our lives we have been going down the same path
in our thinking and emotions until that path has become deeply
worn and very slippery. One step from the top and we instantly
find ourselves sliding down, with no means to stop once started.
Here think of a situation, played out many times, in which we
are resistant to our meditation—putting it off until later, getting
up as soon as it gets difficult, changing our method in the hope
that a different way will work better. We know we do this, but it
does not stop from us fruitlessly playing it out again and again.
When we do something different, we create the first steps in lay-
ing a new path next to the old. Each time we manage to take
this new path it becomes more established and the old path
begins to dry up and finally grass over. Of course, we do not
always manage to take the new one, even after it has become
quite established. Sometimes it is just not possible to avoid our

old ways of behaving and feeling. However, this is not a cause for self-recrimination—we just notice what is happening and do something different. Annie reminds us of the importance of kindness and patience at moments like these:

> It is easy to recognize what we are doing at the cognitive level and intervene, but at a deeper level our story has been about our survival, and getting that to change is very difficult. If I look at myself, all my issues—around my mother, around claustrophobia, around being moved in on—continue to exist. These patterns of survival are who we are. Making changes takes an extraordinarily long time. They only change through tiny drip-drip steps.

Just Awareness

Mindfulness leads us to see that we are neither just our thoughts nor just our emotions. During the MBSR/MBCT courses, we spend a lot of time looking in detail at how we experience things—what goes on in us when something happens. How do we feel when a friend ignores us? Or when we get a promotion? What makes up a pleasant or unpleasant event? By session six of the eight-week mindfulness course, "Thoughts Are Not Facts," it has become apparent that thoughts and emotions, as well as being invaluable, can also distort and restrict our ability to clearly see and respond well to our experience—that having a thought, feeling an emotion, is *just* a thought, *just* an emotion, and does not necessarily mean that what is thought and felt is true.

This is a particularly empowering insight. When we find ourselves struggling with our practice, believing we will be incapable of doing it or that what we are doing is hopeless and wrong, we can, recognizing this belief as a destructive state of mind that emerges under pressure, step back and choose not to identify with it. Furthermore, as we step back, it is clear that our thoughts and emotions are happening within our awareness—like images coming and going in a mirror—and that while they are transitory it seems the mirror, awareness, is not. This is the key insight: we are not our thoughts; we are not our emotions. These all come and go. But awareness itself is the space in which this occurs. Christina Feldman says that this realization is a huge shift. Instead of being mesmerized by specific events in the mirror—my self, my pain, my ways of criticizing my practice—we begin to see that we inhabit a vast web of interconnectivity in which our thoughts, emotions, and actions condition every aspect of what we experience. This is to see things as they really are—not solid, discrete events, but a sea of endless process where our thoughts create our reality. Christina:

> *Encouraging people to see that there may be choices in how they respond is often not something that may have occurred to them. By encouraging people to see process, to see that suffering is actually not a static state of affairs but something that's being recreated moment to moment by the habitual processes in their minds, creates some choice. This thought doesn't automatically occur when you're in the midst of an obsession or a preoccupation or a grand state of resistance—it doesn't occur that there might be another way of being.*

Taking responsibility is empowering: my thoughts, my emotions, my actions in this moment are the source of all my experience. If I am skillful in my choices, then I create situations that benefit myself and others, but if I am unskillful, driven by forces within me of unconscious reactivity, then I create situations that cause me and others pain. A minute's reflection on my life supplies many examples. This view gives me choices. Even though I may be caught up in circumstances that were not of my making, now, right now, it is only I who can choose how to be with this in this moment. It is only I who can be present with my experience as it is.

A Deeper Insight: Key Points

- Sometimes our meditation becomes really stuck and it seems nothing will help it. This is possibly because within our personal history there exist deep hindrances that we are partially or entirely unaware of.
- Traditionally, our personal history has not been given any significance because there is a concern not to encourage getting more caught up in the thoughts, emotions, and behaviors that have already hurt us— not to pour petrol on the fire as it burns out.
- However, our personal history and our sense of self are at the center of all we do, including choosing to practice our meditation.
- The spiritual path is also a personal and emotional path.
- Understanding how we have become who we are—our

personal story—is of value because it gives us insight into how things really are in the present moment.

- Combining the insights of psychotherapy with insight meditation can produce a powerful tool that can be used to unblock our meditation. By constructing a time line we may see patterns of emotional difficulty that alert us to unconscious and painful memories that our meditation threatens to make more conscious.

- When we have these experiences, it is likely that we are having an "amygdala meltdown," signaling that we are under threat. We may know rationally that this is not true, but our emotions are saying something different and louder. And what they say goes.

- The antidote to all this is to acknowledge what is happening in the present moment, to do something different—principally, being present with our *felt sense*—and then to do this repeatedly to build a more skillful, conscious way of being. There are a number of skillful means we can use here, like *letting in nourishment*, *soothing the waters*, *putting out of mind*, and *finding expression*.

- Finally, all our thoughts and feelings about meditation are coming and going like reflections within the mirror of awareness. Knowing this reveals ultimately that we are entirely responsible for ourselves, and accepting this creates the greatest freedom and opportunity for change.

CHAPTER 7

The Damaged Heart

It's not some kind of fluffy, comforting, lovey-dovey concept. In reality, it's the opposite—it's incredibly challenging and it brings you right up against a very key and uncomfortable question—in fact, the most important question of all: do I have the genuine capacity to love myself and others, including those closest to me?

ALEX

An emptiness, a space where before the deep howl resided, quite serene, soft, an unusual quietness . . .

TESS

Imagination can give birth to reality.

PHILIPPA VICK

We have almost reached the end of the afternoon on the one full day of practice that is part of the eight-week mindfulness course. Together, we are practicing a meditation that "inclines the mind" toward developing loving kindness and compassion. Imagining someone easy to feel kindly toward—a child, a partner, a pet—we move on to ourselves, those we do not know, those with whom there is some bad feeling, and finally everyone, including ourselves. Toward all these countless others and ourselves we make the wish, using either a traditional formula that has been recited for twelve hundred years or something of our own that carries the same spirit:

> *May we be free of suffering and the roots of suffering. May we know happiness and the roots of happiness.*

Implicit within this is the essence of the course. The roots of suffering are the conflicted thoughts and emotions that we can all too easily get caught up in. The roots of happiness are our ability to be mindfully present and unconditionally kind. If felt, this can be deeply beautiful; on many occasions people have been moved to tears.

However, on this occasion we have in the group a rather earnest young woman who is seeking our attention and whom the others are clearly feeling anything but kindly toward. Perhaps with memories of church, she insists on whispering the words of my offered aspiration out loud, despite my repeated attempts to say do it, or something of your own, *silently within your own mind*. With each step of the practice—someone dear, herself, someone neutral, someone difficult, everyone—she repeats three or four times in a clearly audible mutter her wish that there may be an end to suffering and its roots and knowledge of happiness and its origins. With each repetition, the irritation in the room builds and builds.

For my part, I do not know quite what to do. I am a mass of conflicting emotions. I feel a responsibility to help the group meditation; my failing and progressively shrill attempt to communicate not to speak aloud is an expression of this. I also feel the group's irritation in myself. This has not been the first time the young woman has chosen a powerful moment to have the whole group notice her. From the disproportionate power of my feelings I recognize how deeply I disapprove of this and how it would be something—however much I may want it—that I would never allow myself to do. Being with this insight is very uncomfortable and humiliating. I also feel some compassion for the young woman; there is something childlike about her whispered prayers—she may do all sorts of things, but in this moment she really does mean what she is saying as well. She *is* wishing all of us happiness and that we all should be free of suffering, and some of us are clearly not wishing her the same back.

A Dangerous Love

I tell this story now because it so clearly shows how there can be an enormous discrepancy between going through the motions of meditations that generate loving kindness and compassion and what may be going on within us, beneath the surface, at the same time. Western teachers writing about mindfulness and loving kindness have become aware of this difference. Talking about the resistance we meet in ourselves to cultivating compassion, Paul Gilbert, author of *The Compassionate Mind* and creator of compassionate mind training, identifies many causes. We may view being compassionate as self-indulgent or being weak and spineless. Or we may feel that we cannot extend compassion and kindness toward ourselves because, being responsible for our own ills, we do not deserve it—as we do not if we are a bad person. More complex still is when we find that loving kindness and compassion are stirring up deep wounds in our psyches, the core wounds that we have visited in previous chapters. We may find that we touch previously unrecognized wells of anger and grief that are connected to feelings of lost, insufficient, or absent belonging and love. More painful still, it may be that those of us who have received both love and cruelty from someone we have been dependent on will find that the presence of loving kindness and compassion is felt as an unbearable threat that must be resisted or escaped from. This is deeply confusing and frightening. Psychoanalyst Valerie Sinason, known for her work with those who have been ritually abused, told me of an experience where she had offered some kindness to a patient, saying that they were now safe. However, tragically, this had the opposite effect, and rather than provide comfort, it created even greater fear. What Valerie did not know was that the patient's hurt had been preceded by seeming love from those who then became the abusers. In the patient's mind, kindness, love, and abuse had become wholly associated and intermingled.

The creators of MBCT, Zindel Segal, Mark Williams, and John Teasdale, most recently made much the same observation. Confronted with the invitation to cultivate loving kindness and compassion, many of us experience painful feelings about our failures in this area in the past and the impossibility of ever doing it right in the future. This may start a cascade of self-denigrating thoughts and emotions that make us even less kind, less compassionate. They suggest that those of us who are especially prone to ruminating about our failures and fears will find kindness particularly hard, and those of us who ruminate and are also afraid of emotionally engaging will be more likely to want to withdraw from our mindfulness course early. When Nina, someone who has already had some exposure to Buddhism and loving-kindness meditations, seems to be struggling with the whole thing of kindness and compassion, I ask her what she is experiencing:

> *I would say you are correct when you say that loving-kindness meditation brings up a lot of feelings for people. For me, probably as a result of having had a very harsh mother, one of the feelings that can come up is anger. What is my anger saying? Something along these lines: "This is all pie in the sky: the world is not full of loving kindness; it's actually dangerous and full of loss. I can't access much kindness for myself a lot of the time, nor can many others. I haven't always got that voice inside of me, and I can't suddenly invent it because I am in a Buddhist meditation group. Mindfulness or Buddhism has got unrealistic expectations of me. I can't possibly live up to them—especially with grandiose statements like 'wishing peace to all sentient beings.' It's all a bit too lofty and unreal."*
>
> *Another feeling it can bring up is sadness around noticing how unkind I am being to myself and others sometimes. As you can see, with all this swirling around it is mightily difficult to focus on loving kindness. As a result of this I might be sitting there feeling a fraud; I am supposed to be full of gentleness and kindness, but in reality I feel more of my own "badness." I am falling short of the required standards. I am clearly a bad person.*
>
> *When you say that deep core wounds peek up through the practice, this is totally obvious to me. These wounds are whirling around for most of the day, and when I sit still they grow stronger and more insistent. . . . The difficulty I have with just sitting is that as people confront their own demons, they can be left quite alone; it's not always a nurturing environment but*

more of an endurance test. It's as if there is no place for feelings there. . . . The difficulty Buddhists have when trying to convey what they have discovered to ordinary Joe Bloggs is that they can sound very self-punishing and not full of compassion for themselves. So when I get in touch with the angry part of me, I criticize Buddhism and Buddhists for being totally out of relationship or antirelational and trying to live up to impossibly high ideals.

Nina's emotional reactions to kindness and compassion are not unusual or particularly extreme. Having experienced her earliest of relationships—that with her mother—as "harsh," she later comes to see the world similarly as "dangerous and full of loss." In earlier chapters we looked at the core wounds such a background can leave us with. As newborn infants we come into the world all set up for and expecting someone there who will give us a safe haven. We know this is happening when we feel loved, seen, heard, and understood. In those moments of gazing, smiling, and laughing with the one who cares for us we know a love that will enable us to recognize, give, and receive love for the rest of our lives. And at those times when we communicate being empty and lonely or when we need some quiet and space, our caring person quickly understands and responds, leaving us with the knowledge that we are held within a benevolent universe that can provide for our needs. However, when our experience is predominantly different from this we can be left with ways of experiencing ourselves and our world that are deeply painful and confusing. Broadly speaking, these less-than-good experiences, or "insecure attachments," can be described as "the indifferent hold," "the overwhelming hold," and "the dangerous hold":

- **The indifferent hold** When we have experienced our initial caregiver as turning away from us, not relating, not present to our needs, we may feel that there is no safe haven and, in response to this, become insensitive to our own needs and the needs of others, capable of ignoring painful situations and repressing distressing emotions. Effectively, as we have been turned away from, we now turn away from ourselves.

- **The overwhelming hold** Alternatively, when we have experienced our caregiver as intrusive and engulfing, placing their needs over ours, flooding us with their emotions, unpredictable and volatile, we may feel that our safe haven is threatened in a different way. As adults we continue to gravitate to answering the emotional needs of others, while being empty in ourselves and prey to our own emotions. As we were used and swamped in emotional chaos, so we now swamp and misuse ourselves.

- **The dangerous hold** This variation, fortunately much less common, when added to the two above, compounds them, making them far more severe. When the one who is meant to care for us is themselves so distressed, disorganized, traumatized, and emotionally absent, we may be left frightened by their presence, caught within the double bind that the one we want to comfort us in our fear and unhappiness is the same as the one who is its cause. Faced with this impossibility and similar emotional traumas in later life, the best we can often do is to vacate ourselves and feel nothing.

Each of these experiences, accumulated during our earliest years and compounded, reaffirmed, and complicated by subsequent events, may be at the root of what hinders our ability to mindfully befriend ourselves just as we are, extending compassion toward our own suffering and feeling a loving kindness that wishes we be well and happy. Nina's clear and insightful understanding of herself demonstrates this. Her experience of a mother she recalls as harsh is repeated in her experience of a world that feels dangerous and full of loss, where she must endure her aloneness, her abandonment, and the absence of love—a world where there is no kindness. She, as we all do when infants, takes responsibility for this. Turning her anger against herself, she feels she is a fraud, not good enough, and bad—all characteristics of the traumatic mothering she has received. Buddhism, practicing mindfulness and its compassionate ideal, when perceived through her wound, is felt as her absent and indifferent mother. What should be caring becomes cruel and without compassion. Nina's core wound, as with all our core wounds, takes what is potentially good and nourishing and makes it into something threatening that must be defended against.

Give Peace a Chance

Philippa Vick, a psychotherapist specializing in trauma and an MBSR/MBCT teacher, talks about our defenses against threat as a sequence of barriers. Our barriers protect us from feeling the original hurt of our insecure attachments, feelings around being emotionally engaged, being cared for, having control, and taking pleasure in success. They reduce our sensitivity and redirect us away from emotional "hot spots." Our barriers are resistant to change. They are like a pair of eyeglasses that color deeply how we experience ourselves and our relationships—how we experience loving kindness and compassion.

- **The insight barrier** When feeling overwhelmed, frightened, and endangered as a baby or a small child, we instinctively shrink away, shut down, and withdraw. If we have had to do this repeatedly, in later life we will fear engaging with our own emotions and the emotions of others, feeling as we did when tiny—that they are dangerous. Thinking and impersonal abstractions are far safer. From behind this barrier, all talk of kindness and compassion feels a long way away; we may be able to intellectually appreciate the theory but at the same time have little or no real sense of what it feels like inside.

- **The nourishment barrier** When the one who mothers us is distant or not there, we can find no safe haven in their attuned love. Slowly, as our expectation dies, we angrily and resentfully adjust to not having our needs met, while still hoping they will be. As adults we know our early loss through depression, emptiness, and feeling bad about ourselves. Having not known loving care, kindness, and compassion, we neither easily recognize it when found nor retain it if received. From behind the nourishment barrier, we long for kindness and compassion, but it never feels enough. We cannot believe it is possible, while desperately wishing that it were so.

- **The response barrier** When feeling that love comes with strings attached, we may defend ourselves through stubborn resistance or by getting on top and being in control. Behind our barriers of endless delaying and sabotaging tactics or pleasing ourselves without regard to anyone else, we fend off feeling wrong or being vulnerable. From within this barrier, loving kindness and compassion are seen as either an irrelevance, barely noticed, or a distinct danger to be avoided. They require the heart to open, and it is just this that this barrier prevents.

- **The completion barrier** This, the last defense in the sequence, becomes necessary when we have felt the need to prolong being little or when we have become a busy grown-up too soon. Though quite different, both experiences create a fear of completing anything— being no longer a child, ending a relationship, an essay, the washing up—or having a succession of jobs and chores that are never done. Behind this barrier, doing more and more, leaving no space, we need never pause and soften.

In some ways, each of these barriers is like a bodyguard— hired to protect us but not going home once the job is done. We now want them out of the way, so we can be less constrained, but they hang about, keeping even our friends away. Philippa

Vick says that these barriers are "different levels of wall" that defend us from feeling vulnerable. Attempting to relax them, allowing ourselves to become more open, creates more anxiety. So that we find alongside our wanting to be mindful, wanting to incline our minds toward loving kindness and compassion, a not wanting that is driven by fear that resists anything changing:

> *What stops us allowing ourselves to feel kindness and compassion is fear and the self-protection of our barriers. Much better to stay with the known devil of invulnerability than the devil of opening to possible goodness. Letting go of old ego protections is felt as far worse, far more frightening, than having to stay in our old threat zones. What makes this worse is that we have a basic belief that an emotion has to feel right if it is OK. So we don't allow and close down against the transformative power of using our thoughts skillfully, of recognizing that energy follows thought, that it is important to not feed destructive patterns of thinking and feeling. That we can experiment with generating feelings of kindness and compassion even if this feels initially odd. For it to be right, it doesn't have to feel right immediately. Imagination can give birth to reality.*

As in the previous chapter, looking at the neurobiology of this may help, as it shows just how impersonal our defenses are. We did not make them up: nature gave them to us and we supplied the details. When we begin to relax a protective barrier erected to defend against the feelings created by the insecure attachments we looked at above, or other painful events that have happened in our past, it may be disturbing because we can feel sudden overwhelming emotions, body sensations, and impulses that we do not necessarily understand. Our instinct is to immediately stop what we are doing—plainly it is making things worse. As long as the barrier is in place, it is just about OK and we can manage our emotions more or less. But when the barrier opens for a moment, what spills out are all the things we do not want to feel.

What does this look like from the brain side? If when we begin to practice mindfulness and cultivate loving kindness and compassion this resonates with something difficult in our past, it can set off the alarm system of the amygdala (see page 208) and the brain network that records painful memories. When this happens, the emotional memories that are made active feel just as they did when they were recorded—this is why they can be so unsettling and distressing, and also so disproportionate to the situation. There is little, if any, conscious awareness of this; it is fast and automatic, and all that is required is a trigger that is somehow unconsciously tied to the circumstances that created the emotions in the first place. Once this has occurred, the amygdala, which is redisposed to spot danger, sends out an alarm that causes other parts of the limbic system (see page 210) to release hormones into the body to enable our fight, flee, or freeze reactions. They also inhibit the reflective awareness of the cortex that, under other circumstances, when not feeling threatened, makes conscious decisions and determines appropriate and skillful ways to behave. Once threatened, however, our more balanced mind tends to believe our emotional memories, rather than reflect and see if what we feel is really happening. We stop noticing that we are experiencing an emotion that *only feels* dangerous and instead completely believe that we are *now actually in danger*. If we have not learned to stand back from our reactivity—perhaps mindfully—we will be swept along by our powerful and fast survival mechanisms that have precedence over our ability to make more considered responses. These only come back once the heat of the moment has died down. Achieving this in a healthy, balanced way is not easy—we are, after all, trying to alter something that has taken millions of years to develop and perfect—but it is possible because we also have an innate ability to consciously recognize what we are feeling. When we intentionally engage this ability through mindfulness, warmed by loving kindness and compassion, we can begin to catch our instantaneous reactions and moderate them with better-informed responses. Karen, who has been practicing mindfulness for a while, describes an experience of exactly this process:

> *After sitting, I was aware of feeling really tired, but I wanted to make the most of my evening and also wait up for my daughter when she got home from work late. So I decided to read an article on "the terrors of love" and then listen to a CD on the five hindrances. Although the article and CD were inspiring, something was being stirred in me, but I chose to ignore it. I lay on the sofa and fell asleep, but it was an agitated, unpleasant sleep and I woke up feeling really disturbed. But by this time Mags was due in, and I didn't want to open the box and so tried to push the feelings aside. Mags then came in and went straight to bed. (So much for waiting up for her.) I had a disturbed night's sleep and woke up feeling like "poop." Again I realized I had a choice: I could avoid it and carry it with me all day or get a bit "closer" to find out what it was about.*
>
> *So after breathing meditation, I sat with it. I realized that what the article had triggered was regret about the choices I've*

made that meant that I haven't experienced physical intimacy for such a long time, and such sadness that I might never again in this lifetime; how much I miss feeling in tune with and trusting of another; how I missed being touched, and touching. Also, the article shocked me as I genuinely didn't know that that is how you express love day to day, and such regret that I didn't. And finally guilt, that I take my husband and what he does for me for granted and give so little back. Reading it I questioned whether I really know how to express love, even though I know I can feel love. I realized that the guilt I can do something about—that's fairly straightforward—but the question of whether I can ever give myself fully to another I'm not so sure about.

Karen has found for herself the best way to befriend her feelings—feelings that can be traced back through her protective barriers to the first years of her life. Recognizing that she had triggered something big, she first tried to ignore what she knew was now bubbling beneath the surface. However, her troubled sleep, horrible feelings on waking, and her self-knowledge told her that here was something that had to be addressed. Completing her mindfulness of breathing, she created an emotional environment in the here and now where she was in control and that felt safe. Resting in this place, she was then able to recognize and stay with extremely painful emotions of loss, guilt, and the shock of her insight into how her ability to express love may be forever impaired. Finally, having faced this and begun to find words for it, she started to integrate it meaningfully into her understanding of herself. We could say Karen took an amygdala meltdown and connected it through her mindfulness of her felt sense to her more reflective, better-understanding cortex.

EXERCISE: MAKING THE CONNECTIONS
What can we do when we feel disturbed by loving kindness and compassion? Remembering that we may be touching something deep in our emotional history, and that this will be felt as an emotional body memory that we have protective barriers against feeling, we can try to be mindfully present in this way:

1. *We create an emotionally safe environment* that enables us to be present in the here and now, as adults in control of our situation. This could be during our meditation practice, on our cushion or seat or anywhere else that feels right.

2. *We go to the felt sense of what concerns us and welcome it.* At this point there may be no particular memories or concerns that we can pinpoint as the problem. This is not important: regurgitating known old memories has limited value and can disturb us further. This is about gently opening to our felt sense and accepting our experience with kindness, curiosity, and no judgment, while being careful not to get overwhelmed. (For the full process of finding and staying with the felt sense see page 143.)

3. *Once we have been present, this experience becomes a memory* that we can recall and that we can use to make sense of our reactions. We may find that our reactions

to extending compassion and our willingness to treat, with kindness, ourselves and others are conditioned by fear, sadness, or anger. Finding this and identifying those reactions as a felt sense, they too can become objects of mindfulness—a mindfulness that contains warmth.

On the Path

Our first steps on the path of loving kindness are often faltering and unsteady. Not knowing whether we are capable of kindness and compassion, we doubt ourselves, imagining that we may be incapable of loving. Alex describes this anxiety: fearing what he may find within himself, yet intuiting that this fear is baseless, he hesitates in his practice of loving kindness:

> *I've been doing the formal practice for almost six months and although introduced to the loving-kindness meditation quite early on I feel very resistant to introducing it into my practice. I understand that it's not some kind of fluffy, comforting, lovey-dovey concept. In reality, it's the opposite. It's incredibly challenging and it brings you right up against a very key and uncomfortable question—in fact, the most important question of all: do I have the genuine capacity to love myself and others, including those closest to me? So I find plenty of excuses not to do the loving-kindness meditation, usually based around the fact that I don't have time to do it following my main practice in*

*the morning. I have to get breakfast on the table, I have to start
getting ready for work, etc. But the real reason, of course, that
stops me is the fear of what I will find: the fear that I won't be
able to find the love in me for those I care most about. And
that is terrifying. Very occasionally, I incorporate the loving-
kindness meditation in my sitting practice, and when I do I
immediately feel myself stumbling, tightening, holding back, not
willing to give myself wholeheartedly to it. Of course, it's the
fear that holds me back. I suspect that if I can stay with that
fear, while giving myself over to the loving-kindness meditation
with all my heart, then the fear might dissolve.*

Not all our resistance to loving kindness and compassion
comes from our childhood. There are many occasions when,
perhaps due to wounds to the heart, we retreat behind our self-
protective barriers. Feeling emotions like resentment, anger,
shame, humiliation, guilt, wounded pride, or moral outrage is
never really comfortable.

I am sitting with Lisa, who is estranged from one of her two
children. There has been a long history of shared unhappiness
and animosity. All Lisa's attempts to make amends, to maintain
contact, have been rebuffed with a wall of silence. We are talking about loving kindness and compassion, and Lisa says how
very difficult it is. I ask how. She replies that while she knows
she should think about her daughter in this way, after all that
has happened she just feels a hard knot of wanting revenge.
"It's evil feeling this," she says. "I so wish it wasn't there." I ask if
it is not hurt that she is feeling. She looks sad as she thinks
about this.

"Yes," she replies, "it is hurt—it feels so unfair." With this I can see and feel Lisa's heart soften a little, and we go on to talk about what Buddhism says about these hurt, contracted places in us. Lisa's daughter wants exactly the same thing as Lisa: they both want to be happy, to not have the horrible feeling that exists between them. Perhaps by going behind the anger, feeling the hurt, we can recognize this and that we are far more connected than we are separate—that even while the wolf of hate is present, the wolf of love is finally proven stronger. Later we return to the subject. Lisa says that her anger has been like an ice dagger from a fairy tale she once read: the dagger has been in her heart, but kindness is replacing it and it feels so much better. Most of us have a version of the story Lisa tells here—places where we have been so unhappy we cannot go there again. Finding a way to bring kindness and compassion to these walled-in places within us may not be initially easy but is finally a relief.

Whatever our wounds, it is also important to remember that as we grow into life even our earliest and most influential experiences can be healed to greater or lesser extents by the relationships that follow. We are amazingly responsive to new experiences, and that which was hurt and arrested can be mended and start to grow again. Whether we angrily assert our invulnerability or find ourselves incapable of receiving, or whether it is all too frightening to be present, in all cases, as we begin to be present to ourselves, befriending our wounds, this change begins. Philippa Vick describes this process as something starting very small but growing more powerful as it gathers momentum:

Our wounds are held very deeply in the unconscious, in the body, and we need to not immediately believe what they tell us.

What has hurt us in the past is not necessarily still present now. Kindness is the most powerful thing in the world. It is like a crack that water begins to trickle and then pour through, or like, what does Leonard Cohen say? "There is a crack in everything. That's how the light gets in." Kindness is that crack. We all have such a deep fear of opening, and we hide in cynicism, which sounds like being intelligent, but it is really just our monkey minds defending themselves against the simplicity of feeling, of presence. To take in loving kindness means a loss of control. A relinquishing of trying to manage everything. It requires opening in the face of self-protective systems of contraction and recognizing that in the present there is no threat.

When we cultivate loving kindness and compassion we often find that it reveals insights into just how closed our hearts have been and how, like Karen, we can be neglectful and unseeing of those closest to us. Evi describes her own experience of this:

When we did a loving-kindness practice recently in our mindfulness group, I had a really strong sense of the fact that my partner shows me unconditional loving kindness and compassion (most of the time!). I was also suddenly aware that though I would say that we have a good relationship and that I love him and he me, I do not generally recognize this gift that he gives me (but take it for granted and push it away). I also recognized that while I show loving kindness to others—my children, aged mother, friends—I often lack loving kindness and compassion in relation to him and even more so in relation to myself. I am very critical of my own and his failings. It did feel like a watershed moment. I felt my stomach churn and tears came to my eyes. Since then I have been trying to be less critical with myself and him, and am feeling happier in my own skin.

Martha has much the same realization, but persevering with the practice, letting her imagination lead her into a new experience, she begins to touch into the unlimited well of compassion that Buddhism believes is present within each of us once what is obscuring it is removed. Starting as no more than the willingness to suspend judgment, no more than imagining that we can feel kindness and compassion, something initially that is only an idea begins to warm and is felt, and from this it spreads out, touching all those around us:

The first time I did a loving-kindness practice, I felt overwhelmed with a sense of sadness as I very quickly realized how unkind and hard I can be on myself (and others). It felt very foreign to be offering loving kindness—I felt quite vulnerable and undeserving in some ways. However, I did persist and began to notice something different happen, where I felt imbued by a very expansive, warm, more gentle feeling that embraced the harder core and softened it. The more I do a loving-kindness practice, the easier it becomes. I no longer feel undeserving of loving kindness; in fact, I recognize how desperate is my need for it at times and how welcome it is.

I have two children, aged eleven and nine, and have talked to them about meditating from time to time, and they are aware that I practice. My eleven-year-old had a very painful experience performing to a crowd, when she was unable to find a "loud voice," despite persistent insistence from a teacher. She was very traumatized by it. As we talked about it one evening,

I explained to her that when I feel angry or upset or hurt I try to breathe love and kindness into the part of me that hurts and suggested that it might be something she could try. A few days later, her brother was describing distress he was feeling about an incident at school. In a calm and moderately loud voice, I was amazed to hear her advise him, "When you are upset, it really helps to be kind to yourself."

Tess describes how difficult opening to loving kindness can be and, at the same time, how powerfully it can help in the healing of old and deep wounds. Having been estranged from her mother for some years, she suddenly realizes in her meditation how much she wants to reconnect:

I went for lunch on Wednesday with Mum. I'm not sure how to explain how it came about—maybe through some kind of magic or the universe hearing my call to her. I think it started before Christmas. My close friend's mother died in early December while I was away. I found her a beautiful angel in the Christmas market and a German candle, but I didn't give it to her. Instead, I sent it to my mum, who I haven't seen for years.

In the last group meditation before Christmas I experienced something I knew I needed to come back to. I felt a pain so deep that I chose, wisely I believe, to leave it covered until a time that I had more space to see it and let it be felt. In the meditation itself we had been asked to first find a source of loving kindness, a source of compassion, for ourselves and see if we could receive it, then to go to a place of hurt within ourselves, sensing where we could feel it in our bodies and then stay mindfully with the pain. Then, as we breathed in, we would bring loving kindness to ourselves, to that pain, and as we breathed out, send that loving kindness to others who feel the same pain as us. There was no way I was going to do that meditation! It was days before Christmas. My husband's parents were arriving in the next couple of days; I knew I wouldn't be able to keep it together. So I sat through the meditation willfully avoiding the pain. I did what I was taught to do by Mum when I went to the dentist: that was to make pain somewhere else in the body to distract from the real pain. She taught me to clasp my hands together and squeeze my thumb and fingers together very hard. The great thing was, nobody knew that you were doing it, so it appears that everything is fine!

And so, after we all left, and even as I drove away, I was tempted to return and tell the person who had led the group what had happened. And through the next few weeks it was on my mind—this nameless, unknown pain that I consciously, actively avoided.

One thing I knew was that we were going to be doing it again, so when I received the e-mail with the date of our next group meditation I was prepared and willing and curious to know it. Well, not exactly willing, but I knew I would not avoid it. This time I turned towards the pain and immediately I could feel a lump in my throat. I stayed with it and it became a constriction of hurt so painful I wanted to cry out, but I couldn't. It was my deep howl that I have carried within me for years, from a primal, dark, secret place so deep inside. And the cry I heard, when I listened, was simply, "I miss my mum, I want my mum"—that was it. When all else has been stripped away—the things that have been said, the wrong things that have been done—I allowed myself to feel for the first time and undefended the real hurt that has always been there. My tears flowed freely.

I told the two people leading the group I needed some time to gather myself before returning home. I also felt that this was something that I could not hold alone and asked if I should seek a therapist to guide me. They kindly provided me with a recommendation and tea. Over the following days I chose to be extremely gentle with my tender self and observe carefully the hurt. I noticed how I was left with an incredibly heavy heart, my whole being felt weighted down. I sat on my cushion feeling this weighty warmth with such sadness for myself and Mum. Though I don't think I told anyone else what I was feeling, it was self-care, and just staying with, rather than pushing away or engaging too much with the outside world. I was letting things be just as they were—no longer "What is this?" but instead, "And this too." On the Saturday I went to dharma dance and danced from the heart—danced for my mum and me. Later, when I looked at my e-mail, there was a very short message from Mum. It said, "I really miss you." I wrote back immediately, "I really miss you too, Mum. Let's meet sometime soon."

With a little careful thought and planning, but also not wishing to delay (I wanted to go with my heart open), we arranged to meet for lunch. We both had to travel some distance and we didn't have long. It was worth it. I waited for Mum at Paddington Station. I knew her train had been severely delayed, but I had no way of knowing how long she would be because I don't think she knows how to use her phone. I dared not leave our meeting place for fear I might miss her. I waited for almost an hour and a half, and then I looked up and spotted her before she saw me. She was looking for our meeting point. She had *traveled all the way alone on a train for the first time in years. She looked older and smaller and bewildered. I cry now as I write this. We had lunch together and talked about nothing in particular; it felt just nice to be together. We walked back across the park and then parted and went our separate ways. I left her with a gift of a small quartz heart that I had been holding for her for most of the time. That evening, very soon after I arrived home, I went out again to our meditation group. In the extended three minutes, during the mindfulness of emotions, I felt curiously emotionless. This surprised me after my day's events. "What is this?" I asked—a numbness? No, it was calm that I realize now is still here. An emptiness—a space where, before, the deep howl lived—quite serene, soft, and an unusual quietness . . .*

A Loving-Kindness and Compassion Meditation

This is the meditation that Tess refers to above. It combines three elements: making a connection with a source of loving kindness and compassion, receiving these qualities into our core wounds, and then extending loving kindness and compassion out to those who are wounded, just like ourselves. This is a powerful practice; if you feel in any way overwhelmed, pace yourself as Tess did:

1. Start with mindfulness of breathing until you feel settled.

2. Next, imagine before you a source of loving kindness and compassion. It may be a person, an animal, or even something abstract like a place or a piece of music. Go slow. Really get a sense of this presence. Accept whatever presents itself, however unlikely.

3. With this source of loving kindness and compassion still present, try to get a felt sense of a place of woundedness within your body. Stay with this felt sense, accepting it with kindness and compassion.

4. Now visualize the source of loving kindness and compassion radiating out these qualities, which, as you breathe in, you deeply receive into yourself. Stay with this for a while, breathing in loving kindness and compassion, noticing what happens to your felt sense.

5. After a while, having received as much loving kindness and compassion as you can, imagine others who have exactly the same wound as you do and who suffer in the same way. With these people in mind, with each out breath extend to them loving kindness and wish that they too should not suffer. Stay with this, exhaling loving kindness and compassion for a while.

6. Now put the two together: breathing in, receive loving kindness and compassion; breathing out, give loving kindness and compassion. Continue in this way for as long as you want.

As with all mindfulness practices, what is most important is to be present with the experience as it is. If you find this practice difficult to do, perhaps creating a resistance in you, then you can choose to go to the felt sense of the resistance—"Where am I feeling this in my body?"—and make this your object of mindfulness, accepting it without judgment, extending kindness and compassion toward yourself. And breathing.

A False Love

How do we know that our loving kindness is not being used as a plaster to cover over resentful, frustrated, angry, or envious feelings—feelings we do not want to acknowledge that we have?

The truth is, we probably cannot ever entirely know how simple or complex our emotions are, but as we become more able to be present with them as a felt sense, their complexity becomes more transparent. From this nonjudgmental acceptance grows the ability to be real.

Likewise, when we practice loving-kindness and compassion-cultivating meditations, implicit within them is the knowledge that it is a hard thing to do. We may be able to wish well for someone we love, but for an enemy? Because of this we need to use our imaginations when we cannot yet truly feel something. This need not be dishonest—as children we all pretended and played at being grown up, and on the back of our imaginations it eventually became so. And so it is with loving kindness and compassion: by creating the possibility, without denying that it is currently only a possibility, it eventually becomes our reality.

What Do We Practice?

Finally, there is a decision to be made whether we include a specific practice of loving kindness in what we do. Zindel Segal, Mark Williams, and John Teasdale, whom we met earlier in the chapter (see page 246), say that because practices that cultivate loving kindness and compassion can also cause emotional disturbance in those of us who are feeling particularly fragile—those of us vulnerable to recurrent depression—they prefer not to teach them directly. Instead, they try to create an atmosphere of kindness and compassion that permeates the entire eight-week course, through the embodiment of these qualities in the teachers and their teaching, and through the mindfulness meditation itself; that is, a practice in which we befriend ourselves with "curiosity, kindness, calmness, and equanimity." They quote Jon Kabat-Zinn, who also says that because his whole clinic has always attempted to embody loving kindness he has never felt it necessary to teach it directly in specific practices (although in his book *Full Catastrophe Living* he does describe a classic loving-kindness meditation taught on the one full day of practice during the MBSR course). They conclude: "If the very act of gently turning towards and attending the present moment is a powerful gesture of kindness and self-care, then all the mindfulness practices in MBSR and MBCT are acts of self-compassion, and there is less need for a single practice exclusively devoted to training this capacity."

Paul Gilbert is also aware that trying to cultivate unconditional friendliness toward ourselves and others can put us in touch with difficult feelings. However, this has not prevented him from providing many exercises and meditations that explicitly develop kindness and compassion. In the face of the type of threats we have looked at here, he recommends that along with mindfulness we redirect our attention to memories that are more compassionate and helpful, that we strengthen our rational minds and reality testing, that we work out where we are perpetuating harmful ways of thinking, and, lastly, that we make choices that help us and others diminish distress and cause us to flourish. This set of "compassionate skills," he says, has some overlap with the Buddhist Noble Eightfold Path and plainly, like the Eightfold Path, it is a set of things to be *done*.

Those of us who come from one of the many Buddhist traditions that believe kindness and compassion are essential may find MBSR and MBCT's caution surprising. Buddhism has never hesitated to incline the mind toward and cultivate the loving-kindness and compassion practices that are found throughout both Early and Theravada Buddhism, as well as at the very center of schools of Mahayana Buddhism that make compassion, along with wisdom, their principal concern. Here, there is no additional consideration for those of us who are perceived as too vulnerable to cultivate an open heart. We all are suffering: it is recognition of this that has brought us to meditation; it is the experience of suffering that continues to motivate us; and it is suffering that we work with in our mindfulness practice. After all, if the practice of mindfulness is the practice of working with our obstacles and hindrances—intellectual and emotional—then we have no choice but to stay present with what is sometimes difficult and distressing.

This commitment to loving-kindness and compassion practices is supported by neuroscientific research. In his article "The Neurobiology of Compassion," in *Wisdom and Compassion in Psychotherapy*, neuroscientist Richard Davidson describes some interesting (if not wholly surprising) results. He gives us three pieces of information. First, imagining a positive outcome for someone else may reduce our levels of the stress hormone cortisol, which, when released frequently and left in our systems, can be damaging. Second, using information provided through EEGs, he found that very established practitioners of loving-kindness and compassion meditations showed high levels of the brain activity associated with the production of conscious awareness. Third, fMRI scans reveal brain activity that may suggest practicing loving-kindness and compassion meditations has the potential to enhance our empathetic responses—particularly being able to feel into what someone else is feeling and have a perspective that includes others as well as ourselves. Those who had been practicing the longest naturally showed the most dramatic results. Many had chalked up tens of thousands of hours. However, even those who practiced just thirty minutes a day for fourteen consecutive days also showed significant changes in the region of the brain that is associated with social emotions. Richard Davidson concludes that practicing kindness and compassion clearly activates parts of the brain that are involved with emotional processing and that when we add to our genetic disposition and the sum of our nurture "lots of intentional practice," compassion training is not only good for ourselves but good for everyone else as well.

In our own teaching we have taken a middle way. Many of the people who have attended our MBSR/MBCT and other courses have no particular interest in Buddhism, and we very clearly say that we have no intention or desire to make conversions. However, this does not mean that Buddhism is a forbidden subject and, along with clearly acknowledging our sources, we also introduce several small practices of loving kindness for those who are interested and would like to explore them further. Those who think kindness and compassion are too sentimental, unrealistic, or idealistic, or just not for them, are at liberty to let these aspirations and meditations go. As Jon Kabat-Zinn says, there is plenty of kindness in the course itself—we need not force feed it. My feeling is that part of the kindness of MBSR, MBCT, and Buddhism is the willingness to give each of us as much time as we need and find the way that best suits us. This gives us space to experiment, make mistakes, and start again and again. As we have seen here, kindness and compassion, along with associated feelings of sympathetic joy, equanimity, and tranquility, can bring up powerful feelings; but working with these feelings—and all other feelings—is at the heart of mindfulness meditation. We can "incline the mind" toward them, implying no more than an aspiration to embody them or jump straight in and start cultivating the feeling of kindness and compassion immediately—the choice is ours. Finally, whether or not we choose to include a specific loving-kindness or compassion practice in our regular meditation, the very act of mindfulness itself will gradually put us in touch with the natural kindness and compassion that is at the heart of it. How this looks when it begins to spread out and is practiced by a whole community is described by Sarah, a doctor who recalls her time working with the Tibetan refugee population at Dharamsala in northern India, the home of the Dalai Lama:

Whenever I think about loving kindness and compassion, I always arrive at the Dalai Lama's teachings in his temple in Dharamsala. When the temple is empty, it feels no more than a rather bleak concrete building. On the days of the teachings it becomes warm and alive. Thousands of people from all walks and ways of life come together without any fuss, large queues, or noise, with the whole environment feeling fluid, with each and every one there having huge respect for not only the Dalai Lama but for each other and the form and order of the event. Sitting on cushions you bring yourself, a reserved place is always respected, anything you leave overnight is there in the morning with everyone standing by the unwritten rules and protocols. Plain bread and tea are passed around; neighbors share the food that they bring, even if they don't share the same language or means. Lunch is a huge basin of rice and dal served free to anyone who wishes to share it. It's all totally uncommercial, with no one trying to advertise, be competitive, or make money. It is just as it is. The Dalai Lama arrives exuding compassion, smiling, engaging, keen to hear everyone's stories and reasons for being there—Tibetans, Buddhists, and inquisitive travelers alike. He then gives his teachings with total engagement, humor, and words that just make you feel normal and that all in the world and in your life is fine.

Thinking about the whole event afterwards brings back the feelings of being totally safe, warm, and secure—where bad

*things don't happen and if anything does happen, it will all be
fine anyway. Neighbors can be trusted and relied upon; everyone is united with a common purpose with no competition or
commercialism, all working for the common good. Life is simple, but having great spiritual depth, quality is not materialism;
expectations are a warm feeling, rather than achievements; and
everyone in the room is contributing.*

*So when life gets fraught, frantic, and difficult, thinking
about the Dalai Lama's teachings brings all the thoughts of loving kindness and compassion alive and real, thence putting the
grasping, greedy world we live in into perspective.*

A Traditional Loving-Kindness and Compassion Meditation

Here is a traditional loving-kindness and compassion meditation. It can be condensed and shortened to fit alongside a
mindfulness meditation, taking just a few minutes, or kept
as something separate, perhaps lasting thirty minutes.
Remember, we need not expect that we will feel every
step—they get harder as they progress. We practice to
"incline our minds" toward loving kindness and compassion, in the knowledge that they will grow in us once we
give them the opportunity. When it comes to people with
whom there is discord, this does not mean we are expecting
ourselves to forgive and forget, rather it is creating the opti-
mum conditions so that what has gone wrong in the past
might not go wrong again.

Start with a short period of mindful breathing to help settle and become calm.

Visualize before yourself someone who is dear and toward whom you can wish well-being and happiness. Go slow; try to find the felt sense of this. This someone can be anyone, even a loved pet—it is the feeling that is important. Then wish (in these words or others that are meaningful to you):

> *May you be free of suffering and the roots of suffering.*
> *May you know happiness and the roots of happiness.*

Next, visualize yourself, or perhaps a particularly wounded or unloved part of yourself, and going slowly, trying to find the feeling, wish:

> *May I be free of suffering and the roots of suffering.*
> *May I know happiness and the roots of happiness.*

Next visualize someone unknown toward whom you have no strong feelings one way or another, someone neutral, and wish:

> *May you be free of suffering and the roots of suffering.*
> *May you know happiness and the roots of happiness.*

Next, visualize someone with whom you feel some discord, even though this may be harder (if new to this, choose first someone not too difficult), and wish:

May you be free of suffering and the roots of suffering.
May you know happiness and the roots of happiness.

And finally include everyone, not forgetting yourself:

May we all be free of suffering and the roots of suffering.
May we all know happiness and the roots of happiness.

End with the breath.

The Damaged Heart: Key Points

- There can be a discrepancy between how it seems when we are practicing loving-kindness and compassion meditations and what is going on beneath the surface.
- Teachers of mindfulness have become aware that these practices can cause varying degrees of psychological disturbance and distress.
- This may be because the practice is being unconsciously associated with the quality of care we received in our infancy from the person who mothered us. When it has not been good enough, it creates "insecure attachments."
- These are "the indifferent hold," "the overwhelming hold," and "the dangerous hold." The first two represent different absences of a safe haven, the third an intensification of either created by fear.

- To protect ourselves from the pain these insecure attachments have caused, and continue to cause, we erect defensive barriers.

- These are the insight, nourishment, response, and completion barriers. Each of these represents a different style of psychophysical contraction—they are like body-guards who will not go home after their job is done.

- The neurobiology of this is that our brain acts as if the practices of loving kindness and compassion—or any-thing connected to them—are a threat. This is because it associates them with memories stemming from our insecure attachments or other traumatic events later in our lives. When this occurs, our ability to think clearly is temporarily lost.

- Not all resistance can be traced back to infancy—there are many other events that cause us to close our hearts.

- However, whatever the source of our hurt, it is impor-tant to remember that we have a remarkable ability to heal ourselves through mindfulness and nurturing self-kindness and compassion.

- There are various opinions about whether it is benefi-cial to practice meditations devoted specifically to cul-tivating loving kindness and compassion. Our position is that we need not decide on this; it can be an option that we can experiment with for ourselves.

- Finally, whatever we decide, because mindfulness takes us closer to how things really are, it will naturally reveal the spontaneous resources of loving kindness and com-passion that are already within us.

CHAPTER 8

It's Not All Pain

*Taking an attitude of being a little bit more fearless is hugely beneficial.
It's really making a difference. You really can look at difficult feelings
without being afraid to be swept away by them.*

BEN

*It gives you a little glimpse that, despite the horrid feelings and
anxieties . . . there is a refuge in the middle of all of that chaos.*

SAM

I just lived moment to moment and it was wonderful. Wonderful.

ROZZIE

am talking with Chris about his meditation six weeks after
completing the eight-week mindfulness course. He is concerned that he has not properly understood the meditation
technique and has compounded his doubt by reading three or
four books on mindfulness and Buddhism that have further
confused him. He asks, "What am I supposed to do? Just stay
present with my breath? Is that it? Is there any more? Is it just
that simple?" The answer is basically yes, it is that simple, but
looking at Chris, just now, it seems the opposite; if anything, he
looks more stressed out. Concerned, I ask if he has had no experience of settling in himself, of feeling still and calm. He replies

yes, but not when he meditates—but occasionally, at the end of the day, just sitting down for an odd unplanned minute, he has come home to himself, feeling momentarily at ease. He says it's a good feeling that has crept up on him unexpectedly.

We could be forgiven by the end of this book if, like Chris, our perception of mindfulness is that it is all about suffering. We have named, looked at, and dived into just about every emotion we spend most of our time avoiding. Like Beauty, we have turned and kissed our Beast. However, while mindfulness brings us up close to our chaotic, out-of-control minds and our sometimes troubling and confusing emotions, it also brings us up close to moments of effortless calm and, sometimes, the clear, space-like awareness in which all these experiences come and go. When we can begin to effortlessly rest in this intrinsic awareness, allowing the contents of our minds to appear and disappear without grasping, aversion, or fear, then we begin to understand the comfort and ease that is at the heart of the practice.

Facing Our Demons

Ben talks to me about his changing relationship to his emotions. He says that whereas before he believed his emotions were an important source of truth, now he has realized that they are not to be taken too seriously, too concretely, because they don't necessarily tell the full truth of something—that they are simply the emotions we are experiencing and can be stepped back from. However, he also tells me that he is a dreamy sort of person who can easily be swept away in his fantasies and imagination, and that mindfulness brings him back to the emotions he is having in the moment. This sounds like a precise and possibly quite difficult balance. How can mindfulness enable us to be fully, consciously present with our emotions but at the same time not take them too seriously? Ben:

Well, what comes to mind is what Pema Chödrön calls "from fear to fearlessness." It's the title of one of her series of teachings, and I found it very powerful because that is more or less what you're saying. It's not about denying emotions; emotions are really there—they're not unreal, but they're just emotions. One of the things that I really find very powerful is this makes me a bit more fearless. It is actually interesting to see what's going on, what problematic emotions are there, what resistances are there, the automatic things that I'm doing. Taking an attitude of being a little bit more fearless is hugely beneficial. It's really making a difference. You really can look at difficult feelings without being afraid to be swept away by them. And by doing that, sometimes other things appear and the whole picture changes.

I had a recent good example of this; it was what I call a milestone experience. I had many difficult feelings about my past and Tromsø, where I once lived. I was very homesick after leaving that place. I always found it very difficult when I came there again because I loved it so much. So how to deal with these emotions? I said to myself, literally, "Well, be a bit fearless. Take it on, look at it, rather than being bothered by it." So while I was there, visiting Tromsø, bothered by the feelings—"It's so great here, so beautiful, and I'm not here; I could have been here; I left and I gave that all up"—I just took those feelings on with an attitude of fearlessness. And within a couple of seconds something happened that was really profound: all these emotions dissolved, and what came out of that was a very clear knowing. It's very difficult to explain this. It's not really a thought, although it had content, but it was the insight, "Why would I bother about having lost something like that? I'm here at the moment. I can be here at any moment. If I want to travel to Tromsø, I can do that. Even my memories are not lost. I have those memories." So there was . . . it's very difficult to explain . . . an experience of everything is there. Nothing is lost—not in the past, nor in the future. There are futures where I can travel there and be there, and I'm here now. So there was a realization, very clear and quiet and beautiful. I'd never had such an experience before, but I knew that I wouldn't have had that without the practice, without taking that attitude of fearlessness.

Ben's discovery of his fearlessness in the face of distressing emotions is also exemplified in Sam when, during a breakdown caused by a major transition in his life, he discovers a refuge in his practice:

It was very helpful to do it when my sister stayed for a few days and we went out for a walk and I felt absolutely dreadful and we came back and sat for five or ten minutes. Just a certain feeling of calm or something arose—that you can get through this. I don't know, I can't put it into words really. . . . It is a glimpse of some sort of freedom, isn't it? Or a glimpse that really everything does pass—the good and the bad and the ugly and the middling and the nasty. You get a little glimpse of things

being all right in the end. . . . At some level you are still there,
or you are still breathing and it gives you a little glimpse that,
despite the horrid feelings and anxieties . . . there is a refuge in
the middle of all of that chaos.

I don't know whether I think or I hope that there is some
still, small point in here somewhere that keeps you going. Wher-
ever it is, I don't know, some stillness, some stillness in the heart
of God—the ineffable, the unknown something, the still, small
voice or whatever it is. So, yes, I think it is worth going on. If
only for the wonderful sense of relief when you don't identify
with your own repetitious, boring thoughts and feelings, and
there is a sense of release and then, yes, that is marvelous.

A Brave Heart

Early Buddhism drew from the world in which the Buddha and
his first students lived. There, on the edge of the jungle, lived
lions, and it was with the fearlessness of these lions in mind that
the Buddha embodied and taught what we now know as Buddhism. Later Buddhism took up this image again, saying that
the lion's roar is the fearless proclamation that anything that
arose in our minds was manure to help the tree of awakening
grow. Everything—all our crazy thoughts and emotions—is
workable and offers opportunities to cultivate mindfulness. This
lionlike courage can also be found in our own practice when we
courageously stay present with what we are experiencing. Willem Kuyken describes a student who has the enormous courage
necessary to stay with a panic attack:

A man comes to mind who had extraordinary courage. It was the end of a twenty-minute sitting practice, and he was soaked in sweat. I said, "Tom, what happened for you in that practice?" and he said, "I started to have a panic attack"—you know, the classic panic attack of, "I'm not going to be able to breathe. I'm going to pass out. I'm going to die here; I'm going to fall and everyone's going to open their eyes and look at me. It's going to be dreadful." With the added thing of, "I can't actually get up from here and escape, which is what I'd very much like to do." And so what he did was to stay in the midst of this. When he had the thought, "I'm going to die here; I'm going to fall over," he said, "This is a thought." When he had a huge amount of heat and sweat in his body, he said, "This is heat. This is sweat." Coming back to the experience, he just did that repeatedly for twenty minutes.

Now, what I find interesting about this is that you can formulate it in so many different ways. You can formulate the change process behaviorally: you can say that was a form of exposure and he wasn't using any safety behavior—he wasn't closing it down. Or you could call it a cognitive intervention, in the sense that actually he had all these thoughts about what would happen, and without the use of any safety behaviors he was able to provide an experimental condition—perhaps because of the confines of being in a group and it being too difficult to get out—where he had to test out some of those beliefs and refute them. But as a mindfulness teacher, the thing that struck me perhaps most about him, in that instance, was just his courage, and just how much courage. Standing firmly there in the face of fear and difficulty, standing like a warrior, not reactive.

Rozzie is another such warrior, a lioness. Having had a viral infection, she was left with much anxiety that seemed to her to have both physical and psychological origins. Her husband told her of a particularly rigorous ten-day mindfulness meditation retreat that he had previously attended, which consisted entirely of long, long days of sitting meditation interspersed with very few short breaks. He also said that mindfulness was about listening to our bodies and tuning in on a very deep level, so she decided that this would be ideal for where she was and, despite not having done any meditation before and being quite terrified, she signed up. I asked her about her retreat, and her answer was as follows:

> *The first problem that came up was sitting still. I don't have a lot of problems sitting cross-legged; it's quite comfortable for me, but when they told me I had to sit for an hour without moving at all, without opening my eyes, then of course problems started to arise: the distractions of the other people around me, wanting to open my eyes, fidgeting, things coming up in my body that began to feel uncomfortable. But actually I very quickly managed to get through that, and I felt that as long as I could keep my eyes closed, that somehow I could remain in my body, without looking outside at what was happening all around me. So the sitting element wasn't too difficult.*
>
> *For me, the trouble began when after three days we started to do the insight meditation. My first hour of sitting completely still was excruciating. My whole body went into heat and pain. I managed because we were told to sit with that pain and try not to move, and what was supposed to happen was that the pain would arise, but then it would disappear—and it did, as*

long as you could sit with it and have the courage not to start moving and shifting around. So I worked really hard to sit with that pain. And I achieved it for about three-quarters of an hour; then I think the last fifteen minutes were just unbearable. That first hour of insight meditation was excruciating but also terribly interesting, because once I came out of the meditation I just burst into floods of tears. During meditation I wasn't experiencing emotional pain; when I was sitting there it was all physical and I didn't have any memories coming up or anything. My brain was quite quiet, except for, "Oh God, this is bloody painful!" But afterwards I burst into tears because of the emotional pain moving through me, although I couldn't identify what that emotion was.

Each time I meditated it brought up different issues, different experiences. I had, quite early on—which was possibly a good and bad thing—a state where my whole body dissolved. And I remembered my husband telling me about this experience because he had also had it. That was amazing, but also a problem because I wanted that again. We were told that it would come again, but then the agony would come again as well, and it was forever changing. Of course nothing stays the same, and you have to go with that. So for a few days that was my difficulty, wanting the wonderful sensations, but not wanting all the agony that came as well. It taught me how to accept and to be very present in whatever arose in me.

I think the most powerful thing for me was what was happening inside my mind. For the first time in my life I managed to achieve a state where my mind—I don't really know what happened to it—quietened down; it really quietened down. I couldn't hold on to my thoughts and that was a very new experience for me. It was like they'd flit: words would come, sentences would come, but I couldn't maintain the train of thought. It would just disappear. It was constantly changing, in and out of states and ideas; images would come up from the past and then just disperse, and I couldn't somehow hold on to them. So that was the most powerful thing for me. Coming from a very, very busy mind, it was very liberating to be able to have my mind just quiet, and with a quiet mind I began to be able to focus more on what was happening internally and to accept this state of peace. Being in the moment and being very present and not worrying about what the next five minutes are going to bring, or what's happened in the past, or what's going to happen tomorrow, I just lived moment to moment, and that was truly wonderful. Wonderful. And the first time I'd ever really experienced that.

Rozzie's first attempt at meditating presented her with two new and previously unknown experiences: the sensation of her whole body dissolving and a state in which she was effortlessly able to rest in her awareness, experiencing a quiet and peaceful mind that was untroubled as thoughts spontaneously arrived and dispersed within it. The first experience is quite common and is probably a result of our concentration deepening. This is a good thing and shows our practice is "working." However, it is also, as Rozzie intuits, a danger if we start wanting more and more of it. Then it is simply a hindrance. The second, far more significant, experience seems to have been a real breakthrough that revealed to Rozzie what Buddhism calls "the nature of mind"—not the chattering mind full of conflicts, but the mirrorlike luminous mind that is spacious and clearly knowing.

This is a real insight and having such an experience is valuable because afterwards it is much easier to recognize a second time. Rozzie also has another exceptional experience: off her cushion and during the night, when she is fighting with sleeplessness and the terrible noise of tinnitus in her ears, it seems that she reaches a healing crisis:

> *My tinnitus was extremely distressing, and at times, before the retreat, the sounds in my head were excruciating—like having trains or water going through my brain. I felt like I was losing my mind and it created a lot of anxiety.*
>
> *One thing that I was really frightened by when I went on the retreat was the silence because for ten days we were in complete silence. When you're suffering from tinnitus, you're desperate to block out the silence and, of course, on the retreat I couldn't do it. So I knew it was going to be a massive thing for me to have to face—to actually face how upsetting the tinnitus was—and that was scary. That was really scary.*
>
> *At times during the meditation the sound would be incredibly loud, and to try to overcome that and actually focus on a much deeper level was a very difficult thing to do. You've not only got your thoughts that get in the way, but you've also got a sound that's going on in your head, and with tinnitus it sort of draws you back into your mind, almost forces you to focus on how horrific it is.*
>
> *The nights were incredibly difficult. We were told that when you start to meditate a lot, often you need less sleep, or there'll be some nights when you can't sleep at all, and we were told that that was absolutely fine: just don't fight it; lie in bed, maybe meditate a bit, it's all fine—it's part of what happens. So*

I kind of accepted that, but there were a couple of nights where I couldn't sleep, and the sounds in my head were extremely distressing. And because of the silence, because of the state I was in, the sound just grew and grew and grew. What was interesting with the tinnitus was that the sounds changed, and I got to a place where I wasn't sure sometimes whether the sounds were external or internal, and that created a very weird experience, because you'll try and listen out, "Is that sound coming from outside? Is it something that's happening in the room? Is it something that's in my head?" And that causes a lot of anxiety—it's a very strange experience.

One particular night that I couldn't sleep, where my ears and the tinnitus were excruciating, was the night where I wanted to escape and literally get in my car and drive home. Drive anywhere but be in this excruciating place inside my head. My right ear was buzzing; it was like having a bee or something stuck in your ear—it traveled from one side of my head to the other and then it settled in my right ear. It was an incredible physical experience; inside my ear it was vibrating. Something was banging against my eardrum. It was a drilling— a drilling, a vibration, a buzzing—and when I put my head on the pillow, I could almost feel the drilling and vibration hitting against the fabric of my pillow. This was just terrifying. It was an incredibly difficult night for me.

I think I probably got about an hour's sleep, something like that. But when I awoke, there was no sound at all. No sound in my ears, whatsoever. And I thought that I had died, because for seven months or so, I had some sound in my head. Completely gone. It was four o'clock in the morning. I got up, I thought, "My God, this is incredible. OK, this is what it's like not to have any sound in your head." I went into the meditation hall and had a wonderful meditation experience, no sound, clear. And all I could think was, "How wonderful—I'm experiencing this peace inside my head again." And, OK, the sound will probably return, but you know, if there is anything I've been learning on the retreat, it's just go with whatever comes and accept, try to accept.

Later on in the day, a sound did return, but it was very quiet—it was in the distance and it was a sound that I could live with. It was nothing in comparison with the night before, when I'd had these excruciating sounds going on in my head. But also, it was nothing in comparison to the sounds that had gone through me during the months previously. So, to me, it was wonderful; it was this sort of peace, really. And, actually, with this peace I could begin to meditate on a much deeper level, without the distraction in my head.

So, yeah, since the retreat the sound has stayed the same. Tinnitus can ebb and flow; it comes and goes and it changes, but it has remained unobtrusive. And another thing I was getting, besides the buzzing and vibrating sensation, was an enormous amount of pressure in my ears, like on board a plane or under water. That too has completely left me, and I haven't had it since. So for me, the meditation has worked on so many different levels. It's something that I have to continue doing, because it's obviously helped with my symptoms. It's helped with me being able to live more in the moment, to me being more present with how things are inside myself and my surroundings. I've benefited on so many different levels—my teaching, my relationships with people. There's more acceptance of who I am. And there's peace—peace, I think, on a certain level, has come from the ten days' retreat, which is really, really wonderful. And, actually, what I've been able to hold on to is this: I'm not analyzing my thoughts all the time. I've spent all of my life trying to work through what's going on in my head and, of course, just going round and round in circles, and I no longer feel the need to do that, which is life changing. It really is.

I know that I let go of a lot of stuff on that retreat: a lot of pain, a lot of loss, a lot of fear—I think fear actually is the biggest word for me: fear of my physical symptoms, fear that I was going to live with this sound forever and how was I going to cope with that? Something happened during those ten days that allowed me to let go. Everything started to quieten down—my brain, my thoughts, the noises in my head, all quietened down. And I would go on the retreat again.

EXERCISE: RECOGNIZING HAPPINESS

We are used to being amused, entertained, and pleasantly distracted, but it may be that we rarely feel pure happiness—a happiness that is felt as something warm and healing that comes from inside and permeates our entire bodies, spreading a deep contentment. Mindfulness is not all pain. As much as it may bring us into relationship with difficult experiences, so it also brings calm, stillness, happiness, and a sense of being deeply at ease. Buddhism uses words like "rapture" and "joy." It is easy to miss or discount such experiences when they happen. Perhaps we are so unused to them that they slip under our radar or perhaps we are afraid we will become attached to them, making them hindrances, so we push them too quickly away (which is to then make them into a different type of hindrance). When we feel the nourishment of our practice, when we feel happiness, it is invaluable to pause and make it the object of our mindfulness. Such *experiences, without our becoming hungry for them, deepen our con-centration and facilitate insight.*

Positive mind states arise like everything else—notice their aris-ing, breathe around them, accepting, entirely present, and when they have gone, adding nothing more, return to the breath.

A Peek Around the Corner

Throughout this book I have written a great deal about the par-adox that for things to change for the better we must start by accepting them as they already are. I have also been cautious not to let too many ideas about what we may gain from mindful-ness meditation take us away from the present and into a fantasy of the future. However, it is not pleasurable and healing feelings that are the problem, but our tendency, through grasping, to turn them into something that creates more unhappiness—the hindrances we explored in chapter 5. Talking about MBCT, Mark Williams and Danny Penman, authors of *Mindfulness: A Practical Guide to Finding Peace in a Frantic World*, list numerous positive changes that happen when we practice mindfulness. Apart from the many health benefits that come from having greater resilience and a stronger physical constitution, the emo-tional rewards include an increase in positive mood, a reduction in the recurrence of depression, a greater enthusiasm for life, less alienation and isolation, and, finally, becoming more our own person. Jon Kabat-Zinn agrees. He says the practice of mindful-ness is both cultivated by, and an expression of, being nonjudgmental, patient, trusting, nonstriving, accepting and allowing, and having a "beginner's mind"—each newly arising moment being greeted with curiosity and fresh "not knowing." These qualities together give us the possibility to rest in our awareness, a refuge from the "toxic elements of thought and emotion and the hard driven suffering that usually arises from them when they are unmet, unexamined, and unwelcomed in awareness."

Buddhism also teaches about the importance of happiness and joy. In the Four Foundations of Mindfulness, joy is both an important part of the experience of mindfulness and one of its rewards. In the story of the Buddha's awakening we learn that, after many years of fasting and other ascetic practices, the "Buddha to be" realized that he was getting nowhere. Then he remembered a time in his youth when beneath an apple tree he had spontaneously felt a deep calm and pleasure. This realization enabled him to understand that wholesome pleasurable experiences—those that are not just about satisfying a bottomless craving—were part of the path, and this proved to be the turning point in his journey. After his awakening, the Buddha said of himself that he was "one that lived in happiness." Elsewhere he describes how delight, joy, and happiness arise and lead to deeper levels of calm and insight that, in turn, lead to the ineffable bliss of awakening. He also said, "Without gladdening the mind when it needs to be gladdened, realization will not be possible." And so it goes on—example after example of just how important happiness and contentment are.

Taking our first steps in mindfulness meditation, we may not yet have experienced what is being described here. However, it is entirely possible that we may have a glimpse of the fruit of our practice before it becomes ripe and ready for eating. Qualities that help our fruit ripen are found throughout Buddhist teachings. The Four Foundations of Mindfulness lists mindfulness and concentration, along with investigation, energy, joy, tranquility, and equanimity—each as a "factor of awakening." Below is another set of qualities, from a later Buddhist text, the Mahāyāna Mahāparinirvāṇa Sūtra (The Great Teaching on the Final Release), which describes eight characteristics of enlightenment: freedom from desire, satisfaction, serenity, diligence, mindfulness, concentration, wisdom, and absence of idle chatter. In the accounts of the novice meditators below, these characteristics are already—though perhaps fleetingly—peeping through.

Satisfaction and Freedom from Desire

Nicky just seems to be full of enthusiasm and appreciation. Not wanting something different from what is happening, she is free of desires; loving what she is doing, she is fully satisfied. Her joy is infectious and, as she inhabits the feelings she describes here, she is free of suffering:

> It is hard to continue, but it shouldn't be because it makes me feel so much better. I can think, "Well, nothing's changed, really," but I do feel I just appreciate things. You know, now I have a day off and I think, "Oooh, I've got a day off work, great!" I don't always go into work thinking, "Oh God, I've got to go to work"; it's just that when I've got a day off I think, "Isn't that nice!" I went to tai chi today, and it's a bizarre old group of people really—and the teacher is, you know, I love

him but he's very strange—and I just thought, "Aren't I lucky to be with these people?" It was just very special. I wouldn't have thought that. And I went to 5Rhythms dance last week, and I couldn't make head nor tail of it really, and part of me was thinking, "God, this is absolutely wonderful—I love it," and another part of me was thinking, "Oh my God, what am I doing here with all these people?" You know, it was a real half and half. And I kept on 'cos I was thinking, "Just be with it," although I also kept thinking, "Oh, is it going to be finishing yet? When is it ended?" I just kept on saying, "Just be with it. Just be with what's happening in this room, at this time, and enjoy it for what it is." So that, to me, is mindfulness . . . it's just teaching me to actually not try to be somewhere else and thinking of the next thing, to be with what you're doing at the time, rather than wanting something else that may be not obtainable or is maybe somewhere else.

Karen speaks likewise of "moments of pure happiness" that, amazingly, are not destroyed by events she has always dreaded and feared:

My "why" I practice has become very real to me, rather than an abstract idea in my head. I actually want and am experiencing moments of pure happiness. (I had a fragment of a dream recently in which someone asked me how I was after Dad dying, and they were surprised when I answered truthfully that I was the happiest I'd ever been. I saw their surprise and explained that Dad passing had somehow set me free, and that though I still grieved for him, it didn't stop me feeling happiness.) I am beginning to see how I have a choice how I react to things,

*which feels amazing given that my worst nightmare—the family
rejection I have been trying to avoid all my life—has happened
and I have lost the only person from my family who I loved
dearly and, tentatively, felt loved by. That's my why, and what
is motivating me to sit come rain or shine.*

Serenity

The most profound serenity is neither contrived nor created; it is
not a passing emotion but a resting in the calm and stillness that
is a characteristic of our awakened nature. Here Sam has an
intimation of it as he lets his preoccupations with himself relax
and drop away:

> *I think it helps me to get a bit less hung up on myself, on my own
> importance, and to realize that it is not just me isolated in this
> world bothering about things. It sometimes gives me a feeling of
> peace or at oneness, that I am just part of things going on, that
> can be rather lovely and perhaps a somewhat sort of humbling
> feeling, if "humbling" is the right word. You are somebody, but
> perhaps no big deal, but keep going and keep being friendly with
> yourself and not giving up.*

Diligence

There is something really fearless and determined about diligence. The Buddha is said to have vowed, as he resolutely sat
himself down on the eve of his awakening: "Let my flesh and
blood dry up, I will not give up. I will not change my posture
until realization has been gained." While this takes it a whole

lot further than most of us will be capable of just now, it is our ability to be diligent that takes us back again and again to our meditation seat. After being impressed by a particularly diligent meditator I wrote this:

> I am talking with Alex (whom we met in the previous chapter). He is really struggling with his practice, finding his way to relax and let his anxiety go. His efforts are really impressive. I am not sure I could work at it as hard he as does. I say to him, "You work at it so hard." He initially takes this the wrong way. "What do you mean? Too hard? Am I working at it too hard?" "No," I reply. "I mean you have really applied yourself to your practice when it would be so much easier to just give up and stop. You have hung in there, doing it every day, and coming here and talking about it, even though you are presently finding it so hard. That's impressive." "Yeah," he replies, "it's really important. Of course I'm working at it."

Mindfulness

Mindfulness is not simply the moment-to-moment awareness that we repeatedly remember to return to in our practice but also the characteristic of awakened perception—being entirely present with what is, not adding anything to how things really are. Sam gives a clear expression of this along with the pleasure of the experience:

> I think sometimes there has been a certain sense of the sitting there just being there and experiencing whatever the feeling or emotion is. It helps it to move on a bit and not just get stuck,

*which I think is very helpful really. And I love the whole thing
of just accepting and experiencing in your own body the emotions, feelings, and whatever comes without either repressing or
acting it out. This seems a very helpful idea, really.*

Concentration

As we still our minds through concentration, they become calm
and peaceful. It is said that with concentration comes freedom
from desires and discontent. Ann would be the very last to
believe that she has any ability to concentrate, but even so she
describes here a brief moment of calm abiding that sometimes
just seems to spontaneously happen:

*You get into one of those states that sometimes happen natu-
rally, of just being. You're tuned into the world around, the
universe around, and you somehow lose that dissatisfaction,
that anxiety, that striving for things to be different.*

Wisdom

Wisdom means to see or know. In the practice of mindfulness
what we come to know and see clearly is the nature of our minds.
This starts with the monkey mind—the mind that will not sit
still and that can create so much discontent and unhappiness.
As we practice, our moment-to-moment awareness enables us to
disengage from our unconscious and automatic reactions, to step
back from identifying with every thought that goes through our
heads and see how our minds cause their own suffering. Then,

as our practice deepens and we begin to find the equanimity to enable us to remain present with whatever experience we are having, good or bad, we begin to sense the deeper levels of mind that are characterized by spaciousness, clarity, and spontaneous compassion. Knowledge of this intrinsic, mirrorlike awareness is the deepest wisdom, and it reveals how things really are: an infinity of utterly interconnected change, in which everything in every moment is dying and being born, and is permeated with consciousness and love. Ben senses this ephemeral quality of his reality, knowing this there is no longer such a pressing need to defend his position:

I now look a bit differently at emotions—like emotions are not that heavy. I'll give you an example in my work. I came to realize how much people hang on to saving face. I find it very useful—and this comes from mindfulness training—not to bother too much about this, not to bother too much about saying to people, "Yeah, I did that wrong. That's my fault. I should have done it differently." Many people would never say that. They would find all kinds of ways to avoid or deny it or package it in some other kind of construction. It seems that for many people the worst thing is to be wrong and lose face. Yet if you really think what happens when you do that—nothing happens. It's actually sometimes very useful. Now I'm not bothered at all by taking the blame for something. This is something that I see as a direct connection with mindfulness. Sure, it's not nice if you have done something wrong and you have to say, "Well, I should have done that better," or "I should have seen this. Sorry guys." It's not nice, but it's also not a disaster. Also, other people appreciate it; it's not a disaster at all. So if you just take a little step back—that's something I've learnt from the mindfulness training.

Sam speaks of how a "certain feeling of freedom may have seeped through from the meditation":

I do like the nice times that come along when there is a feeling of calm or stillness or space, which is hard to speak about, isn't it? But equanimity, certain feelings of calm, acceptance, and stillness that can be very delightful and beautiful and you think, "Oh, this is nice. I do like this." And perhaps that is a tiny glimpse of what the real big boys achieve in the direction of nirvana and shunyata and all that? I don't know. I am just in the foothills, aren't I? There are many, many, many foothills, but I am intrigued by what it does for people who go on for ten, twenty, thirty years. Do the calm and stillness and equanimity increase and do the trivia of life bother you less? I am keen on how it affects the rest of our life, and I notice that, thankfully, I do get a bit less hung up about the trivia—like if the ink runs out on my printer, which it did the other day.

I had a month or so of feeling all calm, and I did a particular painting that is two halves coming together in a circle and it just came about and I was pleased with it and I thought, "Oh yes, that is something to do with meditation and space and calm and acceptance and so on." So I have been having quite a good time with my painting—just been trying to enjoy myself and not make it such a big deal and just play around with the shapes and colors, and I think that a certain feeling of freedom may have seeped through from the meditation.

Absence of Idle Chatter

The eighth characteristic of enlightenment is, surprisingly, something as seemingly simple as letting go of idle chatter—not wasting time with gossip, particularly hurtful, malicious gossip. Yet our chatter—with others and, particularly, inside our own heads—is where conflict and discontent start. Believing and feeding our same old story only sows more seeds for future suffering. What we think and feel is the universe we create and inhabit; becoming more mindful, wise, and compassionate breaks this cycle. Martin Wells talks about someone who puts this into action with considerable success after a shaky start:

> *Someone I know has got family in France, and she was there about five years ago and got into a typical conflict with her mother. Her mother would say things like, "Oh, just fill the kettle a little bit 'cos I'm saving energy," that sort of thing, and then the person I know would say something like, "Well, look, I am forty-nine and I do know how to live my life." And then they'd have a huge row, and she'd come back to England feeling resentful. However, she's been practicing meditation now for a while in between these visits, so when her mother said a similar thing more recently, and she was just about to react, she thought, "What am I defending against here? What am I resisting? What's the fight about, if I say, 'Back off, Mum'?" And she just noticed it, and it dissolved into the ether—as it does. So she said, "Thanks, Mum," quite openheartedly—genuinely thanked her for the advice or the suggestion—and they started to have a very different set of transactions, and when she came back to this country she really missed her mum for the first time. My*

sense was that she'd really understood acceptance and letting
go of egoic defenses and, in the letting go, realized that it's only
the death of that defense, or that egoic conflict, that could lead
to something else—to an improved relationship with her mother
and feeling better about herself.

Learning to Relax

Finally, we might add just one more: the importance of relaxation. Lama Rabsang tells a story of how he, as a monk in a
Buddhist monastery in northern India, took a very long time to
realize that relaxation was the key to mindfulness. Having completed three years of meditation, he was settling down to
complete a further three when his teacher asked him if he would
oversee the discipline of the other monks in the retreat. This
request appalled him. Rather than seeing it as a vote of confidence, he believed it was his misfortune and planned his
escape. With his friends' help he booked a taxi to make his get-
away, but before he succeeded the old retreat master called him
to his room:

> Then downstairs in the monastery was the old retreat master.
> He's eighty-six years old and he calls me in the evening. He told
> me, "Oh, you did very well, your retreat is good, blah, blah,
> blah." Then he says, "For sure, you did everything very well in
> retreat, but I'm not sure what's going on in your meditation."
> Then he said, "Meditation is just relaxing and being aware.
> Just relax," and he showed me like this [Lama Rabsang demon-
> strates relaxed]. And then I go back to my room, my meditation
> cushion. I sit, meditate. Then I suddenly recognized it, why all

*these years have I made meditation so hard and so difficult—
it's not difficult, just let it be . . . [big breath]. Something like
open and let go of everything: there is no meditation—just be
with this present moment and that's it. You know, that moment
we always have. It's just [letting out a big breath] . . . and then
[laughing] I was scared. "What happens now?" I thought.*

EXERCISE: REDEEMING THE BRAGGING BOX

*Many of us are so full of self-criticism and shame that it is almost
impossible to notice and acknowledge when something about our
meditation has gone right for us—when it feels good. The bragging
box exercise asks that we recognize and express something good about
our practice and simultaneously notice what this brings up emotionally for us. For instance, if we have managed to sit three days in a
row when we have only ever managed two before, that is what we
recognize and express: "Three days. Well done!" And as we say this,
we also notice what it brings up: "Yeah, but the practice was rubbish," or "I can't say that: I'll get big-headed," or "Well, three days,
that's nothing. I'll do three months next with no problems." Whatever it is, we also acknowledge this and accept it with kindness: this
is what my mind does with something good. Then we return to what
has worked, what is good, and feeling it as a felt sense, we remain
present, allowing ourselves to let it fully in.*

Choose something really good about your practice—it need
  not be something huge.
Write it down or say it out loud. Say it again. Listen, hear
  it. Again.
Notice what reactions this brings up and then put them
  aside. Name them: "Just thinking."

See if you can get a felt sense for what is good: where do you feel this in your body? Make this your object of mindfulness. Stay with it, let it in. And do it again.

It's Not All Pain: Key Points

- Mindfulness is not all sitting with what is difficult and painful.
- We can face our demons and experience significant changes in how we feel and think.
- Many of us may find a courage to be fully present with ourselves that we previously did not know was there.
- There are many accounts of the joy and happiness that come out of mindfulness.
- Even when these are qualities associated with being awakened, it is possible that we can have a taste of them early in our practice.

CHAPTER 9

Final Words

I know people feel bad; they feel they're somehow failing if they don't sit regularly. I don't think that need be a problem, frankly. I'm more interested in how they're living their lives.

STEPHEN BATCHELOR

I think when people highlight practice over everything else, it just becomes a little bit narcissistic again, you know: my practice, what's going well, what's not going well, why it's not going well; well actually, maybe it's not going so well because it's not coming off the cushion.

CHRISTINA FELDMAN

The end of this eight-week course is the beginning of the rest of your life.

JON KABAT-ZINN

Learning mindfulness in a Buddhist context is usually open-ended, but when our introduction to mindfulness is through an eight-week mindfulness course it comes to an end quite suddenly. The group almost blinks with disbelief—at the start it seemed that it would stretch on forever and now it is over.

Coming to the End

On such evenings, looking around, we can see in each other quite different reactions. Some of us have clearly been changed by what we have done together. Over and over again comes the comment that kindness has been the biggest thing: we stop beating ourselves up so much and experience an increase in acceptance and letting be. Nicky talks about her newly discovered appreciation of her life, being happier with herself and her situation:

> *I don't think it's just the fact that it makes me feel good . . . it does make me feel good . . . but it's just the ability to appreciate things. And that is wonderful. Because I think I've lived a lot of my life not appreciating anything, not being excited by things, always wanting something else. And it's the first time in my life I think that I'm actually . . . I mean not all the time—God, I want to win the lottery and lots of other things—but I just am happier with my lot.*

Jake, though not having established a regular sitting meditation, has nonetheless integrated mindfulness right into the center of his life, finding a new way to be with emotional conflicts that have plagued him for years:

> *Mindfulness has helped to quiet my mind and reduce the anxieties and stresses that the conversations and arguments in my mind invariably led to. My mind has been so much more peaceful, and I can now adopt a state of mind that quiets the conflicts that have troubled me for years and led to so many*

problems and issues. I haven't, per se, taken to sitting medita-
tion sessions on a regular basis as my antidisciplinarian streak
always runs counter to what I should do, but, rather, I have
been able to bring mindfulness into my everyday activities, so
that I feel more in tune with things and my mind doesn't run
away down tracks I don't wish to explore.

Others remark on the radical new perspective that, for
change to happen, we must go closer toward what hurts. Hearing this and beginning to apply it has not been easy: however
intellectually convincing, it initially feels odd and wrong. Ben
talks of it as "a fundamental change. . . . Of letting things happen and letting difficulties also exist":

After a while I started to realize that the way I'm looking at
myself, the way I experience myself and the way I do things, had
changed. There was a fundamental change. It had to do with
more awareness, with getting or having or providing myself with
more space. Of letting things happen and letting difficulties also
exist. I have a very busy job and there are a lot of challenges
there, and I was absolutely horrified when I took on the job as
head of department that I'm doing now—a job I couldn't have
done if I hadn't had this tool of mindfulness and if I wasn't on
this journey.

Elizabeth talks about how her meditation is beginning to
connect her to something that is going on among those she
knows and the wider world—something really precious to her—
and how she hopes it will support her throughout the rest of
her life:

Elizabeth: It's the experience of feeling quite peaceful when I do my meditation, and it also feels good later in the day when I think, "Oh, I did spend half an hour meditating this morning." It's a funny thing, how there's a growing awareness—in the world, in the people around us—of mindfulness and meditation. I kind of like the idea of being part of this discovery, this growing area of interest.

Nigel: That sounds a little like your feeling of spirituality and how we are all connected.

Elizabeth: Yes, it is, which again feels very much part of my scrip—that I want to be included. So what keeps me practicing? That does. Also what keeps me going is that mindfulness is not connected with my work, although that's how I got into it—the idea that when I've stopped work, that this practice can still be there and can still develop and can be with me until the end of my days. That also keeps me going.

Nigel: That mindfulness can be a real resource, a refuge?

Elizabeth: Yeah and, you know, I feel as if there's so much more to learn and discover through my practice. And it's one of the few things left that doesn't necessarily get worse as you get older. I'm getting deafer and my sight's not so good and I'm not as physically capable as I used to be thirty years ago, but mindfulness is something that can be what it is—the fact that it isn't competitive or judgmental or any of those things. I mean, here am I using words like "my eyes are getting worse, I'm getting deafer"—well, there isn't an equivalent in mindfulness, and that's wonderful.

Like Elizabeth, the majority of us intend to continue, but naturally the degree of our commitment varies. As the last week approaches, already our lives have come crowding back, reclaiming the time that was carved out for the course. Continuing to make space for our mindfulness practice is going to be an enormous challenge. Without the regular meetings to keep us on track, we will be on our own and our practice will be much more vulnerable. Those of us who really committed to all the practices right from the start will most likely have formed the strongest "mindfulness habit," and this will help us keep going when alone. Others committed later or perhaps not at all, finding different reasons why they could not really engage with the meditation—possibly the reasons that we have explored in this book. If we know this of ourselves, the end of the course may come as a shock and a wake-up call: we started out with such good intentions, such certainty—what happened?

Others among us will have already made the decision not to continue. This is not necessarily a bad thing and can be for all sorts of reasons: we may just disagree with the whole mindfulness thing, perhaps valuing more the emotional conflict that mindfulness seeks to calm, wanting our struggles to continue in our lives because they seem an important part of the experience of living, an important part of what makes us who we are. Or we may have realized that, even though we still believe mindfulness to be a good thing, we will never find time for it in the life we currently lead—that it can be something for later, when we have more space.

Whatever the reason, the truth is that very many of us do not continue to practice mindfulness once the course has ended. This may be a relief, but it may also evoke disappointment in ourselves and possible further self-condemnation. Willem Kuyken talks about his experience of people coming to the end of their mindfulness courses, the choices they make, and how this sometimes throws up bad feelings:

> *There is a huge variability in the amount people practice. So there are some people who feel at the end of the program . . . as if the tanker has shifted its direction of travel somehow, and they don't need to meditate anymore. Something has softened in their mind, or something has changed in their attitude, but initially they wonder, "Is it OK for this to have happened without me needing to do formal twenty, thirty, forty minutes' practice anymore?" Other people settle into a pattern of practice but have some awareness that actually it's not working for them, that they are striving too much, that they're trying too hard. I think with depression there is a danger of self-condemnation or self-judgment around "I'm not getting this right."*

Elizabeth, despite being committed to her mindfulness practice, nonetheless remains prey to guilty feelings when she falls below her own expectations. Her practice is something that has not yet become a rock-solid habit, and it is this that can cause her problems:

> *It's not a thing that I can rely on that will automatically happen, and that brings its difficulties. All the oughts and shoulds. I feel bad when I "can't" or don't allow myself to meditate. If I get to the end of a day and for one reason or another I haven't, although I thought I would, I can feel burdened by that. Then*

I think, "Right, you didn't do it today; you didn't find a space
because all of the other stuff you prioritized," so I have to let it
go and think tomorrow's another day.

Getting the balance right between on the one hand beating
ourselves up for not practicing and on the other making an
informed, wise, and self-compassionate decision not to continue
is sometimes difficult. We need to be sure we are not secretly
avoiding something because we are scared, yet mindfulness is
not the place for stubborn heroics. What can help with this is
the enormous kindness that goes with mindfulness. Maybe there
can never be an absolute certainty about our motives and this is
OK. Maybe we make the best decision we can in the knowledge
that we can change it either way and at any time later and this
need not be a problem. Rebecca Crane embodies this kindness
when she says:

It doesn't feel a disappointment to me when somebody at the
end of an eight-week course decides, or drifts into the decision,
not to continue. My sense is that once somebody has started to
increase awareness, that is going to be an influence on them for
the rest of their lives. So whether they practice or not, a shift
will have taken place.

Sometimes we cannot know immediately with any certainty
that we will carry on, and along with those of us who have
decided either that we will or will not continue our mindfulness,
there is a third position of not yet knowing. Elizabeth, on finishing her eight-week course, describes herself in this way. It was

not until later, when she found a friend to practice with, that the decision was made:

> When I first started out, I had no idea that I would actually keep going. I'm sure I probably did think, just at the end of the course, "Well, I won't be doing that anymore. That'll do for now; this is not me." I wasn't immediately caught up in it. But I did a few follow-ups, which felt good, and then I think what was very important was to have found another person who lived locally. That was important. So have I had any difficulties in keeping it going? Yes, absolutely, I've had difficulties and continue to.

And the last word goes to Sam. Based upon his own experience, he encourages us, having made our decision to continue, to keep going, however much we are struggling:

> "Don't lose heart," I would say to any aspiring meditator. Not that I see myself as a seasoned old sage—far from it. But keep on sitting. I just think it is a chance to sit and be with yourself and accept whatever comes along, really. Although sometimes it's easier said than done, isn't it? And sometimes it is very distracted and sort of bitty and you think, "Oh, that was hopeless." I suppose it is a hard thing to intellectualize about and analyze, but I just have a feeling that it is a very worthwhile thing to do. Have faith in the process and yourself. Don't give up. Hang on in there.

Disappointment

We may reach the end of a mindfulness course, or our first attempts to meditate alone at home, and feel disappointed. The disappointment may be with the course and what we have been taught, or perhaps with ourselves and our inability to use it. If this happens, it could be that we have arrived at another possibility: to practice mindfulness without recognizing it.

Disappointment arises from there being a gap between what we expected or hoped for and how things are perceived to be. Essentially, disappointment is an absence of acceptance. Often we meet such feelings with automatic behaviors, thoughts, and emotions—frequently blaming ourselves or others. The opportunity here is to mindfully notice the emotions around disappointment and simply drop the story line, do something different, and make the felt sense of disappointment—the feeling of it in our body— our object of mindfulness. In this way disappointment is transformed and our mindfulness practice is back on track.

EXERCISE: WHAT IS YOUR DECISION?

It may be that you read this book because you were trying to decide about your own meditation practice: whether you would continue, resurrect, or let it go. If you are unsure, you can use your felt sense to help you decide or find some clarity that may include not knowing yet. And remember, it is we who introduce unnecessary notions of right and wrong:

Think about starting meditation What does this evoke in
 your body? Where do you feel it? Is there a word, phrase,
 or image that captures this? Stay with this, does it
 remain the same or change? If it changes, follow this
 and repeat the process until it finally settles and rests.

Think about continuing meditating What is the felt sense?
 Use the same process as above. Where do you feel it in
 your body? Word, phrase, or image? Stay with that.

*Think about stopping meditation, perhaps just for the pres-
 ent* What is the felt sense for this? Same process. Stay
 with that.

Record what you have discovered.

*We need not act immediately; we can sleep on something and go
back to it tomorrow, finding our felt sense again. The important
point is that we make our decisions consciously, not driven by habit
or fear, and within an atmosphere of kindness and acceptance.*

Together: With a Little
Help from Our Friends

Since the earliest of times, groups of people have gathered
together to practice mindfulness meditation and listen to
those more experienced in its practice talk about what hinders it and what really helps. Coming to the end of a

mindfulness course, whether secular or Buddhist, presents us with a choice about whether we are going to continue practicing with others or not. Those of us who are not keen on groups and joining things may have immediately decided that groups are not for us, but even if we are OK with groups, perhaps enjoying the support they give, we may feel we cannot find time for one more thing in our hectic lives.

If this is your choice, it might be worth reconsidering. In my experience those who practice mindfulness regularly with others revivify and strengthen their practice, helping it to continue and grow. There is something about sitting with others that deepens the experience—perhaps it is as simple as not being able to get up when we feel it is not going well, or perhaps there is an energy created by the collective concentration. Whatever it is, it certainly helps.

And one more thing I have noticed: After attending a course, we often have become attached to the people in it (well, most of them). Going into a new, wider group, made up of new people, and having to make new relationships may seem daunting. We may think, "I don't know these people. They have probably been meditating for years and I am only a beginner." Noticing this thought (or other similarly disruptive ones) mindfully might be a good idea; remember, thoughts are not facts! A new group quickly becomes familiar, and you will then have taken your place in the wider community of practitioners that has provided a refuge for mindfulness meditators for almost two and a half thousand years.

From Practice to Path

A group of us meet to sit and practice meditation together. Everyone has attended the eight-week mindfulness course at some point during the last six years. Many within the group also have some experience of and involvement with Buddhism. Yet the question of whether we are identified with MBSR, MBCT, or one of the numerous Buddhist schools is simply not an issue. We are all together because we value sitting in a group, and because mindfulness, kindness, and compassion are things that have come to be important in our lives. This is not to say that we are all good at practicing meditation and that we do not continue to struggle with all the obstacles and hindrances we have looked at here. When we talk with each other about our practice, it is clear that it is frequently hard to keep going, and yet the way it affects and influences our lives continues to be deep and pervasive.

This brings us to the end of this book. We have given nearly all our attention to trying to understand why sometimes we cannot meditate—what it is within us that gets in the way and blocks our practice. We have also recognized that there are occasions when the decision *not* to practice can legitimately be a good one—that if we have reached the end of a mindfulness course, be it MBSR, MBCT, or Buddhist, and make this decision, it need not be a cause for self-criticism, shame, or disappointment. Buddhism is useful here because it is not solely focused on practicing meditation: we can be Buddhists and yet not meditate. In fact, in the regions that are Buddhist in their religious orientation—Southeast Asia, China, and the Far

East—the vast majority of Buddhists may pray regularly but virtually never have the sort of formal meditation practice we have talked about here. For them, Buddhism is about the values that increase happiness and diminish suffering, and how those values may be expressed in our daily lives—in all the exchanges we have with others and the planet upon which we all live. When the Buddha taught, he laid out a whole plan in which meditation was just one part. This is the Noble Eightfold Path that describes the skillful means to be ethical and wise, as well as the elements of meditation that help us to achieve this. Taking just one part of this path, whether it is about living an ethically aware and engaged life or about how to practice meditation, is to diminish it as a whole.

Some of this attitude is also present within MBSR and MBCT, although admittedly it is not so clearly spelt out. While it is true that those of us who are drawn to MBSR and MBCT courses are motivated by our own personal need to feel better and find some balance in our lives, it is also true that many of us appreciate that this will have beneficial effects on those around us. Cultivating self-kindness and self-compassion quickly spills into feeling kindness and compassion for everyone else who comes into our orbit. In this sense, implicit within MBSR and MBCT is an ethical element. By simply practicing, being compassionately present, we begin to notice when we are harming others, as well as ourselves, with what we say or do. In my own experience, this sensibility organically unfolds as, through the practice, my sense of being connected to everyone and everything else grows: my actions spread out around me and, if only in infinitesimal ways, become causes in all that follows.

So if kindness and compassion bring their own ethics, what

of wisdom, the other principal concern of the path, apart from meditation? Again, this is implicitly present. The phrase "knowing how things really are" is found throughout this book, and has been defined in a number of ways.

First, it is knowing how things really are in each moment, just as they are, without adding anything else. Within the eight-week mindfulness course this comes into sharp focus in session six, "Thoughts Are Not Facts," which brings together the growing insight that we color our experience with the emotions we are feeling. Many of these emotions are invaluable—kindness, compassion, equanimity—but others that carry us where we have been previously hurt can and do adversely distort our perception. Knowing when this is happening is the beginnings of wisdom.

A second understanding of how things really are goes much deeper. It may be that as we have developed our ability to notice sensations, emotions, and thoughts come and go, we have also recognized the space-like awareness in which this is all happening. This spacious awareness we have called "the nature of mind," and knowing this, being able to rest in it without effort, is wisdom itself. Rebecca Crane describes this whole process as trusting in a deeper connection to our experience, from which will come guidance on how best to live our lives:

> *The end of this eight-week course is the beginning of the rest of your life. We have all taken this time over the last two months to explore our lives in this new way. We now have the rest of our lives to continue this exploration. So we can let ourselves off the hook here! This isn't about trying to make ourselves or our lives better. It is a reminder that we always have this*

opportunity to take a fresh look at our experience, to really sense into how things are for us in this moment—and to trust that this deeper connection to the feel of our experience will offer us guidance in how to move with our lives. Sometimes we will take the opportunity and sometimes we will miss it. This doesn't matter. The key thing is that we always have this opportunity to begin again . . . and again.

Stephen Batchelor considers the ethical and wisdom aspects of the whole path so important that if we are to choose just which part we can really follow, then perhaps integrating compassion and generosity into our lives is the most important. Here he expands the word "practice" to include much more than just a formal sitting meditation:

STEPHEN: I'm not convinced that practice necessitates doing a regular hour a day on a regular basis. That is one form of practice, but something else I emphasize is to broaden the sense of what we mean by "practice." As I understand it, the whole of the Eightfold Path is practice. So I'm very reluctant to single out proficiency or dedication to a particular spiritual exercise as "practice." That is an aspect of it, yes, and a very central aspect of it, but if somebody doesn't meditate daily, I don't feel that they're not practicing, necessarily. It could be that their practice is involved in their work or in their relationships or in their studies or whatever it might be. Practice, I feel, has become reductively identified with performing spiritual exercises.

NIGEL: So if our practice is involved in our work or our
relationship, what sort of practice is that?

STEPHEN: Well, it's a practice of being. Let's say it could be
an ethical practice where people become very
conscious of trying to live a life in which they're
causing less suffering to themselves or others. Or a
practice in which they seek to cultivate compassion or
generosity. The difference is that they try to live their
lives within a framework of values that they're
consciously seeking to realize in every area of their
lives. In fact, some people come on retreats regularly—
once a year, twice a year, or more—but they may not
sit daily at all. I don't see that as a failing. If you look
at most Asians, they don't meditate. And yet I think
many of them are very conscious of Buddhist values,
and they seek to live them out in their world. I think
that's important. I think the danger is that you reduce
the notion of practice to doing meditation and there's a
kind of cut-off from everything else you do in your life.

NIGEL: Meditation and the rest of our lives are not
integrated.

STEPHEN: They're not integrated. When the Buddha
presented the Eightfold Path, every aspect of it was to
be *bhāvanā*'ed [meditated upon]. In Tibetan, that's
gom. How is the word *gom* used in Tibetan? It means
"meditation"; it means sitting on your bum, basically.
It's the same in Theravada countries: when they say,
"I'm going to do my *bhāvanā*," it means "I'm going to
go and sit down cross-legged and watch my breath."
But the word *bhāvanā* is applied to every one of the

eight steps, the Eightfold Path. The whole path has to
be *bhāvanā*'ed—the whole path. The whole of your life
is to be brought into being: the way you speak, the way
you act, the way you work, the way you apply yourself,
the way you see the world, the way you think—all of
that is practice.

So I don't place all the emphasis on sitting meditation, even
though I encourage people to sit regularly. I think it's a
good thing. But I don't think that is the sine qua non. I
know people feel bad; they feel they're somehow failing
if they don't sit regularly, but I don't think that need be
a problem, frankly. I'm more interested in how they're
living their lives; whether they're able to function in
their own inner life, in their relationships, with a
greater degree of attention, of care, with equanimity.

The Noble Eightfold Path

We practice mindfulness so we may be present in our lives.
To be present is not a passive thing but rather a full, intimate engagement with every aspect of ourselves and the
world around us. Buddhism codifies this engagement in the
Noble Eightfold Path, which focuses on the different facets
of life and helps to integrate them in one whole practice:

WISDOM
- *View*: To recognize suffering, as would a doctor;
  understand what causes it; and implement its cure.

- *Intention:* To no longer be driven on automatic pilot and to embrace loving kindness and compassion.

ETHICS
- *Speech:* To be mindful of untruthful, divisive, hurtful, or unconscious ways of speaking.
- *Action:* To be mindful of killing, stealing, and hurting or misusing others sexually.
- *Livelihood:* To earn our living in a way that does not entail harmful speech and action.

MEDITATION
- *Effort:* To skillfully cultivate the mental conditions that favor meditation.
- *Mindfulness:* To cultivate insight into our bodies, sensations, minds, and the nature of how things really are.
- *Concentration:* To cultivate calm abiding.

Christina Feldman says something very similar. Mindfulness is embedded in every aspect of our lives. It is better to not focus solely on our sitting-meditation practice but to be present in the wider concerns of the path as a whole:

CHRISTINA: The Buddha never did just teach meditation, never did just teach formal practice. I think people often miss this—how much the Buddha's emphasis was on the living of an awakened life in which meditation plays one part. But it's really what happens off the cushion, what happens when we open our eyes, that brings in the rest of the Eightfold Path. I think this is one of the obstacles to people sustaining a practice: they see it as a practice, rather than a path, and the Buddha actually taught a path. He didn't just teach a practice. He taught wise understanding, wise thought, wise speech, wise action, wise livelihood—all the ways that we engage with the world—as well as wise effort, wise mindfulness, and wise intention. I think when people just talk about practice, it's a very limited slice of what the Buddha taught. Practice is there to support awakening in our lives, but Buddhism really talks about the path. It never talks just about "practice"—it talks about cultivation, about the bringing into being in every area and every dimension in our lives. I think when people highlight practice over everything else, it just becomes a little bit narcissistic again, you know: my practice, what's going well, what's not going well, why it's not going well. Well, actually, maybe it's not going so well because it's not coming off the cushion.

NIGEL: Is it possible, then, to follow the path without wise effort, mindfulness, and concentration?

CHRISTINA: No, I don't think so. I don't think so.

NIGEL: So the ethical, meditation, and wisdom aspects of the path all have to be there.

CHRISTINA: They all have to be there; otherwise we have a sort of vague mindfulness and so it will not make any difference. I mean the formal practice part is like the muscle of the path: we're developing capacities for concentration, for wise effort, for mindfulness—it's the muscle of the path. This is actually what makes a path something that can be manifested, so we should never underestimate the need for that muscular development. It is just as you say: this is the way we develop different inclinations of heart; this is the way that we create new neural pathways; this is the way that we develop capacity—and capacity is essential for taking on the rest of the path. If anything, I think one of the biggest problems people have is to isolate practice outside of the context of the path. Then how does your practice deepen when we've done our half an hour today and then think, that's my practice done, and it doesn't matter what happens when I open my eyes or when I move into the world and move into relationship with people. This is where the path is cultivated, and I think there is, if that's approached wisely, a much greater level of inspiration about that undertaking—that the path is about awakening my life.

EXERCISE: THE WIDER PATH

Take a few minutes to reflect on your life, your relationships, employment, the choices you make. You may have started mindfulness to make your life better: how, if at all, has it done this? How is your mindfulness practice reaching into your life and affecting it?

How have my relationships been affected? Find an example.
How has my work been affected? Find an example.

How have my choices, my values, what I consider important been affected? Find examples.

Having taken this inventory, are there any changes that it
may now be time to make?

Path Advice

So what do those who have contributed to this book have to
say about staying on the path? What keeps us going when it
gets tough?

SARAH: Commit to sitting for a short period rather than a
long period that is unmanageable.

GESHE TASHI TSERING: One of the main causes people
give up doing meditation is because they want an
experience. They want to gain the result within a
short period that is not going to happen. When we
talk about meditation, we're talking about working
with our minds—the wild, unsubdued, untrained
mind. To work with that mind needs time.

WILLEM KUYKEN: It's about nourishment. We know you
need your five a day and you need to exercise. Well, we
need to nourish the mind in exactly the same way.

SAM: The more you keep on doing it, a certain sense of
basic wisdom arises. Sometimes I do feel a bit wiser
and calmer and I think: stop doing those habitual
things because it's not getting you anywhere and really

try another path that would, perhaps, be much more interesting. And that's the hidden wisdom popping up, and I think that's due to meditation.

BEN: Just do it and don't make a big fuss about it; it shouldn't be something holy. From the Buddhist teachers we learn don't make a big deal out of Buddhism, and I think that's also true for mindfulness. When you talk to people about it they say, "Oh, you're meditating, oh . . . ," as if it's special, but actually it's like taking a shower. I think that—and the key is really to keep doing it, no matter what happens, whether it's going all over the place or not. Every session is different. Sometimes I'm completely carried away by lots of sticky thoughts and sometimes I'm not. There's no such thing as a lousy meditation, so don't give up. Also, don't get discouraged by it because sometimes you just sit and you have a very "good" experience, things are very concentrated and that's great, and maybe it lasts ten seconds, but it doesn't matter. It doesn't matter, as long as you just do your practice. Every practice is different, every time, so don't bother about whether it's good or not. I think that helps a lot.

RUTH: You will be hit by all kinds of stuff and that's normal.

FRANKLYN SILLS: Find a place that is not beating yourself up but just being patient. I think that's a big one.

ELIZABETH: The bit that I value most is the complete lack of judgment. It's all fine: it's interesting and it's all important, even when it's crap or when it feels hard, and it's all absolutely normal as well. This is what everybody feels.

CLARA: I think that one of the things that helps is a structure. Part of me likes having a structure; part of me fights against it. So if I can accept the structure, then I think that's very useful. And then loosening up and taking it into my everyday life, just bringing my awareness back to the moment, whatever is happening in the moment. That helps. I think having a kind of awareness of mortality helps also, that's a motivator, and something about having an inspirational teacher and knowing a bit about him and about what his struggles have been and seeing how he's coped in his life. What else? Something about just keeping at it and understanding what the resistance is about.

LAMA RABSANG: It's difficult to be satisfied with this precious moment and just let it be; instead, we're looking for something. In meditation we want to see some kind of special light or to have some kind of special experience—some special openness when we think, "Wow, that's what we're looking for." Looking for something special creates lots of struggle. We have to learn to let go of wanting special experiences. Everything's easy when you learn that all the ordinary experiences in meditation are enough.

ANN: I'd say keep at it. I do find keeping in touch with a group of other people—it doesn't have to be the same group—very helpful. Like touching base, sharing thoughts, reflections, experiences. I do find that very, very, very helpful—very nourishing, really.

CHRISTINA FELDMAN: Well, I would give you a quote
from Ajahn Sumedho. When somebody asked him a
question about sustaining practice and how much they
should practice, he said, "Well, you know, half an hour
a day is plenty, except if you're very busy, then you
need an hour!"

TSOKNYI RINPOCHE: Start. Just simply do it. Don't think
why, how—just do it. In order to move, just move. You
can ask, "Why move, why not move?" There are
thousands of reasons to move, thousands of reasons
not to move. But you know in your heart it's good to
do. So just do it. Just do it. And then slowly, slowly,
something has a pleasurable taste, and then you do it.

MARTHA: Keep calm and carry on regardless!

REBECCA CRANE: Just do it! Without expectations.

MARTIN WELLS: Hang on in there—it's worth it. And it
will be tough; it will involve the sort of surrender and
relinquishing that you maybe never experienced before.

TESS: To stay, that is the key.

PHILIPPA VICK: The most important thing for practice is
practice.

ELLEN: Don't give up.

EXERCISE: ADVICE FOR YOURSELF
*The last exercise: what advice would you give yourself in light of
what you now know of yourself and the things you particularly
struggle with?*

Write it down, put it in a self-addressed envelope, and give
it to a friend to post to you in one month's time.

When it arrives read it and, more importantly, act on it. It is your wisdom gathered on the path.

Final Words: Key Points

- At some point all of us face the decision whether to continue practicing mindfulness or not.
- This is a complex decision and is best accompanied by much kindness and self-compassion. No decision is final; we can afford to take our time and change our minds.
- As Sam says, "Don't lose heart. Don't give up. Hang on in there."
- There is much more than just mindfulness practice; there is a whole life-embracing path that consists of ethical, meditational, and wisdom aspects. In Buddhism this is called the Noble Eightfold Path.
- The essence of the path is the integration of mindfulness, kindness, and compassion into every aspect of our lives. A practice that continues until the day we die.

Quick-Fix Chart for the Struggling Meditator

PROBLEM	POSSIBLE SOLUTION
Not wanting to meditate: feeling resistance to the thought of meditation or not wanting to meditate once started	• Try sitting with the resistance as your object of mindfulness—you will usually find it dissolves. • Try checking your motivation: Have "oughts" and "shoulds" crept in? Is there another part of you that does not want to do it? Do you have doubts and misgivings you are not recognizing? Mindfulness includes, with kindness, every part of us. Pushing resistance aside generally makes it stronger. Be curious rather than tough. • Try talking to someone about your meditation; don't become isolated with a problem someone else has had and solved.

PROBLEM	POSSIBLE SOLUTION
Can't meditate every day: irregular pattern of meditation leading to not meditating	• Try meditating at the same time and in the same place for the same amount of time every day. • Try to meditate, not when you feel like it, but, like brushing your teeth, just do it regardless of how you feel.
Physical pain: pain in the shoulders, back, buttocks, and legs	• Change position and adjust your seat so it is more comfortable and supportive; there is no need to heroically endure pain. • Try making the sensations of the pain your object of mindfulness. Again, there is no value in heroically continuing and thus creating a deep aversion later. Stay with it for a while and then change position.
Strange physical sensations: like tingling, floating, hands or other body parts appearing to disappear	• This is nothing special—like everything else it comes, stays, and goes. Don't get caught up in it. • Make sure you are not breathing too hard, too deeply—this causes hyperventilating. Breathe normally.

PROBLEM	POSSIBLE SOLUTION
Feeling sleepy: eyes will not stay open, drifting into dreams and fantasies, head lolling, strong desire to lie down	• Try being mindful of the experience of sleepiness itself. • Try sitting up a bit straighter. Open your eyes, or, if they are already open, lift your gaze higher. • Try doing something more physical like walking meditation, yoga postures, or breathing exercises for a while before returning to sitting meditation. • Make sure you are not eating immediately before meditation and that the room has air and is light. Try not to turn it into a battle—know how to intentionally give in occasionally and it not be a defeat. We all feel sleepy sometimes.
Feeling distracted: this is the big one: attention jumping all over the place, constantly carried away by thoughts, flooded by memories, caught up in fantasies, even stopping meditating and wandering off to do something else without consciously intending to—this happens to everyone all the time	• Try naming the distraction "thinking," in a kind voice at the back of the mind. This clearly reestablishes the object of mindfulness. • Try a few intentionally quick and deep breaths. • Try naming the breath "in," and "out" or "rising," and "falling."

PROBLEM	POSSIBLE SOLUTION
	• Try counting the breaths up to ten and then starting again. Count the in breath.
	• Try using a breath poem: "Breathing in, I have arrived. Breathing out, I am home."
	• Try remembering why you value meditation, why you have chosen to practice today. Say it to yourself in words.
	• Most important, remember that mindfulness meditation includes distraction and is not trying to create a calm, thought-free trance. Noticing the distraction mindfully and returning to the breath or the body sensations *is* the practice. A distraction you are mindfully aware of (a thought, emotion, or sensation) is not a distraction—it is your object of mindfulness.
Obsessing: caught up in a thought process that goes round and round, and that you can't stop—particularly with painful, self-destructive, or aggressive, vengeful thoughts	• Try practicing this loving-kindness and compassion meditation: "May I know happiness and the roots of happiness. "May I be free of suffering and the roots of suffering.

PROBLEM	POSSIBLE SOLUTION
	"May all beings know happiness and the roots of happiness. "May all beings be free of suffering and the roots of suffering." If your obsession involves self-hatred, emphasize yourself. If about another, emphasize that person or situation.
Boredom: feeling disengaged, fidgety, looking for stimulation in the meditation	• Try reapplying yourself—if you are bored, this means you have drifted away from your practice of mindfulness. • Try being mindful of the experience of boredom itself. What exactly is it like?
Fear: physical sensations, emotions and thoughts that cause agitation, anxiety, fear, and terror; these may arise from: a. experiences from the past, either remembered or not previously consciously known—traumatic memories, for instance (first arrow)	• Try staying mindfully aware of the physical sensations of the fear without falling into the storyline. You can support this by breathing around the fear so that the fear is not the sole object of your mindfulness. • If the fear is very strong, then choose another object of mindfulness—it could be your big toe—and concentrate on it. When you have calmed down, you can then return to the fear.

PROBLEM	POSSIBLE SOLUTION
b. unskillful meditation that fixates on the content of the experience and thus adds to the intensity of the fear (second arrow) c. the ego's basic fear that it will be annihilated—the deep fear all meditators may sometimes face	• Most important, do not try to use the mindfulness as a means to make the fear go away. Being present with fear is very good. Stop fighting and it will slowly go away of its own accord.
Disappointment: feeling that it is not working, that you can't do it (this is sometimes connected to trying too hard) or feeling discouraged, not wanting to continue	• Try making the sensation of disappointment the object of mindfulness. Do not believe the thought. • Try reviewing your expectations of yourself and meditation. Have they become unrealistic for the stage you are at? • Try cultivating loving kindness for yourself and be patient. Develop a sense of humor.

PROBLEM	POSSIBLE SOLUTION
Guilt: of three kinds—feeling guilty that: a. you are taking time away from family and/or work b. you are giving time to yourself c. you have not meditated at all or enough	• Try making the sensation of guilt the object of mindfulness, turning toward guilt with curiosity and loving kindness. • Try to not believe the storyline.
Fantastic meditation: feelings of great calm, bliss, clarity, spaciousness—not bad in themselves, but easily grasped at and dangerous because they can create expectations	• Try being unmoved—these experiences of meditation will also come, stay, and go. Practice appreciating not just them but also the quality of "nothing special."
"Stupid" meditation: a seductively happy stupor where the mind is contentedly dull with few thoughts and disengaged from the body—possibly a side effect of deepening concentration	• Try making the sensations of stupid meditation the object of mindfulness. Resist seduction. • Try checking your posture—have you slumped?
Creative inspirations: sudden brilliant flashes of insight and understanding, visions, and creative projects	• A particularly seductive kind of distraction. Try noting it and return to your object of mindfulness. If it is really brilliant, it will be there when you finish. • If you can't resist, try quickly writing it down for later—do this only as a last resort.

PROBLEM	POSSIBLE SOLUTION
Not recognizing successes: looking at your practice through your old eyes, as something not good enough; judging yourself negatively or ungenerously, as you have been judged by others in your life; not giving yourself a break—not saying well done for just sticking at it, irrespective of results	• These are all expressions of old, outworn, narrow, and mean narratives. Recognizing them as such, let them go by not following with further thoughts—not pouring gasoline on the fire. • Recognize these beliefs as a felt sense and use this as the object of mindfulness, seeing how the felt sense arises, stays, and dissolves. • Practice generosity toward yourself. Generate warmness and appreciation.
Numbing: a dull, disengaged state that is not noticed and therefore may be a prolonged state of disengagement	• Once noticed, check what is within or beneath it at a felt-sense level. Whatever you find, make this your object of mindfulness.

On Mindfulness and Psychological Trauma

Sometimes while wearing my mindfulness-teacher hat, I notice that a person who is describing their difficulties with practicing mindfulness is actually describing the symptoms of an emotional trauma. These may include intrusive and frightening memories; disturbing, volatile, and uncontrollable emotions; or, alternatively, an unnatural feeling of being disconnected, emotionally numb to themselves and others. They may also feel depressed, unable to concentrate, edgy and agitated, and suffer from insomnia and nightmares.

There is no exact pattern to this. Each of us, to some extent, experiences trauma in different ways, but the one thing that is universal is that it is *normal* to react to *abnormal* circumstances and events in these ways. To be traumatized is not to be mad or bad.

Within the world of psychotherapy, mindfulness has come to be one of the key elements in the newer cutting-edge therapies for trauma. For example, EMDR, sensorimotor psychotherapy, Somatic Experiencing (SE), and the work of Babette Rothschild all encourage a mindful relationship to the traumatic experience, as this enables us to allow the trauma to work itself through our systems without causing further trauma by reigniting and identifying with overwhelming emotions and thoughts.

Though we usually practice mindfulness alone or sitting with others in groups, in cases such as these having someone alongside who can help us retain our mindfulness and who knows the process of undoing trauma is invaluable—perhaps even essential. Therefore, if you suspect—possibly from something you have encountered in your meditation—that you are experiencing trauma, I would encourage you to seek help from a properly qualified psychotherapist or counselor who knows specifically how to work in this area. They will be able to help you remain mindfully present with your traumatic experience in a way that you might find impossible on your own. Struggling away with a mindfulness practice that is touching on trauma is extremely difficult and painful, and will in all likelihood cause you to stop. This is both unnecessary and unskillful when help is available. Being mindful includes being mindful of your real capacity and choosing to act.

How to Practice Mindfulness Meditation

Most people reading this book will already have learned how to practice mindfulness meditation—either from a course or from some of the excellent CDs that now come with many books on mindfulness. However, if this is not the case, here is a method you might try for doing a mindfulness meditation focused on breathing. If this is your first go, try just ten minutes:

Get comfortable, so you are not straining to keep yourself in the position you choose. Cross-legged on the floor or seated on an upright chair are equally fine.

Closing your eyes or resting them with soft focus on the floor in front of you, place your attention on the sounds happening within and around you, without reaching out toward them or thinking about them. Just let them come to you.

After a few minutes, turn your attention to your breath, noticing whether you are breathing in or breathing out. Do not change the breath in any way. Leave it exactly as it is . . .

Now notice where you are feeling your breath most strongly. This may be at the tip of the nose and the top lip, in the throat and chest, or in your abdomen. Perhaps choosing either the nose or the abdomen, choose one place to rest your awareness for the rest of this session.

Now, as you feel the breath, inwardly name it, perhaps "in" and "out," or "rising" and "falling." This is to help with concentration—the sensation of the breath remains the most important thing to be aware of.

Now, as you follow the breath, notice how at the top of the inhalation and at the bottom of the exhalation there may be a small pause as it changes over. In this pause have a sense of being in your body, a body that is breathing.

Finally, when thoughts fill the mind, when you become caught up in them and are carried away—when you realize this has happened—in a kind voice in the back of the mind, name this "thinking," and simply return to the breath. You may do this countless times during each sitting.

And continue . . .

As the sitting comes to an end, return to the sounds inside and outside of yourself, for a minute or two, then open your eyes if they have been closed, and carry some of your mindful awareness into the act of getting up and doing what is next.

Further Reading

The following are books I have referred to in the text. As such, they may be useful sources of information.

Daniel Coyle, *The Talent Code* (New York: Bantam, 2009)

Richard Davidson, "The Neurobiology of Compassion," in *Wisdom and Compassion in Psychotherapy* (New York & London: Guildford Press, 2012)

Paul Gilbert, *The Compassionate Mind* (London: Constable, 2009)

Rick Hanson and Richard Mendius, *Buddha's Brain* (Oakland: New Harbinger Publications, 2009)

Jon Kabat-Zinn, "Why Mindfulness Matters," in *The Mindfulness Revolution* (Boston & London: Shambhala, 2011)

Jon Kabat-Zinn, *Mindfulness for Beginners* (Boulder, CO: Sounds True, 2012)

Barry Magid, *Ending the Pursuit of Happiness: A Zen Guide* (Boston: Wisdom Publications, 2008)

Zindel Segal, Mark Williams, and John Teasdale, *Mindfulness-Based Cognitive Therapy for Depression* (New York & London: Guildford Press, 2013)

Daniel J. Siegel, *The Mindful Therapist: A Clinician's Guide to Mindsight and Neural Integration* (New York & London: W. W. Norton and Company, 2010)

Chögyam Trungpa, *Cutting Through Spiritual Materialism* (Boston & London: Shambhala, 1973)

Alan Wallace, *The Attention Revolution* (Boston: Wisdom Publications, 2006)

John Welwood, *Toward a Psychology of Awakening: Buddhism, Psychotherapy, and the Path of Personal and Spiritual Transformation* (Boston & London: Shambhala, 2000)

Mark Williams and Danny Penman, *Mindfulness: A Practical Guide to Finding Peace in a Frantic World* (London: Piatkus, 2011)

Index